Inside the Torii Gate

The Journal of an Exchange Student in Japan

Jonathan Jüri Buchanan

The Beresford Press

Inside the Torii Gate: The Journal of an Exchange Student in Japan

Publisher: The Beresford Press
Cover Design: Jason Croteau and Larissa Buchanan

Canadian Cataloguing in Publication Data

Buchanan, Jonathan Jüri, 1974-
Inside the Torii Gate: the journal of an exchange student in Japan

ISBN 0-9683945-0-7

1. Japan 2. Education -- Japan 3. Buchanan, Jonathan Jüri, 1974-
4. Canadian students -- Japan -- Biography. 5. Students, Foreign -- Japan -- Biography. I. Title.

LB1696.6.J3B83 1998 952.04'9 C98-901260-3

The Beresford Press
400 Walmer Road, Suite 724, Toronto, ON M5P 2X7

Printed and bound in Canada

To Japan,
to Trinity and Reitaku,
and
to my family,
for making everything possible.

Acknowledgements

The Japanese were always very gracious toward me, going to great lengths to make me feel at ease in their country and welcome in their homes. I am indebted to all of the people who offered their friendship and invited me into their homes and their hearts.

Many people have helped shaped my views of Japan and it has been a great experience learning from all of them, including my teachers, fellow students and friends in Japan as well as my teachers, professors and Japanese friends in Canada. I am grateful for their inspiration and encouragement.

I wish to thank Trinity College School and the Hiroike Institute of Education for providing me with the opportunity to study for a year in Japan. And I owe a debt of gratitude to the Trinity Guild for financial assistance toward some of my expenses.

I also want to thank my family for their support and assistance with the book.

Notes to the Reader

With few exceptions, I have protected the identity of the Japanese people in my book by using pseudonyms. I often refer to my friends by their given names, even though I always addressed them by their last name, either with the suffix *san* for seniors or *kun* for equals and juniors. However, I was addressed by my given name in the more informal Western manner either as Jon-*san* or Jon-*kun* depending on the age and the status of the speaker. Quite often, I was simply called Jon.

I have also followed the custom for books using Japanese words by placing them in italics and using the appropriate macrons except for Japanese words that are familiar to English speakers and the names of cities, including Tokyo and Kyoto. A glossary provides a quick reference to the Japanese words used in the text.

The value of items is given in yen which is the Japanese currency. While I was in Japan, the average cost of ¥100 was $0.81 Cdn or $0.69 US.

JAPAN

Hokkaido
Honshu
Japan Sea
Nikko
Kanazawa
Suwa
Kashiwa
Tokyo
Kyoto
Yokohama
Hiroshima
Kobe
Nara
Osaka
Fukuoka
Nagasaki
Beppu
Shikoku
Kyushu
Pacific Ocean

CONTENTS

Before The Exchange

Two roads diverged in a wood,
And I,
I took the one less travelled by,
And that has made all the difference.

Robert Frost
"The Road Not Taken"

The call came just a few days before my 16th birthday, in the middle of March from Mr. Rodger Wright, the headmaster at Trinity College School, confirming that Reitaku High School was expecting me on April 8, 1990. I could hardly believe my good luck. There were just three weeks left before I would leave for the Empire of the Rising Sun, Nippon, Zipangu (the country of gold), or simply, Japan. I would be more than a tourist, an outsider, venturing inside the *torii* gate. Enrolled at Reitaku High School for a year, I would be living with 550 students in a dormitory setting and sharing the day-to-day experiences of a teenager in Japan.

The Japanese school year begins in April and it was almost too late to make all of the arrangements. Reitaku High School had been notified in October of my interest in the exchange program. Then, we waited, and waited, and waited for a decision.

Finally, my parents expressed their concerns to Mr. Wright and he responded to them in a letter dated February 28, 1990:

> The Japanese work in mysterious ways and only now do we have the formal acknowledgement of Jonathan's participation in the programme. As you will see by the correspondence between Michio Nonaka [Chairman of the Exchange Program Committee] and me, Reitaku is willing to accept Jonathan if we say he is O.K. I have done that and I anticipate a formal acceptance any time now.

Apparently, there had been some misunderstanding about a few of the teachers' comments on my report cards, which Mr. Nonaka had scrutinized very carefully. Accepting a foreign student at an all-Japanese high school was a decision that was not going to be made lightly.

Besides, the Japanese have always worried about outside influences, although I hardly considered myself a threat.

In a letter to Mr. Wright dated February 12, 1990, the chairman of the Exchange Program Committee had written:

> We are willing to accept him at Reitaku if everything is cleared; however, we'd like to know a little more about him. We could not get a complete picture of Jonathan Buchanan from the advisor's comments. We are rather concerned about the following comments [from the teachers] and are wondering if you could please elaborate on them:
>
> "I am sure that he will not write superficial answers on the English exam again. I trust that he will take heed of what Mr. Gleeson has to say and that he will pay more attention to his math homework."
>
> Also, please could you give more information on the Housemaster's comment, "It is in the athletic and social aspects of life, here, that we like to see development, and Jon is certainly showing this."
>
> We are sorry to ask so many questions, but we want to make sure that he will fit in at Reitaku. Of course, if you think there is no problem with these comments, we will welcome Jonathan Buchanan from April this year.

Mr. Wright sent this response by fax on February 20 to Mr. Nonaka:

> Thank you for your letter and your interest in Jonathan Buchanan. It is very good of you to want this exchange to be a success in every way; and, so, I appreciate your concerns about a few cryptic comments on Jonathan's report. I assure you there is nothing to worry about. Jonathan is an exceptionally bright boy with a very dry sense of humour. His teachers are

> merely prodding him for an even higher calibre of work.
>
> Initially at TCS, Jonathan was uncommonly shy. Being awkward at sports, too, he was a bit of a loner. Now, in his 4th year at TCS, he has many friends and has found his niche in cross-country running and on skiing teams where he trains harder than anyone else. He is always helping other boys with their work and is a sought after roommate. Hence, his Housemaster's comments about the athletic and social development is merely a reflection of the great progress he has made in this area. He is an ideal candidate for this exchange.

Finally, Mr. Nonaka responded on March 12:

> Thank you so much for the letter dated February 20. I understand about Jonathan Buchanan clearly. Because of your letter, our anxiety about him is cleared. We are ready to accept him from April.

I will always be grateful to Mr. Wright for setting the record straight and to Mr. Nonaka for accepting my headmaster's word that I was a suitable candidate.

On March 23, Mr. Wright wrote to the Japanese Consulate and included the following comments in his letter of support for my visa application:

> Jonathan is ideally suited for this exchange. Besides his high standard of deportment and scholastic ability, he has a disarming sense of humour and personality which, although enigmatic, is nevertheless endearing.

I'm not sure about the "endearing" part, but I would discover soon enough that the key to survival in Japan depends on an unfailing "sense of humour" more than anything else.

Arrival in Japan

And there came,
Breaking through the mist,
Roaring through the sea,
Four black dragons,
Spitting fire.
And I ran,
Cursing through the fields,
Calling the alarm,
Shouting to the world,
"Four black dragons,
Spitting fire!"
And the earth trembled
And the sky cracked
And I thought it was the end of the world!

Stephen Sondheim
"Four Black Dragons"
Pacific Overtures

The sun, shining high up in the sky, nourishes all things (with an impartial spirit of benevolence).

The meaning of the word
Reitaku translated from the
Chinese classics.

Historically, the Japanese have always been suspicious of foreigners and their motives. The hostility toward strangers and fear of outside influences kept Japan almost completely isolated for more than two centuries.

Japan's strict isolationist policy had been decreed in 1639 by Iemitsu, the third shogun in the powerful Tokugawa family. He was concerned that Portuguese and Spanish missionaries were undermining traditional Japanese values as well as his own political power. The Portuguese had discovered Japan in 1543 when one of their ships, headed for China, was blown off course during a typhoon and shipwrecked on the southern island of Kyushu. Japanese warlords were fascinated by their muskets and soon, Portuguese ships sailed regularly to Japan with goods for trade. A Jesuit priest, Francis Xavier, who arrived in 1549, wrote to his sponsors that "the people whom we have met so far are the best who have been discovered and it seems to me that we shall never find among heathens another race to equal the Japanese."

Nevertheless, Iemitsu felt threatened by the growing number of Christian converts, particularly among the *daimyô* (feudal lords). He expelled the "barbarians," banned all Christian activities and required every Japanese family to register with a Buddhist temple. Japanese citizens were forbidden to travel outside their country and anyone who was abroad at the time was not allowed to return home. The new laws were enforced with the death penalty.

Japan remained virtually closed, except for a handful of Dutch sea merchants. The Japanese tolerated the Dutch because they were interested only in trade, supplying guns, clocks, eyeglasses, tobacco and valuable silks from China. The Dutch also provided important information about scientific and technical discoveries from the other side of the world. Despite the so-called "friendly" relations, the Dutch seamen were confined to Dejima, an island across from Nagasaki, to prevent them from mingling freely with the Japanese people. The island was connected to the mainland by a narrow causeway that was closed after dark.

Eventually, the Americans forced Japan to open its doors once again. On July 8, 1853, Admiral Matthew Perry sailed boldly into Edo Bay (modern Tokyo Bay) determined to use gunboat diplomacy, if necessary, to establish trade relations with the Japanese.

Hundreds of threatening samurai, in medieval ceremonial dress with swords drawn, lined the shore. The Marine band played "Hail Columbia" while Franklin Buchanan, captain of the warship *Susquehanna*, presented greetings from President Fillmore to the reluctant *daimyô* of Uraga.

The Japanese were hardly in a position to argue with "four black dragons spitting fire" in Edo Bay since their economy was in shambles. Unable to mount an effective defence, the bankrupt shogunate reluctantly agreed to some of the American demands. For the first time in more than 200 years, the Japanese gave in to foreign pressure. Although the imperial court and many of the *daimyô* opposed the decision, several trade treaties were signed during the next few years.

At first, the Japanese resisted the foreign intrusion as much as possible and trade relations developed very slowly between the two countries. In 1867, however, the Tokugawa shogunate was overthrown. The new political leaders abolished the feudal caste system and restored the authority of the emperor. Young Emperor Meiji eagerly embraced many Western ideas to create a modern, industrial country. In 1873, the restrictions against Christianity were also dropped and missionaries from all over the world, including Canada and the United States, began arriving in Japan to set up churches, schools and medical clinics.

Despite the foreign "invasion," the Japanese people have stubbornly kept their language, religion and culture intact. Even the Allied Occupation after World War II had little impact on their traditions or values. The complexities of the language, religion and customs continue to be a barrier between the Japanese and the rest of us. Nonetheless, one of the biggest concerns facing Japan today is the vulnerability of its young people to Western influences imported through television shows, movies and music. The slow erosion of some traditions is frightening for the older generations.

≈

The skies were clear and I stared below at the endless stretches of ice and snow of the Great White North of Canada and Alaska before we began our North Pacific crossing. We flew west from one time zone to the next, almost as fast as the earth was spinning on its axis. Fortunately, the plane was not full and I had both the aisle and window seat to myself, so I managed to stretch out comfortably during the 13-hour flight.

There were only a few Westerners on board and most of them appeared to be businessmen. In recent years, the high cost of visiting Japan has edged out the fear of eating sushi as the number one reason for tourists staying away and the language barrier ranks close behind.

I enjoyed the Japanese meals on board, especially the sushi. The elegantly prepared portions of raw fish, cucumber and rice, flavoured with sweet wine vinegar and wrapped in seaweed, were served with *soba* (buckwheat noodles) and traditional green tea. Using chopsticks, I carefully picked up each morsel of food. Japanese *hashi* are shorter than Chinese chopsticks and easier to manipulate. I was determined to learn how to handle them properly despite newspaper claims that the ability to use chopsticks properly has become a lost art, even in Japan.

For months, I had dreamed of going to Japan. After four years of boarding school, I wanted to travel and experience something different. Trinity College School had a fine reputation and attracted students from across Canada and throughout the world. But we were stuck out in the middle of nowhere. Since 1868, the school has occupied a large campus in the small, rural town of Port Hope, Ontario, about 60 miles east of Toronto. The area was great for three of my favourite activities: running, cross-country skiing and indulging in Jim's pizza. Still, I had my reservations about sticking it out for seven straight years.

Fortunately, Trinity offered exchange programs in countries all over the world, including Australia, England, France, South Africa, Switzerland and India. Each country offered exciting new opportunities but I was drawn to Japan. I wanted to experience a different culture and learn a new language. I was also curious about Japan's educational system. Why did Japanese teenagers perform consistently higher than Western teens on standardized tests? Were their schools better than ours? Were they really so different from us?

I studied the literature from Reitaku again. The school's brochure was filled with photos of smiling students participating in a number of academic, sports and social activities. Private boarding schools are rare in Japan, so spending a year at Reitaku was an unusual opportunity. Established in 1950 by the Hiroike Institute of Education, Reitaku is the oldest residential school with a solid reputation for its progressive programs and creative concepts. "Though we expect our students to aspire to high standards of academic achievement," wrote the late headmaster Sentaro Hiroike, "we place even greater emphasis on the development of individual personality and originality of character. We hope that, through your three years with us, you will discover your full potential as a young, international-minded person, and learn how to be as sociable, co-operative, sincere and creative as possible." High moral standards and values prepared Reitaku's students "to face university and the everchanging world beyond" with "happy faces and a true sense of responsibility."

I couldn't help smiling since I remembered reading something similar in a brochure for Trinity. However, I'm not sure whether or not any of my classmates would have swallowed the most important precept put forward by Dr. Hiroike, which dealt with self-denial and personal sacrifice: "Under God, govern yourselves in the spirit of self-renunciation." Even more intriguing was the bit about rules being kept to a "minimum while ensuring an orderly environment."

Like Trinity, Reitaku is a highly respectable school with excellent academic standards. Many of the students are on the elite university track with dreams of getting into Tokyo University and other prestigious schools. The staff place a strong emphasis on all aspects of school life, not just the 3 R's, "read, remember and regurgitate." Reitaku also promotes the "all-round" student by providing a wide variety of programs in sports and the arts. Both schools share time-honoured traditions that play a very important role in creating a strong sense of camaraderie among the students.

The roots of Trinity's exchange program go back more than a century. Reverend Arthur Lloyd, one of the school's first headmasters, had been a missionary in Japan and brought back a student with him to study at Trinity in 1891. But the current exchange to Japan was new, initiated by our economics teacher, Mr. Mac Campbell, who visited Reitaku High School back in 1985. However, the concept of such a program was very unusual for the Japanese and it took three years to finalize the arrangements.

And yet, the students at Trinity showed little enthusiasm for the new program. Without a doubt, the timing was awkward. The exchange began in April to coincide with the Japanese school year, which interrupted the regular academic program at Trinity. The exchange was also long, lasting a full calendar year. Most students were intimidated by the idea of spending an entire year in a country with a foreign language and culture. And the cost! Although there were no additional school fees, my parents were still responsible for airfare, travel during the holidays, medical insurance and other expenses.

Perhaps the most challenging aspect of the exchange program was the agreement between two families on opposite sides of the world to share the responsibility for a foreign student during school breaks and holidays. During my year in Japan, a Reitaku student, Kazuo Takada, would be attending Trinity as well as spending time with my family in Elliot Lake, a small mining community in Northern Ontario.

Marcus Morton was the only student from Trinity who had been to Japan so far. Although he enjoyed his year, Marcus admitted that the cultural differences and the language barrier made life very difficult at times. He also warned me that Reitaku had a lot of very restrictive rules despite what the brochure said. But I didn't give his warning a second thought. Trinity had plenty of rules and they had never been a problem for me. I was really keen on going to Reitaku and pumped him for as much information as possible.

I also read about the Japanese and their customs and traditions. I was not about to embarrass either school because of my ignorance. I even tried to teach myself a few basic expressions: *dôzo* (please), *dômo* or *arigatô* (thanks), *dômo arigatô* or *arigatô gozaimasu* (polite thanks), or *dômo arigatô gozaimasu* if you want to be very polite. I figured that other expressions, such as *gomen nasai* (I am sorry), might be useful as well.

As we crossed the International Date Line, we lost a day and I set my watch ahead to April 8. That's when reality began to set in and for the first time, I felt somewhat anxious. Would my Japanese classmates accept a *gaijin* (foreigner) in their midst? Or would they ostracize me because I was different? A year could be an awfully long time if the exchange didn't work out as well as I hoped...and prayed.

The weather was overcast as our plane finally approached the coastal waters of Japan. Suddenly, we descended through the thick clouds and I could see the whitecaps on the menacing blackish blue waves of the Pacific. Not my idea of a welcoming sight. But within minutes, we were flying low over rich green fields, golf courses, divided highways and a floral display spelling out NARITA in large block Roman letters. The area around the airport looked very similar to California and it was hard to believe that I was actually in Japan.

≈

In the terminal, a sea of Asian faces surrounded me and the language was incomprehensible. At customs, there were separate lines for residents and non-residents and I lined up with the handful of foreigners who were on my flight. The immigration officer carefully examined the hastily prepared documents stuffed in my passport, including the long letter from my headmaster, Mr. Wright, who wrote about my "enigmatic but endearing" personality. I was grateful that the immigration officer did not bother to ask any questions.

After retrieving my luggage, I found the assigned meeting place where I was greeted by Merwyn, a Brit who was teaching English at Reitaku, and Nonaka-sensei, the chairman of the Exchange Committee. (In Japan, all teachers are respectfully called *sensei,* which means master.)

Both Merwyn and Nonaka-sensei shook my hand and asked a few polite questions about my flight. I quickly mastered the customary foreigner's greeting, a half-bow, followed by extending my hand. I also found out that the Japanese prefer a loose handshake to a firm grip. They avoid physical contact as much as possible and view some of our customary greetings such as embracing and backslapping as vulgar and repulsive.

We pushed our way through the crowded airport. Outside, the air was hot and sticky, a sharp contrast to the frigid temperatures I left behind in Canada. As we piled my luggage into the trunk of Nonaka-sensei's Nissan Sentra, I noticed that all of the cars in the parking lot were either white or a light colour. In a country where people strive to be alike, it must be a nightmare finding one's car in a parking lot. Even more surprising was the fact that all of them were relatively new and spotlessly clean. There wasn't a speck of rust on any of them.

Japan has become the ultimate throwaway society where people buy five million cars each year. Frequent mandatory maintenance checks and inspection policies are expensive, not to mention the cost of repairs. So most of the used cars are loaded onto freighters and shipped to other, less prosperous countries in Asia as well as Latin and South America.

We drove past small family farms along a narrow highway that was unbelievably cluttered with billboards. Many of them were familiar, advertising McDonald's, Kentucky Fried Chicken and Denny's. I was hardly experiencing culture shock but I found driving on the left-hand side of the road very unnerving, especially with trucks hurtling toward me on what seemed to be the wrong side of the road.

My initiation into Japanese culture took place at Narita-san Shinshô-ji, a famous Buddhist temple dating back to AD 940. Despite the striking contrasts in their lives, the Japanese have managed to maintain a sense of harmony between the old and the new. Traditional rituals such as temple worship are not ignored by a society influenced by conspicuous consumption.

Narita-san is a large wooded sanctuary in the midst of the congested and chaotic sprawl of urban growth. A colourful pagoda built in 1711 dominates the carefully manicured grounds crowded with Japanese visitors and pilgrims.

We participated in ancient rituals, running our hands through the scented smoke rising from an urn to cleanse our souls and throwing coins into a bin as we made a wish. We left our shoes neatly lined up with dozens of other pairs at the entrance of each building, which housed various temple treasures along with intricate carvings of the 500 disciples of Buddha, paintings, calligraphy and a giant revolving cabinet with the sacred scrolls of the Buddhist Sutra. We joined other pilgrims seeking enlightenment from Buddha's teachings by pushing the carousel around.

At Narita-san, ancient traditions have kept pace with advances in technology. Here, Buddhist priests exorcise new cars from the powers of evil. After all, driving in Japan can be a perilous experience and many people believe that the blessings improve their odds.

Generally speaking, the Japanese are not superstitious. Just the same, buying fortunes from vending machines at temples and shrines is a popular pastime. These fortunes range from "bad luck" to "great luck." My fortune read "great luck in all of my future endeavours." I'm not very superstitious either, but I was pleased with such a good omen and slipped the paper into my wallet.

We ate lunch at a small family-owned restaurant near the temple. Most restaurants in Japan are modest establishments seating 16 or less but the food is usually very good and reasonably priced, about ¥650 ($5.25 Cdn or $4.50 US) for a complete meal. A real bargain considering there is no tipping or service charge.

Once again, we took off our shoes and placed them beside our private booth, where we sat on cushions around a low table. Shoes are always removed at traditional restaurants where floors are covered with thick straw-woven *tatami* mats.

Hot Oolong tea was brought to our table as soon as we sat down. During the summer months, iced *mugi-cha* (barley tea) is served instead. We were also given *oshibori*, hot towels for cleaning our hands and face before the meal. However, there were no napkins or serviettes on the table. Hopefully, I wasn't going to spill anything.

Service was quick and efficient as the waitress placed individual trays in front of us containing a traditional Japanese lunch. The main course, *karê-raisu* (curried rice), was lamb in a rich brown, rather than a yellow, curried sauce, served on a bed of rice. Each tray also contained a small bowl of soup and several dishes with condiments, including sliced ginger, shreds of hot pepper and *daikon* (a delicious white radish). We began with the soup, picking out the vegetables with our chopsticks and then, drinking the broth straight out of the bowl.

The food was delicious but I was relieved when the meal was over. For some time, I had been trying to ignore the sharp burning pain running up and down my legs. Throughout the meal, I attempted, without much success, to find a comfortable position. Sitting cross-legged was awkward but stretching out my legs under the low table didn't work either. Neither Nonaka-sensei nor Merwyn seemed to experience the same discomfort. Was it because they were much shorter than me? Or maybe I just needed more practice?

On our way back to the car, we stopped at a public washroom, politely called *otearai* (honourable hand-wash) by women, a *benjo* (excretion place) by men, or simply *toire* (toilet). Public washrooms are very common in Japan, and can be either spotlessly clean or grungy. As I headed toward one of the stalls, Merwyn called through the open doorway to tell me that I was in the women's section and pointed out the urinals as well as another set of stalls on the other side of the large open room.

"Oops!"

Luckily, I was alone in the *benjo*. I didn't need to suffer the embarrassment of meeting up with a woman in a public washroom. Needless to say, I wasn't prepared for the concept of a unisex washroom, even though Merwyn assured me that Japanese women don't pay attention to the men standing at the urinals. Really?

As we drove back to the school, the clouds lifted and soon, the sun was shining on the collection of farms and houses along the highway. But this was not a time for a pleasant drive in the country.

Generally speaking, the Japanese are very aggressive drivers and Nonaka-sensei was no exception. He used a network of narrow service roads to avoid the congestion on the highway beside us. As soon as the flow of traffic improved, he pulled onto the highway. Within minutes, however, we were caught in the middle of a traffic jam. Nonaka-sensei slammed on his brakes but the reflexes of the driver behind us were not quick enough to avoid a rear-end collision. Both Nonaka-sensei and the other driver pulled over to the gravel shoulder to examine the damage, a minor fender bender. They bowed politely, exchanged business cards and quietly discussed the incident for about five minutes. Then they bowed again and we proceeded on our way to Reitaku. Regardless of the severity of most accidents, disputes rarely end up in court.

≈

Kashiwa is a community of 300,000 residents, less than an hour by commuter train from Tokyo. The outskirts of the town were similar to the suburbs of our large cities with plenty of trees (*Kashiwa* means "oak leaf") and open green spaces. We passed many comfortable homes, which were an interesting combination of Japanese and European styles. But the houses were small and some of them had a tiny garden with neatly raked pebbles, a few plants and dwarf trees. Otherwise, the space in front of most homes was sacrificed for a parking area since there were no garages or carports. In Japan, you cannot purchase a car unless you have a private parking space.

Like Trinity with its large campus, well isolated from the rest of the community, the Hiroike Institute of Education occupies 110 acres of prime suburban land. Except for a high chain-link fence surrounding the property, the grounds resembled a tourist resort. The winding streets of the campus were lined with cherry trees that had been in full bloom a week earlier. But all traces of the delicate pink blossoms had vanished. There were a number of buildings on the spacious grounds as well as an outdoor swimming pool and a nine-hole golf course. A luxurious hotel catered to visiting parents and people who attended the conferences at the Institute of Moralogy, which was founded in 1926 by Dr. Chikuro Hiroike.

The professor was a highly successful educator and philosopher who created a new moral science, called Moralogy, which is not to be confused with a religious cult. Hiroike believed that true happiness can be achieved by applying high moral standards to one's daily life, regardless of personal religious beliefs. After Dr. Hiroike's death in 1938, his son, Chibusa, established Moralogy centres across Japan, in Brazil and the United States. He also built Reitaku High School and Reitaku University "to develop and nurture the best in young Japanese men and women." Today, Mototaka Hiroike, the great-grandson of the founder of Moralogy, is president of Hiroike Institute.

Trinity, on the other hand, is affiliated with the Anglican Church and the school's devout traditions have continued over the years, even though the students come from a variety of ethnic backgrounds with diverse religious beliefs.

≈

The boys' residence was an unimpressive concrete structure housing 300 students as well as a small housekeeping staff. At a respectable distance from the boys' dormitory building, approximately 250 girls lived in three separate residences. Another chain-link fence surrounded the girl's compound.

Merwyn took me on a tour of the boys' residence. We left our shoes in the foyer where everyone had a designated spot to park their outdoor footwear. Each of the nine dormitories was separated into five units and each unit contained a living area and a study room. The cramped dorms were promoted as a place "where students begin to understand the co-operation and respect for others and thus begin to build a strong set of values, which will support them for the rest of their lives."

The main room was painted stark white, with a large bay window overlooking the school grounds. The floor was covered in *tatami* mats but the spacious room was practically bare except for a few shelves along the wall and a low table. A maze of mobiles for drying laundry hung from the ceiling. Futons and personal belongings were stored in closets, which lined the length of the opposite wall. I couldn't believe the emptiness of the room, considering that five or six students shared the space.

A sliding door separated the living quarters from the study area. Drab grey steel dividers extended from the floor to ceiling, separating the claustrophobic study cubicles, which contained a steel desk, a steel bookcase and a reclining steel chair. A frayed curtain could be drawn across for privacy. Posters of rock stars, sports heroes and even some scantily clad women broke up the monotony of the steel grey furnishings. At the end of the room, sunlight brightened up the dreariness of the cubicles belonging to the third-year students who were entitled to the choice spots beside the windows.

At Trinity, two students from the same grade were assigned to each room, which was usually crammed with a stereo, computers, a small fridge and sometimes, a couch. The walls, even some of the ceilings, were plastered with posters, again of rock stars, sports heroes and attractive women in skimpy bathing suits or very tight dresses, as long as they were not "sexually suggestive beyond any standard normally apparent in everyday Canadian life." We certainly had a broad interpretation of Canadian standards. The softer side of the jocks at Trinity was reflected by the number of stuffed animals in the dorms, won at the annual midway in Port Hope. Although we were expected to keep our rooms neat, dirty laundry had a tendency to pile up in the corners and personal belongings were often strewn about. Occasionally, there were room checks and we made an effort to clean up. But most of the time, our sloppy habits prevailed.

In Japan, the *ofuro* (bathing room) and *toire* (toilet room) are usually separate. Before entering the *toire,* we put on the plastic slippers that were lined up outside the door. Separate slippers are always reserved for the toilet room in homes and buildings where you are required to take your shoes off at the entrance. Even house slippers must be replaced with the proper footwear for the *toire*.

A single Western-style toilet had also been installed in the *toire* of each dormitory. Instructions in Japanese were still posted on the seat cover. "Sit down on the seat, facing away from the flush handle, excrete and flush." Many Japanese still believe that the squat-style toilet, which is nothing more than a porcelain basin sunk in the floor or on a raised platform, is more hygienic than a Western-style toilet because there is no contact between the body and the toilet seat. There was no graffiti to be seen anywhere but I was intrigued by the photocopy of a map of the world taped to the wall of one of the stalls so that precious moments would not be lost while studying for a test.

The new Western-style toilets were certainly popular, but comfort was not the only reason for their appeal. The unmistakable smell of stale cigarette smoke hung in the air. Standing on the toilet lid had become a convenient way to sneak a smoke since students could keep watch over the stall door in case the dormitory leader walked in. I have seen as many as four smokers crowd into the stall at the same time, puffing away on their cigarettes. Of course, smoking is absolutely prohibited in all schools in Japan and Reitaku is no exception. And yet, none of the students seemed to care if someone was breaking the rules. Smoking was very common among the male students.

In a room adjacent to the *toire*, a long trough was set up along the wall with cold water taps and liquid soap dispensers for washing our hands. There were also small, computerized washing machines, which were free of charge for the students, but no dryers. Instead, we hung our wet clothes to dry from mobiles hanging from the ceiling of our rooms. During *tsuyu* (the rainy season), the air was always sticky and everything took forever to dry. I don't have any fond memories of limp laundry hanging from the racks. Some of the boys avoided doing laundry as much as possible and sent their shirts to the dry cleaners.

Trinity had a laundry service on the school premises where we dropped off our dirty clothes once a week, and picked everything up two days later, neatly folded. However, socks and school sweatsuits mysteriously disappeared with regular frequency.

In the *ofuro* downstairs, Merwyn explained the bathing ritual. The *ofuro* was a very large tiled room containing a hot tub the size of a small swimming pool and a smaller cold tub. Piles of small stools and basins were stacked in the corner. The walls were lined with mirrors as well as individual faucets and showerheads for washing. Another row of faucets had been placed in the middle of the room. The Japanese are fanatics about cleanliness and everyone follows the ancient dictates of Shintoism, prescribing daily bathing and purification. They scrub themselves clean and carefully rinse off all traces of lather before enjoying a soak in the tub, hot enough to cook a lobster.

At Trinity, the bathrooms were considerably less interesting. Each washroom in the residences contained several toilets, a couple of showers and a bathtub.

Smoking in the washrooms was rare because the rest of us refused to put up with it. Graffiti was a more serious problem. Whenever such desecration of our living space occurred, we brought up the issue at our house meetings and offenders were ordered to get rid of the offensive drawings. Graffiti was also a problem in the washrooms of the classroom blocks. Inside some of the stalls, lewd doodles included the acknowledgements of the "great tits" of one of our favourite female teachers.

At the Reitaku dormitory office, Merwyn introduced me to Kitasaka-san, the housemother, who was a nurse in her early fifties, and the four staff members who served as house and groundskeepers, chauffeurs and counsellors. None of them spoke any English but they reassured me with their smiles that I could count on their assistance at any time. The dorm office also served as a student affairs centre, bank, travel agency, living room and infirmary.

On one of the tables, there were several Japanese comic books called *manga*, full of highly detailed black and white drawings on coloured paper. Some of them were as thick as a Sears catalogue. Comics are extremely popular in a country that probably has the highest literacy rate in the world. Businessmen read them on the commuter trains and politicians have been photographed with a *manga* placed discreetly on their knee during a dull debate in the Diet, which is the Japanese parliament.

There is an enormous selection for all ages and interests, including adventure, romance, office dramas and pornography, even the lurid *ero-guro* (erotic and grotesque) variety. Some of the popular themes are extremely bizarre, providing a cheap thrill. And yet, Japan has one of the lowest crime rates in the world.

Comic caricatures have been discovered on the walls of early Buddhist temples and in the Shôsô-in, an eighth century treasure house in Nara. In the 17th century, *manga* became an important means of educating the people about Buddhism. Today, major companies use comics as a public relations tool; others use the *manga* format to explain technical data to their workforce. *Manga* is big business with annual sales exceeding US $2 billion and all of the top cartoon artists are multi-millionaires.

While at Reitaku, I discovered that not all students pursue a formidable homework schedule. Many of the first-year students spent much of their study hour reading comic books in the privacy of their cubicles. Students at Trinity also read cartoons during their spare time, but there was no comparison between a slim volume, even a Treasury, of *The Far Side* by Gary Larson, and the thick *manga* devoured by Japanese teens.

Along with the *manga* and a few magazines on the table in the dorm office, there was also a copy of *Sankei Shimbun*, one of the many national newspapers. The Japanese are obsessed with world events and the front page was always filled with colour photographs and news stories from all over the globe. Japanese newspapers are smaller than ours because they do not carry classified ads, comics and editorial features. However, even the national editions carry full pages of TV listings.

While we were still in the office, Randall walked in. He had graduated from Trinity the previous year and had taken some classes at Reitaku High School during the past two terms before enrolling in the Japanese language course at Reitaku University. Although I had met Randall at Trinity, I would never have recognized him with his shoulder-length hair. Long hair was quite fashionable with foreign students in Japan, especially if they had limited finances. A man's haircut cost ¥3000, much more than at home. Randall was not on a tight budget, but he liked to be fashionable just the same.

≈

On our way to dinner in the school cafeteria, first-year students were shouting a chorus of "*Chiwa! Chiwa! Chiwa!*" almost loud enough to make our ears bleed. In Japanese society, the recognition of rank is very important at all times. Even at school, students were expected to properly greet each and every one of their superiors, including senior students. The result was a very loud blend of greetings which became rather annoying after a while. I didn't realize that the students were being rude with their abbreviation of "*Konnichiwa!*" until assembly that evening when they were reminded that only the correct greeting was acceptable.

Instead of saying "Hello," the Japanese refer to the time of day. Before 9:30 a.m. or so, "*Ohayô gozaimasu*" (it is early) is the proper greeting. "*Konnichiwa*" (this day) is used between 9:30 a.m. and 5:30 p.m., followed by "*Kombanwa*" (this evening).

The cafeteria at Reitaku was similar to lunch areas in most Western high schools with long tables set in an orderly fashion, but the tables were very narrow in comparison, creating a more congested and noisier atmosphere. A display case in the foyer contained the different meal choices from each of the A, B and C counters. For dinner, I chose a noodle dish which looked quite appetizing. The flavours were strange, but the meal was pretty good.

I never ceased to be amazed by the tremendous variety of unusual foods served in the cafeteria. Even after I had been in Japan for a while, I was not always sure what was on the plate in front of me. It would have been impolite to ask, especially when dining as a guest in a private home or restaurant. In any case, the portions at school were small and I was usually famished. As long as the food was edible, I ate it. Randall also liked exotic food and agreed with me that the meals at Reitaku were an improvement over Trinity, although both of us would have appreciated much larger portions. Not surprisingly, the meals at both Reitaku and Trinity improved considerably when our parents were visiting the school.

Sashimi, thinly sliced raw fish, served with *shôyu* (soy sauce) and *wasabi* (a pungent green horseradish), which were mixed together, was always popular. Octopus with sliced cucumber was also very tasty and often served as a side dish. *Kombu* or *nore* (seaweed), harvested in the waters off Chile and the northernmost island of Hokkaido, was a common ingredient in soups and sushi. Occasionally, we were served so-called Western dishes, such as spaghetti with seaweed and herring roe. I doubt that many of my friends at Trinity would have lined up for fish eggs. To tell you the truth, they were not fond of fish, period. But grilled *unagi* (eel) was my favourite. Unfortunately, like all delicacies, it wasn't served often enough.

Fish and soybeans are the main source of protein in the Japanese diet. Throughout most of their history, the Japanese did not eat meat because Buddhist priests were opposed to raising animals for food. Beef, pork and chicken were eventually introduced in the late 19th century when Japan began to adopt Western ways. A vegetarian diet is not very practical in Japan since most dishes include fish or meat as one of the ingredients. And it is almost impossible to order a specially prepared meal in Japanese restaurants.

Rice is sacred and the Japanese are generally not satisfied unless they have had at least one bowl of the sticky, short-grain *gohan* each day. In fact, the meaning of *gohan* is meal. Although rice can get pretty boring when it is served three times a day, I was usually too hungry to pass it up.

Not everything served in the cafeteria was edible. The dark red *umeboshi* (pickled plums) were absolutely revolting. *Umeboshi* are salty and sour in flavour and are usually served with large quantities of rice. The Japanese have been eating them faithfully for centuries, especially at breakfast, believing that the pickled plums will keep them healthy.

Other exotic and unusual items were readily available at local convenience stores. *Calpis* definitely has to be tried before passing judgement. Forget the name and the fact that is made from milk fermented with sugar. It just tastes great. *Pocari Sweat* is a popular sports drink, even though it doesn't sound very appealing. And *Creap* (from "cream powder") is the name of a coffee whitener. The name says it all.

At Trinity, we were served some pretty revolting selections as well. I was never even tempted to try *bologna à la chef*, a rather hideous concoction of bologna slices and processed cheese, dipped in egg, breaded and deep fried. If the food wasn't edible, we filled up at the salad bar. Desserts were usually okay, even though the lemon snow had the aroma of dishwashing detergent and the texture of petroleum jelly.

Dezâto (dessert) is not a typical part of a Japanese meal, except at Western-style restaurants and Reitaku. We were usually served either a piece of cake, well-wrapped in clear plastic, fruit (always peeled and sliced), an ice cream bar (at lunch) or coffee jelly (at dinner). Sometimes, we were served *yôkan*, a cube of sweet soybean paste, which was a special treat.

Before every meal, we bowed our heads and put our hands together to say, "*Itadakimasu*" (I humbly receive). After finishing our meal, we bowed our heads once again, saying "*Gochisô sama deshita*" (That was a real feast).

≈

Evening assembly was held promptly at 7:10 p.m. in the *tatami* meeting room of each dormitory. We were expected to show up in our school uniform and changing back into dress shirts and grey flannels was a real hassle. During assembly, we sat with our legs tucked underneath our bodies in a kneeling position, in well-disciplined, perfectly straight rows like the samurai warriors listening to orders from their warlords. The first-year students sat in the first row, the second-year students in the second row and the third-year students in the back.

Nonaka-sensei introduced me to the 30 students in my dormitory who politely applauded. Still, I felt out of place, a stranger in a strange land. Japan is a homogeneous society with one people, one language and one culture. I was an outsider, and yet, by special invitation, part of a very distinct group.

Takahashi-san, a third-year student who was the dormitory leader, read the announcements placed on a low table in front of him. I was kneeling behind Itoh-sensei, the staff advisor for the dormitory, who gave a short inspirational talk using the word "*gambatte*" several times which means "persevere and do your best." *Gambatte* is probably one of the most frequently used words in the Japanese language and the key slogan at all schools.

Following Itoh-sensei's pep talk, one of the first-year students read from a 31-day perpetual Moralogy calendar. The messages were similar to the golden rule philosophy of Christianity, urging us to act in the interests of others rather then ourselves. Assembly ended after we sang one of the school's many songs. Everyone was grateful for short assemblies because the *seiza* position was extremely uncomfortable, even painful, as the circulation of blood to the legs was completely cut-off after a few minutes.

Before I was allowed to escape to my room and crash for the night, Merwyn handed me an introduction in Japanese to memorize and recite in front of the entire student body the following day at morning assembly.

"You have to be kidding," I wearily complained, exhausted from the lack of sleep. But Merwyn ignored my protests and carefully explained how to pronounce each word. We rehearsed the speech a few times before he finally let me go to bed.

Nonaka-sensei had arranged for me to have a room of my own during the first term. These private rooms were usually reserved for foreign teachers, housekeeping staff and the teacher on duty. Although the room was small, I was grateful for the luxury of a real bed, a couch, a cabinet, a desk and a chair. But most of all, I appreciated the privacy. The walls were bare except for a map of Tokyo in English and a map of the world in Japanese. Unlike our maps with the Atlantic Ocean in the middle and Japan located on the outer reaches, Japanese maps have the

Pacific Ocean in the middle, putting Japan in a much more prominent position, practically in the centre of the universe.

The Rising Sun

Do all things without murmuring or disputings.

Philippians 2:14

Halfway up we passed under the archway of a stone *torii.* Years ago I read a story about a gate between the past and the future: from one direction, the traveller enters the past, from the other direction, the future.

Peregrine Hodson
A Circle Round the Sun

According to ancient myths, a giant catfish lies dozing under Japan. Every now and then, it stirs, sending rumblings throughout the land. Japan is a chain of volcanic islands with numerous fault lines in the earth's crust running throughout the country. More than 1,500 earthquakes occur each year. The majority of them are just tremors, resulting in little or no damage. Tokyo itself sits on a major fault line, and on September 1, 1923, the Great Kanto Earthquake killed more than 100,000 people. Although modern buildings and expressways are designed to withstand heavy tremors, the fear of another major earthquake in the Tokyo area is very real. Familiarity with earthquakes has not made people less fearful since each small tremor means that they are closer to the next big one. Tokyo has been experiencing major earthquakes every 60 years and another one is long overdue. Even minor rumblings can be scary while lying in bed at night, listening to the windows rattle.

≈

I was woken up in the middle of the night by students running around in the corridors, making a lot of noise and banging on my door. One of them was peering through the frosted glass window, presumably checking up on me. But I couldn't understand what they were shouting about and I was too tired to get up. Soon enough, the noise settled down and I went back to sleep.

The next morning, I woke up from a deep sleep. At first, I thought I was still dreaming -- I couldn't believe I was actually in Japan. I was also suffering from jet lag and had trouble orienting myself to the time of day. Sunlight filtered through the thin curtains of my room but when I looked at my watch, it was only 5:30 a.m. Shifting gears was not going to be easy. Adjusting my internal clock was one thing but adapting to Japanese ways was going to take some time.

Later, I learned that a minor earthquake had caused all of the raucous in the hallway. No wonder everyone was shaken up. It was just as well that I slept through the tremors, at least on my first night.

I checked my watch again. I still had an hour to memorize the short message I was supposed to give in Japanese. But I had never been any good at public speaking and I wasn't sure how I was going to remember the strange words in front of the students and teachers. If there was ever an anxious moment while I was in Japan, this was it.

The first morning bell rang promptly at 6:30 a.m. All students took their turn ringing the bell when their room was responsible for bell duty. Sometimes, they got carried away and it was pretty annoying listening to the clanging bell over and over again. If it was raining, we ignored the bell, slept until 7:00 a.m., and then headed directly to the dining hall for breakfast.

At 6:40 a.m., the bell rang again. It was time to move and I met the rest of my dormitory in front of the residence. Nobody bothered to change. Needless to say, we were a pretty dishevelled bunch of slobs still dressed in the same T-shirt and sweat pants we slept in.

A member of each of the nine dormitories carried a colourful flag with his dormitory number on it, either in Chinese or Arabic numerals. We quickly arranged ourselves behind the flag-bearer in specific formation according to our rank, starting with the first-year students. When the 6:50 a.m. bell rang, we jogged in orderly fashion with the other boys' dormitories to the large open grounds in front of the Moralogy lecture building. Along the way, the flag-bearer shouted "*Haito!*" (a Japanization of "Fight!") and the first-year students echoed him.

By the time we arrived at the grounds, the girls were already there in their organized groups, neatly dressed in their green and white phys ed uniforms. The Japanese have a thing about being "number one." Beating us to the assembly grounds was one of many subtle examples of the behaviour demonstrated by girls who were no longer content to play the traditional secondary role in Japanese society.

As soon as we were assembled on the grounds, the martial music blared over the speaker system along with instructions for calisthenics. I tried my best to keep up with the actions of the boys in front of me, as they stretched every conceivable muscle in their bodies, bouncing up and down, swaying from side to side and around and around. Everyone, though, was a bit out of synch so early in the morning.

After five minutes of exercises, we sang the national anthem while two students raised the Japanese flag. Following the anthem, we bowed in the direction of the Rising Sun and greeted it, saying, "*Ohayô gozaimasu.*" (Good morning.) Next, we bowed toward our hometown, repeating, "*Ohayô gozaimasu*" in a time-honoured tradition of paying homage to our ancestral roots. Then, we crowded close together so we could hear the announcements and a short inspirational talk from a senior member of the faculty.

When all of the formalities were over, Nonaka-sensei asked me to come forward and introduce myself to the students and teachers. I stared across the sea of curious faces watching me and immediately forgot the message I had so carefully memorized. I was still in a daze but I was also awake enough to feel awfully silly with everyone waiting for me to say something.

Nonaka-sensei came to the rescue and whispered the words in my ear. Somehow, I managed to repeat them, saying the following in Japanese: "Good morning. My name is Jonathan Buchanan, but you can call me 'Jon.' I am an exchange student from Trinity College School in Canada and I will be here for one year. I am pleased to meet you."

At some point during my short speech, the students started to laugh. I didn't blame them since my pronunciation must have been dreadful. At least they had a sense of humour. Another good omen. As soon as the ordeal was over, we left the grounds within our well-organized groups and jogged to the cafeteria where breakfast was served.

Morning assembly is also a common practice with Japanese businesses to motivate their employees. At the beginning of each day, everyone gets together in factories and offices, exchanges greetings and listens to a pep talk and the day's agenda from one of the senior managers.

At Trinity, our mornings began with chapel service after breakfast, even though many of the students did not belong to the Anglican Church. Still, everyone was expected to show up in proper classroom dress, which meant trousers, shirt, tie and jacket. We sang traditional hymns, recited prayers and listened to a short "inspirational" sermon by the chaplain, which was followed by announcements. Our headmaster, Mr. Wright, also took this opportunity to lecture us if a major incident had occurred at the school, such as drug or alcohol use.

Many Canadian public schools still carry a moral or religious message over the public address system, followed by the national anthem and school announcements first thing in the morning. Otherwise, every effort has been made to eliminate religious teachings from the curriculum, with the exception of parochial schools. American students cite the Pledge of Allegiance, sometimes followed by inspirational lines of their school pledge, such as: "I know I'm capable of success. I can learn and I can achieve. It's in myself I must believe."

At Reitaku, we always ate breakfast with our dormitory groups at designated tables. I was surprised by such a relaxed dress code in the dining hall. But I was even more startled by the Western breakfast in front of me. I objected as soon as I saw another student raise a bowl of miso soup to his lips, but it was no use. At the beginning of each month, students sign up for the Japanese or Western breakfast and most of them chose the latter. The staff assumed that I would want the same and automatically signed me up as well. I was disappointed when I learned that I would have to wait until the beginning of the next month for Japanese fare. I also found it hard to believe that there was no flexibility in the system to change the choice of menu during the month. But this was Japan. Rules were not made to be broken. Obviously, there were not going to be any special concessions for a *gaijin* in the cafeteria. It was a lesson that I would learn over and over again.

A typical Japanese breakfast began with miso soup, made from fermented soybean paste with seaweed and was actually quite good. Honest. Miso soup has been the central dish in the Japanese breakfast menu for centuries because it is rich in protein. Rice was also served, either with seafood or seaweed seasoning on the side. Specials included an egg dish if we were lucky but it was always served on a bed of finely shredded raw cabbage. Yecch! Another popular special was *nattô*, a beige-coloured, sticky paste of partially fermented soybeans, which was not very appetizing to look at, smell or taste, especially first thing in the morning. "Gross" is probably an understatement. Most of the people who lived in the warmer, southern regions of Japan sympathized with my dislike for *nattô*, while some northerners and even foreign students were extremely fond of it.

For almost a month, I suffered with the Western breakfast. The daily special was also served on a bed of raw cabbage. Instead of rice and miso soup, our trays contained white bread with processed cheese, margarine or hazelnut spread and milk. Corn flakes were also served every other day.

Both breakfasts were eaten mainly with chopsticks. The students tackled fried eggs with remarkable dexterity. Great skill was required to master this bizarre feat and I never managed to develop the same proficiency as my dorm mates. We also used chopsticks to pick out morsels of food from the miso soup before drinking the broth from the bowl. There was no need to worry about slurping since it was considered polite and a sign of appreciation by the Japanese.

And of course, there was all the tea we could drink. However, the tea served in the cafeteria was a sad imitation of the delicious traditional green tea. And I soon discovered why. One evening, I was responsible for setting the teapots on each table. As I grabbed a couple of tea bags out of a box, one of the students told me that we were supposed to recycle, pointing to a bin full of soggy old tea bags collected earlier that day.

"Recycle?"

Muttering a few choice obscene remarks under my breath, I dutifully put back the fresh bags and picked up the soggy seconds. How could they do this to me? Serving tea was such a sacred ritual in Japan. As far as I was concerned, recycling tea bags was taking the "Waste not, want not" principle a bit too far. No wonder the tea at Reitaku was awful.

Regardless of which breakfast the students chose, they always devoured the food with incredible speed. When we were studying for exams, there was no time to lose and the food disappeared even faster from the plates. I learned to eat quickly so the others would not have to wait for me.

Breakfast was my first opportunity to get to know some of the other boys in my dormitory, including Takebe-san, my dorm leader. Naturally, he was sizing me up by asking a number of personal questions. Although his pronunciation of English was poor, it was certainly comprehensible.

"What sports do you play?"

"Running and cross-country skiing."

"What are your hobbies?"

"Music and travel."

"Are you a virgin?"

"Uh?"

Did they assume that all Western teenagers were promiscuous? I smiled and exaggerated my romantic escapades with various girls. Why should I disappoint them? But my dorm mates caught on soon enough and realized that I was joking.

After finishing our meal, we took our trays to the disposal area and separated the dishes and debris into various bins. A large bilingual sign was posted on the wall, depicting a crying cartoon figure saying, "Please don't make us cry. Separate the waste." Glass milk bottles were placed in crates; disposable chopsticks, paper and plastic were thrown into one large pail; tin foil into another; and cutlery into a special container. Any leftover food was dumped into a trough and the dishes were placed in a vat full of dishwater. But there was very little waste since most of the students ate everything on their tray.

For centuries, the frugal lifestyle of the Japanese dominated their eating habits. Farmers tried to grow as much food as possible on their small rural plots but there were always shortages in the tiny mountainous country populated by millions of people. No one could afford to waste food. Even the samurai were expected to leave their bowls and plates clean. Despite the prosperity of recent years and an abundance of imported food from all over the world, the Japanese still consider a plate with unfinished food unsightly. In our society, it is quite acceptable, even polite, to leave some food on a plate.

At Trinity, attendance at breakfast was compulsory, except for senior students. Proper attire for everyone in the dining hall was classroom dress and the only exceptions were sports teams leaving for a meet before chapel.

The breakfast menu varied considerably from day to day, and choices included scrambled, fried or hard-boiled eggs; ham or sausage; and pancakes, French toast or waffles. Toast and cereal were available daily. There was plenty to choose from, even though the choice was essentially between grease and sugar. Some of the guys piled the food onto their plates as if breakfast was the only meal of the day. More often than not, there wasn't much left for the students who slept in and arrived at the last minute.

When we were finished eating, we just left our trays at the kitchen counter and the staff cleaned up after us. The amount of waste food left on the plates was scandalous. In chapel one day, we were informed that approximately $400 worth of food was being thrown out every day, enough to feed another 80 students at our school. The dining hall steward appealed to the students to change their wasteful ways but his request fell on deaf ears.

≈

When breakfast was over at Reitaku, we returned to our dormitories as a group. We had less than an hour before classes began at 8:10 a.m. This short break was one of few opportunities in the day when we actually had a few minutes to ourselves. Some of the students listened to music, either Japanese pop or Western heavy metal blaring out of their fancy double-cassette CD players. Others read the newspaper to check out baseball statistics for their favourite teams. And a few even studied before getting dressed for classes. I liked to listen to a Top 40 radio station, J-WAVE, which had programs in English and French as well as Japanese.

I was always amazed by the amount of time some of the boys spent in front of the mirror combing their *torendi na* (trendy) hairstyles. Twenty minutes was not unusual for this ritual. The heady scent of cologne also permeated through the room. When I was at Reitaku, deodorant was not readily available in Japan. As a rule, the Japanese believed that they did not sweat as much as Westerners who ate more meat. I'm not so sure. Just the same, my dorm mates didn't hesitate to tell me that they hated the smell of my deodorant. Even my Irish Spring soap was *kusé*, which simply means "it reeks." Just before I ran out of my supply of deodorant, my room leader came to the rescue with a Bravas Hair Stick. Presumably, the spicy floral scent was more to his liking. Later, I discovered that I could replenish my Mennen Speed Stick thanks to a friend who had connections at the local American army base just outside of Tokyo.

When the 8:05 a.m. bell rang, everyone rushed downstairs in full uniform. The Japanese are punctual to the nanosecond. At Reitaku, schedules were strictly adhered to by everyone except for a few of the first-year students and myself. But we learned our lesson soon enough when we discovered that all of the doors to the classroom building were locked promptly at 8:10 a.m., except for the main entrance. Instead of sneaking through the back door, late students were forced to suffer the humiliation of entering through the front door, past the staff and teachers walking through the area.

While I was in Japan, a 15-year-old girl was killed by a heavy steel gate at another private school when she tried to squeeze through at the last minute as it was closing. The tragic story was reported by the press around the world as an example of some of the inhumane practices of the Japanese educational system. At Reitaku, many of us were shocked by the incident. Although our rules were very strict by North American standards, they were quite lenient when compared to other schools in Japan.

Nearly all Japanese students wear uniforms, regardless of whether they attend public or private junior high and senior high schools. Some of the more progressive private schools in the country, such as Reitaku, have introduced uniforms similar to those of Western private schools. We wore dark blue blazers, white shirts and a school tie along with grey flannel trousers for boys and grey, below-the-knee length skirts for girls. The school's crest was a large gothic "R" stitched onto the pocket of the blazer. First-year students also wore a plastic nametag with a red bar for easy identification. Prior to 1986, the boys' uniform at Reitaku resembled 19th century German military attire with tight fitting black jackets buttoned up to the neck. Girls wore a uniform similar to the formal dress of the British Naval Academy.

Our dress code at Reitaku was strict. Only the clothing issued by the school was acceptable and substitutions were not permitted. Shoes and socks were the only exceptions to the rule since they were not issued by the school. As a result, some daring soul took advantage of the situation and started a new trend by showing up with socks with fancy patterns. I wondered if there was an intention to shock the teachers or if it was an attempt to impress the girls. In any case, it was a welcome break from the regimentation. Most styles of shoes were acceptable except running shoes, and even these were occasionally seen on the feet of teachers and students in uniform. However, we did not wear shoes in the classroom building with its bright blue carpeted floors. Instead, we left our shoes in small cubbyholes in the foyer. Unlike the dormitory, where we usually walked around in stocking feet, slippers (with our names printed on masking tape) were mandatory in the classroom building. First-year students wore brown slippers, second-year students wore green slippers and third-year students wore blue slippers. The colour coding provided an easy way to identify the status of each student. Even guests were expected to don a heavily padded pair of red slippers when they were visiting the school.

For most of the year, I walked around in my socks because the school couldn't find a spare pair of slippers in size 10. I was reprimanded by some of the teachers a number of times until someone finally searched through a box of old slippers and found the right size. By then, I had worn out several pairs of socks. As soon as holes developed, the socks were pitched. While I was in Japan, I never saw anyone walk around with holes in his or her socks.

The dress code was even stricter at many of the Japanese public and private schools. Students were also expected to have the proper hair length: marine cut for boys and short hair for girls. Long hair for both sexes was discouraged at Reitaku but a few students dared to stand out by having longer hair than the accepted norm. Curled, permed or dyed hair was out of the question. Make-up and jewelry were not acceptable either.

We were also supposed to be in uniform whenever we were off the school property, even if we were just riding a bike in Kashiwa or going to Tokyo for the day. Once I saw a Reitaku student change from his school uniform to casual clothes in the washroom of the local train station before going on a movie date in Tokyo. I presume it was common practice. We were also expected to be in proper dress when attending a baseball game if Reitaku was in the championships. At least Reitaku had a decent uniform compared to some of the other schools and I wasn't embarrassed to be seen in it.

Many private and parochial schools in North America have uniforms, but the way students wear them seems to defeat the purpose of a dress code. The crumpled and dishevelled look prevails for boys while girls often have shirttails hanging out and skirts hiked well above their knees. While I was at Reitaku, such abuse of the dress code didn't exist. Today, it is not uncommon to see boy's shirttails hanging over their pants and girl's skirts shortened above the knee.

At Trinity, our formal "Sunday" dress, which was worn on special occasions, consisted of a navy blazer with a school crest sewn on the pocket, white shirt, school tie, grey flannels and black shoes. Since our uniforms were not issued by the school, students wore a wide variety of shades of grey flannels. Even the blazers were cut in different styles. We also had a clothing exchange where we could purchase used blazers and trousers. Such a thought would shock some Japanese since they have an aversion to buying secondhand goods, except for CDs.

We were free to wear any combination of sports jacket, pants, shirt and tie to class, with the exception of clothing made from plaid or denim material. Long hair was tolerated and a few of the male students showed up at graduation wearing a ponytail. But we were expected to be clean-shaven and generally neat about our appearance. Earrings were common, but the boys were not allowed to wear them either with "classroom" or "Sunday" dress. So many of them covered up the offending earring with a Band-Aid!

During my first week at Reitaku, I was measured for the school uniform and issued a blazer, several white shirts, both long and short-sleeved, along with winter and summer-weight grey flannels. The pants were a little too big for me. Presumably, the tailor assumed that I was still growing and wanted to make sure that the clothes would last throughout the year. At least I didn't look like a few of the first-year students, who resembled clowns with their baggy duds.

≈

I was amused when Nonaka-sensei informed me that I would be "hanging out" in the English office when I was not in class. I suppose he wanted to make sure that someone was keeping an eye on me at all times. High school students were not allowed in the residence during the school day and my language classes at Reitaku University were not scheduled to begin until the following week.

For a temporary prison, the English office was pleasant enough. The large area set aside for the 11 English teachers was a good indication of their status at the school. The office was well-equipped, with an air conditioner (a real luxury during the hot and humid summer months), refrigerator, coffee maker, computer, word processor, an electric typewriter, a well-stocked library, a television and a VCR. There was even a couch for Merwyn and another teacher, Mita-sensei, who both liked to catch some Z's in between classes. Fresh-brewed coffee and green tea were available every morning. If only I could have added a closet and lived there!

I glanced through the English-language paper, titled the *Mainichi Daily News* (literal translation: *The Everyday Daily News*). Although I wished the paper had a decent comic section, I was impressed with the in-depth reporting of Canadian news along with everything else that was happening around the world. The sports pages reported that the Toronto Maple Leafs were losing to the St. Louis

Blues in the first round of the Stanley Cup playoffs. I wasn't thrilled by the loss but at least we made the playoffs. The sports section even carried an unusual story about a couple making out in their room at the SkyDome Hotel in Toronto during a baseball game, oblivious to the television cameras penetrating their large window overlooking the ball field. Fortunately for them, the cameramen did not broadcast any pictures over the network but they still reported the titillating story to their audience.

Reitaku High School subscribed to a number of American publications as well, including *Time*, *Newsweek*, *USA Today* and the Japanese version of *Sesame Street.* (I'm not sure if it had much of a readership.) Reitaku University also subscribed to the *US News and World Report*, *The Atlantic* and *The Economist*. Unfortunately, *The New York Times* was bought at the discount rate and sent by surface mail, arriving about four weeks late.

Although English is a compulsory subject in all Japanese junior and senior high schools, the conversational skills of the students are usually very poor. The Japanese complicate matters by teaching obscure rules from outdated texts. Even I would have difficulty with some of their tests. No wonder there is little enthusiasm for the subject. By the time students are in their final year of high school, their only concern is passing the compulsory English component of the tough university entrance exams.

At Reitaku, there was a strong emphasis on English language skills. The teachers had excellent credentials and many of them were fluent. Sano-sensei approached me one day and asked if I would like to assist him with his conversational English class, which was an optional subject for third-year students as well as a club activity.

Girls, in particular, were really keen on improving their conversational skills and made up 80 percent of the English Speaking Society. Their knowledge of grammar was surprisingly good but their pronunciation of the some words was rather odd. I enjoyed helping out with these classes that enabled students to focus on their conversational skills through various role-playing activities.

During my year at Reitaku, I got to know the English teachers very well since I spent most of my spare time in their office. I always appreciated their kindness and, in particular, their sensitivity as far as my need for a certain amount of freedom and independence. No doubt, they realized that the transition was difficult for me and they went out of their way to make sure I felt comfortable in my surroundings. I was also encouraged to visit the teachers' common room, which was out of bounds to other students.

Many of the teachers were very inquisitive about the educational system back home. I remember how shocked they were to discover that North American teachers greeted each other by their given names. At Reitaku, teachers addressed each other by their surnames and used the suffix *sensei* if they were speaking to a senior colleague or simply *san* if they were junior or equal.

≈

The Japanese believe that a strong, healthy body is important so that the students can endure the stress and strain of their *Gambatte!* lifestyle. So I should not have been surprised by the annual medical check-up held in the classroom building after lunch one day. Everyone was required to meet in their homeroom and we went down to the foyer as a group to get weighed, measured and have our eyes tested.

I had trouble figuring out how to fill out my health card. There were no English teachers in sight so I looked at the other students' cards only to discover some very curious birth dates. Everyone seemed to be born sometime in the year 48 or 49. That would mean that they were almost as old as my parents! Later, I learned that the Japanese still use the *gengô* system where time is measured by an emperor's reign. The ascension of a new emperor marks the dawn of a new era. Like some of the others, I was born in the year 49 of Showa, Emperor Hirohito's reign. No wonder I had problems understanding the day's date on the chalkboard which read 2-4-12 for April 12 of the second year of Heisei, Emperor Akihito's reign.

The checkup was reminiscent of similar weigh-ins at summer camp. I weighed in at 60 kilograms (132 pounds) and measured taller than anyone else at 178 centimetres (5'10"). When I left Reitaku a year later, I had grown almost five centimetres (two inches), but remained the same weight.

Today, the average height of a 16-year-old Japanese male is 170 centimetres (5'7") and the average weight is 61 kilograms (134 pounds). The average height of a 16-year-old girl is 158 centimetres (5'2") and the average weight is 53 kilograms (117 pounds). According to Japan's Health and Welfare Ministry, which records the average height of people to the tenth of a millimetre, the height of the Japanese male has increased almost 10 centimetres (4 inches) and the height of a female almost 7.5 centimetres (3 inches) in the past 30 years. This remarkable growth spurt is believed to be the result of drinking milk and the popularity of Western food, especially hamburgers and pizza. Others argue that sitting in chairs enables legs to grow longer, while kneeling on *tatami* mats hinders growth. Whatever the reason, the Japanese are catching up to us.

In Japan, boys are generally thin, and some are almost anorexic looking. Girls, on the other hand, are often a bit overweight. Their biggest weaknesses are chocolate, cookies and ice cream. I could hardly blame them. Japanese chocolate is exceptionally good.

The health check-up held the following week for the university students was even more extensive. A number of classrooms had been set aside as mini-clinics with a medical staff, which included several doctors and nurses. The male and female students were directed to separate rooms where we had our blood drawn and were given an electrocardiogram test. When the results were mailed to us, I was surprised by the range of blood tests. Even our cholesterol levels were checked. I presume the school also got a copy of our test results. Otherwise, why would they bother with the expense? I wondered if they were checking for the HIV virus as well. The Japanese are paranoid about the spread of AIDS and blame Westerners, particularly black foreigners, for the AIDS epidemic in the world.

≈

Every Friday afternoon, the entire student body is mobilized to carry out most of the janitorial jobs at the school. Even the teachers take turns cleaning their offices. At a time when Trinity and other North American private schools are in danger of pricing themselves out of the market, the Japanese have a better handle on keeping operating costs under control. The school year for a boarder at Trinity costs $25,000 while Reitaku is approximately half as much. But then, the students at Reitaku do more than just their own laundry.

However, there are other reasons why Japanese students are assigned menial housekeeping tasks in most schools. By sharing the load, they are expected to learn to appreciate the importance of teamwork, a skill they will need later on, regardless of which profession they choose.

Cleaning has also been a standard ingredient of the spiritual education and discipline embedded into the Japanese psyche from an early age. Both the Shinto and Buddhist religions support the philosophy that no job is too menial for anyone.

Housekeeping duties, which included cleaning the classrooms and washrooms, vacuuming the carpeted floors, dusting, collecting garbage and washing windows, were assigned in the dormitory on a rotational basis. All of us took turns performing the most unpleasant tasks such as cleaning the toilets. Third-year students delegated, supervised and occasionally helped out with the work. The rest of us carried out the tasks based on our rank within the group. And rank was always based on seniority. A dorm leader, appointed by the teachers, was in charge of the five rooms in his section and reported directly to the housekeeping staff. Ultimately, it was his responsibility that standards were not compromised by sloppy attitudes and lazy students.

We were also responsible for cleaning our dormitories every evening before assembly. At the beginning of the summer, we were out on the grounds at 6:45 a.m. picking weeds before breakfast. Once again, everyone was expected to pitch in.

The first-year students had additional chores and they were always up before the 6:30 a.m. wakeup bell, vacuuming the halls and cleaning the study areas. After breakfast, they cleaned the bedrooms. Even on Sundays.

From the beginning, Reitaku adopted a number of the traditions of the British public school. The enslaving of the first-year students to the service of senior students was solidly entrenched while I was there. This practice has also been common at other boarding schools and military academies in many countries. Even at Trinity, 30 years ago, the new boys had to wake up earlier than anyone else to shine the prefects' shoes, make their beds and take care of a number of menial chores. Trinity gradually phased out such a barbarian practice and finally abolished it altogether in 1988.

After four years of boarding school, I understood the hierarchy of position. Nevertheless, I wasn't prepared for the rigid adherence to such a feudal system of subservience. As a second-year student, I was also entitled to the services of the first-year students but I wasn't accustomed to asking someone else to take care of my errands. The senior students certainly took advantage of their position and I suppose they had earned the right to do so.

Times were changing, even in Japan. At Reitaku, the plight of the first-year students had eased considerably in recent years with the second-year and even the third-year students sharing some of the chores. For many years, the first-year students did all of the cleaning, including shining the third-year students' shoes "out of respect" for them. I'm sure they cheered when running shoes became acceptable footwear around the campus.

Predictably, I did not enjoy these extra-curricular activities any more than the other students. So much for team spirit. It was drudge work. Still, no one ever complained. Ever since I left Japan, I haven't wanted to touch a vacuum cleaner again. But that's unlikely. In our society, men are expected to help out at home. In Japan, however, men rarely assist with domestic chores.

At Trinity, the housekeeping staff takes care of all the cleaning requirements of the school. We used to be responsible for vacuuming our own rooms but the practice was abandoned when the job wasn't getting done properly. Needless to say, we were expected to keep our own rooms reasonably neat and tidy. In fact, cleaning of the rooms was scheduled between 7:30 and 8:00 every morning except Sunday. But that was a joke. Most of us only made an effort when there was an inspection and then we simply shoved most of our belongings into the closet.

≈

After classes were over for the day, we headed off to a sports or club activity. Everyone at Reitaku was required to participate in one of the activities offered at the school, which were all coed except for rugby and baseball; the girls played softball instead. Students who did not wish to take part in sports had a choice of clubs, including: the English Speaking Society, Japanese calligraphy, *cha-no-yu* (traditional tea ceremony), photography, classical music, Japanese or English drama. In Japan, hobbies have always been considered necessary for a sense of spiritual completeness. Even samurai were encouraged by their *daimyô* to write haiku, short 17-syllable poems, and participate in the contemplative art of *cha-no-yu*.

However, there were no social service clubs at Reitaku similar to the ones at Trinity. The Japanese students did not become involved with volunteer work, such as senior citizen visitations in the community, nor did they get involved with fund-raising activities for charities and Third World countries. In all fairness to the students at Reitaku, there wasn't enough time for additional activities. At Trinity, we had a tremendous variety of clubs, including Driver Education and Amnesty International. These were scheduled on Thursdays after classes, instead of sports, so we were not forced to choose one over the other.

Participation in a sport five days a week was mandatory at Trinity. I was proof positive that you didn't have to be a "jock" to become a respectable athlete. When I arrived at Trinity, I was undoubtedly the scrawniest, most uncoordinated boy the school had seen and my choices were limited. Team sports such as football, hockey and volleyball were out of the question. I didn't want others to suffer from my shortcomings. Cross-country running was my only safe bet. In the winter, I joined the Nordic ski team, and in the spring, I ran middle-distance in track and field. Western public high schools also have sports and other extra-curricular activities after school. Participation, though, is voluntary and many students never get involved.

The emphasis on fitness at Reitaku was astonishing. I wasn't prepared for the fact that the students were just as serious about their commitment to sports as they were to their studies. Thanks to my training at Trinity, I was in reasonably good shape but I was no match when it came to the rest of the class. All of the students, including the girls, were in excellent physical condition.

I chose *kendô*, a Japanese style of fencing with bamboo swords. For centuries, the warring samurai fought with long metal swords introduced from China in the sixth century AD. They trained rigorously to withstand pain and physical hardship. During the peaceful era of the Tokugawa Shogunate, bamboo swords and protective gear were introduced and training took on a new role. Under the influence of Buddhist and Confucian teachings, *kendô* became associated with spiritual and moral development as well as technical refinement.

During the Allied Occupation, all martial arts were banned from public schools and the Americans successfully substituted basketball and volleyball. *Yakyû* (baseball), introduced by American missionaries in 1873, was already popular. Today, there is renewed interest in the martial arts and they are taught in all schools to help students develop *shitsuke*, the sense of fair play, loyalty, self-discipline and honour, not to mention *gaman-tsuyoi*, a strong stoic personality.

Kendô is the oldest of the martial arts in Japan and is a very difficult sport to master, requiring good coordination of the arms and legs as well as great strength in the arm muscles. Marcus had already warned me about the long hours and brutal regimen of *kendô* practice, which usually began with warm-up stretches, followed by running two laps around the school campus (two kilometres or a little over a mile). Then there were more stretches before we changed into the traditional protective gear designed in the 18th century.

The *kendô* uniform consisted of a *keigoki* (tunic), which was blue for boys and white for girls, over a black *hakama* (long, divided skirt). Then we put on close to 20 pounds of leather armour and a wide blue belt with strands of stiff protective fabric to prevent accidental castration. Over the belt, we hung a navy-coloured cotton sack personalized with our name in white leather *kanji* characters. Traditionally, the samurai did not wear underwear under their *hakama* and neither did we. At first, I wasn't very comfortable with the idea but I got used to it. After all, the *hakama* was almost down to my ankles.

After more warm-up exercises, swinging a *shinai* (bamboo sword) over our heads, we found our positions. In a single orderly line, with the male captains at one end, followed by the senior boys, followed by the female captains, followed by the senior girls, all the way down to the first-year students, we kneeled on the polished wooden floor. Facing our coaches, we bowed formally, with our foreheads touching the floor and our hands placed flat in front of our faces, just like the samurai who knelt respectfully in the presence of their lords hundreds of years ago. "*Sensei, onegaishimasu*," we uttered in unison. "Teacher, please do us the favour (of teaching us)." Then, we put on our *men* (helmet) and *kote* (gloves) and began our drills.

During the first few months, the new students, including myself, spent much of the time swinging the *shinai* back and forth over our heads to build up arm strength and improve coordination. We also did countless push-ups, sit-ups and weightlifting. As soon as our group was in reasonable physical shape, we were given our gear and joined the others in their drills.

I was not fond of the leather headgear, especially after sweating in it for an hour or two. The locker room odour of the helmet was practically enough to knock me out, especially in the heat of summer, not to mention the stench of the *kendô* hall itself. But the helmet was designed to prevent serious injury as we bopped each other over the head as often as possible. Scratching my nose or wiping the sweat off my forehead was impossible because the mask consisted of a series of horizontal steel bars, less than a centimetre (half an inch) apart. Adjusting the helmet was also cumbersome because the two ties were behind the head. If it wasn't a perfect fit, inevitably, I developed blisters by the end of practice.

The object of *kendô* was not to whack the daylights out of each other but to strike or jab three principal parts of the body. The movements were not made at random, but followed the same rhythm *jo, ha, kyû, zanshin* (slow, fast, faster, stop) which governs everything in the arts, from scooping tea in *cha-no-yu* to the intricate steps of the Noh dance. In the first movement, *jo*, we faced our opponents. The girls greeted me with a look of fierce determination; the boys sneered at me with an evil grin. In the second movement, *ha*, we advanced toward each other, disarming our opponents' psyche with piercing shrieks. The shouting was both terrifying and unnerving as I tried to concentrate on my moves. But I never mastered fear like a true samurai, who could not afford to lose his sense of inner calm in the face of death. By the third movement, *kyû*, we were furiously aiming to hit each other on the head, the hips or the gloves. *Zanshin* often came quickly when I found myself at the receiving end of my opponent's *shinai*, pointed at my neck.

Without a doubt, the protective armour prevented serious injury. Just the same, a dull blow from an opponent's *shinai* was quite painful. Even worse, was a blow from a first-year male student who had not mastered the grace of swordsmanship. Often, he struck at poorly armed and vulnerable areas of my body with his *shinai*. Half in pain and half in rage, I retaliated with all my might. In spite of my uncoordinated fencing effort, sometimes I managed to strike back.

Kendô classes were both physically and mentally exhausting. The schedule was gruelling and the routine was often boring, particularly when my teammates emphasized technique instead of merely fighting each other. Practice usually lasted two-and-a-half hours, for at least six out of seven days. Fortunately, the bruises eventually disappeared. In Japan, it seems that nothing of significance can be accomplished without suffering to some extent. I thought of quitting more than once. As a novice and the least experienced member of the *kendô* club, I felt awkward and clumsy. I was tormented by the fact that I would never be as good as anyone else, regardless of how hard I pushed myself. Still, all of the members of our team shared a strong sense of camaraderie, so I persevered. By the end of the year, I was hardly a master of *kendô*. But participating in one of the ancient martial arts connected me not only with Japan's mysterious past but also with the country's competitive spirit. In all aspects of life, the Japanese strive to be number one.

Competitive school teams take sports very seriously and squeeze in as many practice hours as they can, including Sunday mornings. For them, winning is everything. When the girls' *kendô* team was defeated in a championship, they huddled together and cried bitterly over their loss. Girls were not the only ones who got emotional after losing a match. I also saw defeated baseball teams express their sense of shame openly in the middle of the ball field.

Dinner was served right after practice and I sat with members of the *kendô* team in my warm-up clothes. I had settled into a distinct pattern of eating each meal with a specific group. At Reitaku, I ate breakfast with my dorm mates, lunch with my university classmates and dinner with the *kendô* team. In Japan, the routine is much the same in the offices and factories. The work team is also a close-knit group who socialize with each other after work.

At Trinity, wearing a sweaty tracksuit to the dining hall was unacceptable. We were expected to shower and dress for dinner. Groups were loosely formed and we rarely sat with the same students at each meal. Only students from Hong Kong sat together on a regular basis.

≈

During the first week, I applied for an alien registration card, a requirement for any foreigner staying in Japan for more than 90 days. Nonaka-sensei drove me to City Hall, a very large and impressive building for a rather small suburban community. I filled out the application form and handed it to the clerk with my passport. He scrutinized them for some time before handing them back. Apparently, there was a problem with my middle name, Jüri. The version on the passport did not have the two dots, or umlaut, over the "u." I explained that the passport office had neglected to add the umlaut, even though it was on my birth certificate, which I showed to the clerk. But the Japanese are sticklers for detail. As far as they are concerned, if it is not in the passport, it doesn't exist. The clerk was not going to make an exception and my name appeared on the alien registration card without the umlaut.

I was also fingerprinted. There is a joke among foreigners that all *gaijin* are common criminals because fingerprints as well as a photograph are required on the alien registration card. Japan is the only country in the world requiring routine fingerprinting of aliens, but not its own citizens. This has been a sore point with the Koreans, who have no rights to citizenship even though many of their families have lived in Japan for several generations. Today, third-generation Koreans no longer have to carry an alien registration card but citizenship rights are still out of their reach unless they marry a Japanese citizen.

≈

In Japan, doctors don't make house calls, but bankers do. Nonaka-sensei arranged an appointment with a bank official who visited me at the school so I could set up an account with the local Chiba Bank, which has branches throughout Chiba Prefecture. I filled out all of the required documents, showed him my passport and provided my student status.

The Japanese require a *hanko* (personal seal) with their surname if they wish to open a bank account. The *hanko* is a custom borrowed from the Chinese and takes the place of a signature on all legal documents, including bank withdrawal slips. Although foreigners do not need a *hanko*, Nonaka-sensei thought I should have one anyway.

These personal seals, made from soapstone or ceramic, are sold at stationery stores. With a name like Jonathan Buchanan, I needed a custom-made *hanko*, which only cost ¥1000. Buchanan was much too complicated, so Nonaka-sensei decided to use my first name, and had the *kanji* (Chinese characters) set for *jo-na-san* (the "th" sound does not exist in Japanese). Loosely translated, my name means "like a crab apple tree in the mountains." Actually, the suffix *san* is only used with last names, not with given names. However, the bankcard issued by Chiba Bank had my full name written in Roman letters.

Bank machines are everywhere, though very few, even in Tokyo and other major cities, are hooked up to an international system for the benefit of tourists. An account at a Japanese bank is essential for convenient cash withdrawals at ABM machines. The graphics are exceptionally good and an image of a female clerk is shown at the start and finish of each transaction. But it takes a bit of guesswork to punch the right buttons because all of the instructions are in Japanese.

In Japan, cash machines do not operate on a 24-hour basis. When they were first introduced, ABMs could only be accessed during normal banking hours, from 9 a.m. to 6 p.m., Monday through Friday and from 9 a.m. to 2 p.m. on Saturdays. Gradually, banks have extended the hours for cash machines. Now they can be accessed from 9 a.m. to 5 p.m. on Saturdays, Sundays and holidays, but there is a ¥105 surcharge for using the ABMs during the extended hours.

During the first few months, I relied on foreign bank drafts sent by my parents. Unfortunately, the process of cashing them was complicated and I always had to wait a few days before receiving the funds. So I started using my Visa card for cash advances. This was easier, though not necessarily convenient, since the local Chiba Bank did not accept international Visa cards and neither did the cash machines in Kashiwa. In fact, very few banks in Japan will issue funds from foreign bankcards. Cashing traveller's cheques in Canadian dollars can also be a real challenge. Quite often, the best bet is the local post office.

In Kashiwa, I had no choice but to go to a downtown branch of another financial institution, Sumitomo Bank, the second largest bank in the world. The Japanese excel at personal service in all of their banks and treat their "honoured guest" in a far more civilized manner than our banking institutions. Every bank has an elderly security guard on staff who always bows as he opens the door. Inside, customers take a number and sit down on one of the comfortable couches with a newspaper or magazine while waiting. Most of the employees do not speak English and a junior clerk is often called upon to assist with foreign transactions because he or she still remembers enough English from high school.

"Cash, *onegaishimasu.*" I always said, as I asked the teller for money and handed over my Visa and alien registration cards. Usually I waited for about ten minutes while my request was being processed. When the teller handed me the money, I quickly stuffed the wad of ¥10,000 bills in my wallet. Counting money in front of the clerk is considered rude in Japan.

Once, I waited for a very long time for my cash advance. Finally, a bank officer came over and returned my alien registration card but not my Visa card. The bank officer indicated that my credit card was no longer valid, but did not provide me with an explanation. I was very distressed when I left the bank without any funds and wondered why my Visa card had been confiscated.

Fortunately, I was not travelling at the time and I was able to borrow some emergency funds from Nonaka-sensei. Apparently, there had been a mix-up at my bank back home where my card was cancelled by mistake. A few days later, a new Visa card arrived by Priority Post along with a letter of apology from the bank manager.

Credit cards have not had the same impact in Japan as in Canada and the United States. Traditionally, personal debt was frowned upon because Confucius taught that borrowing was shameful. Even today, most transactions are in cash since small family-owned businesses, including restaurants, inns and hotels, do not accept credit cards.

≈

Following dinner on my second day at Reitaku, Randall invited me to go downtown with him. Naturally, I was eager to join him. After all, I had just arrived in Japan and I wanted to see as much as possible. I had no idea that my absence from evening assembly would be a concern. At Trinity, attendance at our evening house meetings was compulsory, but no one said anything if you missed an occasional meeting. In any case, I presumed that Randall knew the rules so I wasn't at all concerned about skipping assembly.

The sun had already set by the time we left the campus. In the Land of the Rising Sun, everyone is at the mercy of the farmer's clock. The sun rises before 5 a.m. and sets by 7 p.m. I never got used to the sun setting so early in the evenings, especially in the summer.

In the darkness, downtown Kashiwa looked like the set of Gotham City in the movie *Batman*. The buildings were ugly and seemed to be arranged in no particular order. And yet, it appeared as if the entire mess of buildings was carefully calculated, like a movie set.

We entered a record store using an escalator down into a large shop, with a wide selection of CDs and LPs of both

Western and Japanese music. Although the Walkman was designed in Japan, pre-recorded cassette tapes were surprisingly hard to find. Instead, record stores sold blank tapes advertising "CD Sound" or "Made for CD" in English. CDs ranged between ¥1200 for a used import and ¥3500 for a new Japanese recording. Ouch! At the time, the price of all Japanese recordings was strictly regulated and there were no discounts on new merchandise. However, used CDs were readily available in most record shops.

Hard rock groups such as Bon Jovi and Van Halen were popular with Japanese teens, even though they didn't understand the lyrics. But who listens to the lyrics? The Beatles were always a favourite with the girls and an LP of *Hard Day's Night* was selling for ¥5000. The store featured a wide selection of American and British music magazines and books, including, *Rolling Stones, A to Z,* for ¥2800.

We also spent some time at a video arcade where all games cost only ¥50. A real bargain after looking around in the record shops. Video games are far more popular in Japan than anywhere else in the world. The graphics are also much better and the games last longer. In Tokyo, multi-storey video arcades cater mainly to high school and college students. Video arcades are also popular hangouts for punks with their dyed orange hair and offbeat dress code.

Heading down one of the side streets, we passed one vending machine after another. In a country where vandalism doesn't exist, *jidanhambeki* (vending machines) are everywhere. These machines dispense an astonishing variety of items, including soft drinks, canned tea and coffee (both hot and cold, depending on the season), yogurt drinks, beer, miniature bottles of sake, ice cream, batteries, shampoo, CDs and condoms. One could also buy panty hose (new for women and used for men with a fetish for that sort of thing). So, I was hardly surprised with the variety of pornographic magazines for sale. The ultra-soft porn is protected by a special wrapping with the words, "Let's keep dirty things away from our children's eyes and keep this a healthy society." However, newspaper vending machines, which seem to dominate major street corners in North America, are nowhere to be found in Japan.

We bought Jolt colas for a ¥100 coin each at a *jidanhambeki*. Jolt is one of the many American inventions that the Japanese believe originated in their own country. And why not? Japan is the perfect market for a drink that boasts all the flavour and double the caffeine of Coke or Pepsi.

Power drinks, which are advertised on television by Arnold Schwarzenegger, are extremely popular with the *sarariman* (male, white-collar employees in Japanese companies) heading off to work after a night on the town carousing with his fellow employees. These power drinks contain enough protein and caffeine to prime exhausted *sararimen* for another day on the job.

As soon as we were back at the school, Randall was called into the dormitory office where Itoh-sensei and Kitasaka-san were waiting for him. The Japanese usually prefer to avoid such confrontations but that was not the case at Reitaku. Whenever we were out of line, we were confronted by at least two or three people in charge.

Apparently, my absence from evening assembly was a serious breach of house rules. Of course, Randall should have known better. Just the same, he apologized, reassuring Itoh-sensei and Kitasaka-san that it would never happen again. Still, he was pretty cool about being hauled out on the carpet as if it was no big deal. Early on, I realized that all rules were to be taken very seriously. And I wasn't about to test the system. Well, not during the first few weeks.

≈

From Sunday to Friday, the evening routine was always the same. We returned to the dormitory after dinner and most of the students had their bath before getting dressed for evening assembly. Cleaning of the dormitories was squeezed in between 6:50 and 7:10 p.m. As soon as assembly was over, everyone quickly changed into their casual clothes and headed off to their individual cubicles to study.

During the first term, I usually studied in my own room and then headed off to the *ofuro* when I had the place to myself. I enjoyed the bathing ritual and spent a long time soaking in the hot tub, allowing the soothing heat of the water to relax my body, not to mention my aching muscles from *kendô* practice.

Later in the evening, I usually dropped in at the dormitory office to watch television and socialize with the housekeeping staff. They were exceptionally friendly and always made me feel very welcome. Communication was never a problem while watching a rugby or baseball game. One night, they ordered food from a local take-out restaurant and offered me some as well. I wasn't about to turn them down, so I joined them at the table. Before I went back to the dorm, Kitasaka-san took me aside and gave me a pair of chopsticks and a small plastic frog. Apparently, my handling of the *hashi* needed some improvement. I thanked her and took them with me so that I could practice in the privacy of my room.

Sometimes, I studied with Randall, usually in the dorm office, because his room was a mess. The floor was often covered with clothes and the walls were plastered with maps obtained either at tourist information centres or ripped off the advertisement boards of the Chiyoda subway line, which ran through Kashiwa.

Curfew was at 9:50 every night, announced by the bell and a first-year student yelling, *"TENKO!!!!!!!"* (roll call) through the hallways. We lined up outside of our rooms and our presence was checked by the student on duty. As soon as everyone was accounted for, we bowed respectfully to the school, saying, "*Oyasumi nasai*" (rest well) and then we bowed in the direction of our homes, repeating "*Oyasumi nasai.*" From an early age, Japanese children learn to love their hometown, to protect their land, culture and traditions, and to be aware of their responsibility as Japanese citizens.

We also had to drag our bodies out of bed for *tenko* at 6:40 a.m. every Sunday, the only morning during the week when there were no classes. At first, I thought it was a cruel joke. After the roll call, everyone went back to bed, except for the first-year students, who had cleaning duties, and the basketball team, which always practiced early Sunday mornings. During the first term, it wasn't always possible to get to sleep again, especially with the droning noise of the vacuum cleaner and the frequent announcements over the P.A. system in the hallway. As time went on, I learned, like my fellow second and third-year students to sleep through the commotion. At least, we had the luxury of sleeping in.

At Trinity, we had to show up for Sunday chapel service at 9:30 a.m. wearing our school blazer, shirt, tie and grey flannels. Sometimes, chapel was scheduled in the evening, either right before or after dinner. But I didn't dare sleep too late in any case. Brunch, the best meal of the week, was served promptly at 10 a.m.

When the first term was over at Reitaku, I joined one of the five rooms and lost all of my special privileges. From then on, my activities were just as restricted as everyone else's. The close-knit lifestyle of the group and the confinement within the dormitory made it difficult to develop a friendship with anyone who was not in my dorm, homeroom or on the *kendô* team. Occasionally, I visited another dorm, where someone had the same interests as me in music or sports, but generally speaking, opportunities to socialize with others did not exist. And forget about a relationship, even a casual one, with a girl. Sure, we had moments for friendly conversations during the day. Moments, mind you and we were the lucky ones. Socializing between boys and girls was strictly forbidden at some private high schools.

The social bonding required later on in life begins in the dorm. During study break at 9:50 p.m., every night except Sunday, we had a *paati* (party) to ease some of the pressure-cooker existence of high school life. Our room leader, Takebe-san, was in charge and he knew how to have a good time, so our *paati* was always a lively affair.

The two first-year students were responsible for picking up snacks at the local convenience stores from the ¥1000 each of us contributed at the beginning of the month. *Sembei*, rice crackers spiced with seaweed salt, were always a popular snack. The first-year students served the food along with bottled milk and yogurt, which were delivered nightly to our dormitory. Sometimes, they even made iced coffee for the group.

We also shared our goodies in the care packages from home. Once, I had been given a box of grapes, beautifully packaged for gift-giving. (Fruit is very expensive in Japan and is often given as a gift.) When I started to munch on the grapes, everyone had a horrified look on their faces. I was wondering what was up when Takebe-san explained that I would suffer from severe stomach cramps if I ate the peel of the grape. Everyone else was painstakingly peeling each grape with a knife. I didn't want them to worry about me, so I followed suit, though I found the task of peeling each grape rather silly and awfully tedious.

The first-year students were also responsible for the entertainment, playing the CDs and telling funny stories. I was amazed how they managed to tell so many different stories throughout the year without repeating any of them. During the second term, Saitoh-kun (*kun*, instead of *san*, is used for juniors) was the only first-year student in our room and often had to shoulder all of the responsibilities. Sometimes, Takebe-san asked the second-year students to pitch in. I didn't mind helping out with the chores, but storytelling was not my forte. Particularly in Japanese.

The custom of relating amusing anecdotes began in the 1600s when men dressed as women to entertain guests at parties. In 1780, these male geishas were replaced by women, who broadened the definition of entertainment.

Predictably, girls were a very hot topic. Even though Japanese boys talked about girls and sex very freely, as far as I know, none of my dorm mates had ever kissed a girl.

On Saturday nights, we always played card games, especially Uno, which was very popular with the group. Western teens might have considered our card games a rather childish form of entertainment. Chances are, however, they wouldn't be stuck in a dorm room with their buddies every Saturday night. At Trinity, card games such as euchre or "Asshole" were very popular but usually played during dull moments at lunch hour or long bus rides to sports events.

My roommates at Reitaku, however, took their card games very seriously. The stakes were restricted to food items and the loser usually had to buy a cake for the following Saturday. Everyone was always impressed when someone managed to coax one of the girls to bake a cake in her home economics class. But I didn't have good connections. When I lost, I took the easy way out and bought a cake from a local store.

These evening sessions enhanced my Japanese vocabulary significantly because of the variety of obscenities frequently used by my roommates. Although there are no "swear words" in the Japanese-English dictionary, the English-Japanese version contains plenty of slang, including a whole host of words labelled as "vulgar." During these parties, my roommates often tried to talk dirty, even when they did not know the specific meaning of some of the words. "Fuck" was a common expression and I was always amused when it was used completely out of context, usually illustrated with an extended middle finger. Needless to say, they appreciated my assistance when I corrected their grammar. "It's 'fuck you,' not 'fuck'," I explained. They were also fascinated with my American slang dictionary with all of its four-letter words. The book mysteriously disappeared before the end of the year.

At Trinity, sometimes we ordered a pizza from Jim's after evening study was over at 9:30 p.m. Two pizzas with several toppings only cost nine dollars and were delivered to the residence. (In Japan, the price for a pizza delivered to the house was an extravagant ¥3000.) Occasionally, we ordered after the 10:45 p.m. curfew and we were always asked by the person taking the order, "Will there be any problem receiving the pizza?" As long as the housemaster wasn't at the door when the sacred pie was delivered, there was no problem. If we were caught, the pizza was surrendered to the ever-ravenous prefects after we paid for it. Most nights, however, we couldn't afford a pizza. Instead, we spent our spare time in each other's rooms or watched TV in the common room. There was always someone watching TV during the evenings, even during study hour. And it was not uncommon to find one of the students asleep on the couch early in the mornings.

The *paati* at Reitaku always ended promptly at 10:20 p.m. The first-year students quickly cleaned up the room and studying resumed in earnest, especially for the third-year students who were preparing for the dreaded university entrance exams. Reitaku had strict rules about everything except "lights out." Officially, lights were supposed to be turned off at midnight but serious students were allowed to study in their cubicles as late as they liked. It was not unusual for many of them to fall asleep at their desks studying for *shiken jigoku* (examination hell). Competition to get into a good university was fierce, with at least ten applicants for every space. The maxim, "Pass with four, fail with five," had special meaning. Many of them would not risk sleeping five hours when an extra hour of study could make the difference between pass and fail.

The Devil's Language

The Japanese have rights and ceremonies so different from those of all other nations that it seems that they are deliberately trying to be unlike any other people.

Alessandro Valignano
Jesuit Priest, 16th century

Our local authorities on the language look at me with indulgent pity when I announce that I mean to learn it.

Mary Crawford Fraser
The Wife of a Diplomat in Japan, 1889

We can always fool the foreigners.

Old Chinese proverb

The Japanese language is elusive and ambiguous. There are three different alphabets or sets of characters to learn, *kanji, katakana* and *hiragana*. Mastering each one is an unbelievable exercise in patience and perseverance. No wonder the early missionaries referred to Japanese as the devil's language.

Kanji are Chinese characters and the only direct link between Japanese and any other language. The Chinese developed these ideograms more than 3,000 years ago and it is the only ancient form of writing which has survived to the present day. The Japanese were introduced to *kanji* in the sixth century when Buddhist monks braved the treacherous trip across the Japan Sea in search of new converts. China's other neighbours, Korea and Vietnam, also adopted *kanji* characters. Korea is slowly phasing them out and Vietnam has dropped them altogether. The reason for discarding *kanji* is simple: the ancient script is extremely difficult to learn. *Kanji* is more than an alphabet. Each character represents a concept, which is enough to confuse Westerners who are trying to grapple with a new language.

More than 50,000 *kanji* exist in the Japanese language but only 1,945 are officially specified by the government for everyday use. Until 1989, elementary school children were required to learn 996 characters. Now, the number has been increased slightly to 1,006. The remaining *kanji* are taught in junior high school and high school.

The two Japanese phonetic alphabets, *katakana* and *hiragana* have 46 characters each, adding to the heavy burden of memorization. The Japanese had already been using *kanji* characters for almost 300 years when they developed *katakana*, a square-looking syllabic system in the ninth century. *Katakana* has been used to write foreign words incorporated into the Japanese language such as place names, technical terms and even some computer commands. Most Western restaurant menus are written in *katakana* and *romaji* (Roman letters).

The *hiragana* alphabet was created by Buddhist monks during the Heian Period (795-1185) to simplify the written language. Monks also taught *hiragana* to the ladies of the court, who kept diaries, wrote poetry and even novels. In 1006, Lady Murasaki Shikibu wrote *Genji Monogatari* (*The Tale of Genji*), describing the erotic pleasures noblemen shared with their mistresses. This monumental work, consisting of 54 chapters and more than 1,000 pages, is considered by scholars to be the world's first novel.

In addition to the frustration of sorting out the various alphabets, the Japanese language has many levels of politeness, depending on the social standing, age and gender of the speaker and the person spoken to, as well as the relationship between them. Despite the efforts during the Meiji Restoration (1868-1912) and Allied Occupation (1945-1951) to make everyone equal, the structure of the language still reflects the fear and servility experienced by the lower classes and women during the feudal era.

≈

I spent the first term learning the fundamentals of the Japanese language and culture at Reitaku University, a relatively small school with only 700 students. The university had specialized in languages, including Chinese, English, French, German and Japanese, for many years. In 1988, a new department was created, called *Bekka* (literally meaning "different department"), to teach Japanese to foreign students.

We were certainly a mixed bag of *bekkasei,* as we were called, ranging in age from 16 to 40, from Hong Kong, Taiwan, Korea, Bangladesh, Sri Lanka, the Philippines, China, Germany, the United States and Canada. In a country where almost everyone looks the same, we were a highly cosmopolitan group. Although we represented many nationalities, we were all *gaijin* as far as the Japanese were concerned.

On the first day of our orientation course, everyone was dressed in casual clothes, except me. Officially, I was a Reitaku high school student, so I had to wear the school uniform to classes every day. Predictably, I felt rather conspicuous in my blue blazer, white shirt, school tie and grey flannels when everyone else showed up in jeans and a T-shirt. There was no point arguing with Nonaka-sensei. Rules were rules and I was expected to comply.

Classes began at 9 a.m. every morning from Monday to Saturday. No one was thrilled by the fact that *Bekka* was the only university department at Reitaku with Saturday classes.

Most of the students had already studied Japanese so all of the courses were introduced in Japanese. For the first few days, I was totally lost. Naturally, I didn't have a clue what the other students were laughing about when one of the professors made a few witty comments. After class, Randall informed me that a test would be given to determine the placement of the students according to their knowledge of the language. Until then, I had to rely on others to tell me what was going on.

I was placed in the lowest level along with Randall and others who spoke English reasonably fluently. Most of them were upset because they had been placed in a class according to their English-speaking, instead of Japanese-speaking skills. Although they complained bitterly to our class advisor, Oguchi-sensei, she did not allow any changes and they remained in the bottom-set.

Oguchi-sensei was always primly dressed in a light-coloured blouse and dark skirt. Unlike the rest of our teachers, she had a good sense of humour and her classes were a welcome break from the monotonous drone of some of the other teachers. However, she did not appreciate students skipping class or challenging her teaching methods.

Whenever students were not satisfied with a response, they badgered the teacher incessantly. Such behaviour was in stark contrast to the high school classes I attended during the next semester where none of the students dared interrupt the lecture by asking questions and certainly not, to criticize the teaching methods. In Japan, *sensei* means "master" and such a position of authority deserves respect.

Learning Japanese was not easy. One would almost think there was a conspiracy to make it as difficult as possible for others to learn. We began with an introduction to the *hiragana* alphabet. By the end of the first day, we were fully immersed in the rote system of learning for which the Japanese are famous. There was also a quiz on the blackboard to see who could fill in the most blanks of the 46-character alphabet.

The next day, we learned variations on the *hiragana* alphabet in order to turn a *ka* into a softer *ga,* a *ta* into *da,* a *sa* into *za* and so on. The quizzes were a daily event and during the first few weeks, I did very poorly. I wondered if I would ever remember so many complicated symbols. After studying them for hours, the images blurred together and everything looked similar. I quickly became discouraged with my lack of progress. Learning Japanese was going to be far more difficult than learning other languages, such as French and Latin.

Uritani-sensei assisted with the teaching of the *hiragana* alphabet using large flash cards. Always impeccably dressed in a conservative grey suit, white shirt and dark tie, he was far more serious than Oguchi-sensei. He also had an extraordinary lisp and we had trouble understanding what he was saying, especially in English. He amused us one day by pronouncing "fax machine" as a "fucks machine." Otherwise, he was a bore and most of his classes were a drag, especially on Saturday mornings.

We spent the first few weeks concentrating on basic words like *neko* (cat) and *inu* (dog), even though there were few domestic animals in Kashiwa. By the fifth week, we graduated to more useful words, such as *denwa* (telephone) and *yûbin-kyoku* (post office).

While I was learning Japanese, I began to have a better idea of why the Japanese have so many problems with English. For one thing, they have tremendous difficulty distinguishing between the "l" and "r" sounds. More often than not, the Japanese will substitute the "r" sound for an "l" because they do not have an "l" sound in their language. Or they just mix them up. When General Douglas MacArthur, Supreme Commander during the Allied Occupation, was proposed for the United States presidency in the early 1950s, apparently a huge banner had been strung across the Ginza in Tokyo by well-wishers with the following words: "We play for MacArthur's erection."

So, I can't understand why Toyota has given names to many of its most popular models that the Japanese can not pronounce properly, such as Corolla, Celica and Tercel. Toyota's luxury station wagon in Japan is the Crown Royal Saloon, an impossible combination. The Japanese also like to stick vowels between consonants. McDonald's Restaurant, which is extremely popular in Japan, is called *Makudonarudo*.

On the other hand, Westerners aren't that great with Japanese words. Sake and karate are usually pronounced as "sah-kee" and "ka-rah-tee" instead of the correct "sah-kay" and "kar-rah-tay." The worst offender is karaoke, which is usually pronounced "carry-okey" instead of "kah-ra-okay." Mrs. Oguchi made some pretty interesting facial expressions when we called her Ohguchi-sensei (big-mouthed teacher) instead of Oguchi-sensei (small-mouthed teacher). No wonder misunderstandings occur so easily.

Good intuition can be a real asset. In time, I discovered that the smallest nuances, even facial gestures and the tone of voice, often conveyed the message more accurately than spoken words. I also learned that neat handwriting is absolutely essential. Every character must be meticulously constructed. Fortunately, no one in our class was left-handed. The *kanji* and *kana* scripts are designed to be written in the right-hand direction and the emphasis on the strokes can not be properly duplicated by a left-handed individual. In Japan, all children are required to write with their right hand as soon as they start school. There are no exceptions to this rule.

For decades, many Westerners have hoped that the Japanese will eventually adopt *romaji* letters for common usage and reserve *kanji* and the other complicated *kana* alphabets for official documents and scholarly works. However, it is unlikely that the Japanese will give up their traditional way of writing for the convenience of others.

Certainly not, when there has been a recent revival in the teaching of even more *kanji* characters in the schools.

Learning Japanese is more than just memorizing countless *kanji* and *kana* characters. There are so many different words that can be used to say the same thing. To complicate matters even further, there are numerous words which have similar sounds but radically different meanings. Take the word *seikô* for example. Most people immediately recognize the trade name for quality watches imported from Japan. The same word (though written with different characters) can mean either "success," "immaturity" or "sex."

The Japanese language allows people to take the easy way out to avoid confrontation and humiliation. When the Japanese respond to a question with a phrase such as, "We will consider it with a forward-looking attitude," they are simply being gracious. Harmonious relationships are protected in a society where it is impolite to use the word "no," let alone say something like, "I don't agree with you." Many foreign businessmen are fooled by the polite language of the Japanese who expect others to understand that a positive response does not necessarily mean "yes."

In fact, the most misunderstood word in the Japanese language is *hai*. Dictionaries and language guides for foreign travellers translate the word as "yes." Sometimes, *hai* is a simple "yes" answer, but not always. Often, it just means, "I hear you" or "I'm listening." In any case, the Japanese do not want to offend visitors or guests with a direct "no." A number of years ago, a student at the International Christian University in Tokyo wrote an award-winning thesis titled, "19 Ways of Saying 'No' Without Actually Saying 'No.'"

Then, there is the careful acknowledgement of rank when addressing someone, especially in business transactions. In the Japanese language, there is no equivalent of the polite "Mister" or "Sir." Instead, the Japanese learn the honorific language from an early age, choosing from a multitude of special endings for all names to indicate proper respect for social distinctions and higher status.

At the university, we learned the honorific language of *keigo* for speaking. There are four levels of politeness and it is extremely important to understand the subtle differences. For example, the formal expressions used during a conversation with a superior are very different than the words used to humble oneself before a superior. Traditionally, *keigo* was used more often by women, but the custom is slowly disappearing. Although women are generally more polite and docile in their speech, the girls at Reitaku were no longer using all of the traditional conventions during a conversation. On the other hand, the speech patterns of the boys were quite different from the girls and their manner of speaking was rather abrupt.

One of my classmates constantly criticized the way Japanese was taught at Reitaku. At 33, Ken was a former rat-racer who had worked in the financial district of New York City before escaping to Japan where he managed to get a job at the city hall in Fukuoka for a year. Reasonably fluent in Japanese, Ken was a very serious student who hoped to become a teacher. He believed that we should be taught colloquial Japanese as well as the formal or polite version, which was part of the curriculum. One day, Ken got into a lively discussion with Oguchi-sensei about the merits of learning everyday usage. I agreed with all of his arguments. Polite conversation may be useful during business transactions, but it was useless as far as understanding my dorm mates. However, Oguchi-sensei was reluctant to stray from the curriculum since she was afraid that we would confuse the two versions. And she was probably right.

Just the same, Ken persevered with his Japanese language studies. He was attending Reitaku University on a full scholarship so there wasn't much of a choice. I was also at Reitaku to learn as much as possible and I too, persevered, even though I had a hard time keeping up with the others.

Every week, we were faced with a torturous *tesuto* (test), where I managed to invent new *kanji* as well as new grammatical structures. I barely passed these tests which were a constant reminder of my own ineptitude with the Japanese language.

≈

During lunch, I joined the handful of *bekkasei* who chose to eat in the school cafeteria. Most of my classmates preferred to prepare their own meals in the dormitory kitchens or eat at a local restaurant. Many of them complained about the food at Reitaku though Randall and I were generally satisfied with the meals.

Occasionally, some of us skipped an afternoon class and headed off to Kashiwa for lunch where one of the back streets was lined with a variety of Western eateries, including Kentucky Fried Chicken, Baskin-Robbins and Mister Donut. We chose spots with generous servings of food, like Shakey's for its lunch buffet featuring pizza, spaghetti (with curry or pesto sauce) and fried potatoes for ¥570, which was cheap by anyone's standards. Not gourmet fare, mind you, but edible. The best item on the menu was pizza with seaweed and ginger. Other choices included the California Ocean Special, an unlikely concoction of shrimp, cheese and salad dressing with a garnish of sliced raw cabbage. Like typical university students, we pigged out and barely managed to trudge back to the train station, but not before stopping at Baskin-Robbins for an *aisu kuriimu* (ice cream).

The *bekkasei* became a tight-knit group and sometimes we went out together in the evenings. We usually chose small, inexpensive restaurants, like Matsumoto. The popular watering hole, was more commonly called *Jiji-Baba* by the university students, which was loosely translated as "the old geezer and the hag," a rather crude reference to the owners.

One night, there were too many of us to squeeze into one of the smaller joints so we ended up in the Casual Club. We sat at low tables in a private booth and entertained ourselves by plugging the video jukebox with ¥100 coins to watch "Y.M.C.A." by the Village People and "Love Shack" by the B-52's from a catalogue of 200 videos. Bar fare consisted of *onigiri* (rice balls wrapped in seaweed), *yakitori* (chicken kabobs), squid, octopus and other delicacies. The Casual Club was considerably more expensive than our usual haunts and Randall was kind enough to loan me ¥2500 to cover my portion of the tab. Although Randall was under strict orders from Nonaka-sensei to keep an eye on me, he still let me order a beer when we were out together. In any case, I learned to be careful. After all, I still had to show up at school sober for *tenko* at 9:50 p.m.

Everyone complained bitterly about the curfew hours. All of the *bekkasei*, with three exceptions, lived in the university dormitory. The girls had to be back at 10:00 p.m., when the doors to their dormitory were locked. The curfew for residents of the men's dormitory was an hour later. Although their building remained open all night with a staff member on security, the gate to the university compound was locked at 11:00 p.m. But the guys quickly discovered a hole in the fence, which enabled them to sneak in after hours. Many of them took advantage of the freedom to come and go as they pleased.

Not surprisingly, the American students were having the greatest difficulty adjusting to all of the restrictions. Robert, a 19-year-old student from San Diego, whined about everything. He wasn't happy with his tiny room, which was crammed with his personal belongings including a stereo, TV and a comfortable vibrating chair, which responded to the sounds from his television set. Robert hated Japanese food and never ate in the school cafeteria. He also complained constantly about the "dumb" language with three alphabets and dozens of ways to pronounce a *kanji* character. Of course, Robert was exaggerating. There are at least two different ways, and never more than 20. Despite all of his muttering, Robert was hooked on *manga* and wanted to expand his knowledge of the language. Still, he left school before the end of the year without mastering even the basics.

Others were stoic, tackling all of the challenges of life in Japan with a *gaman* spirit. Many of them already had a good command of the language even though they were stuck in the bottom-set with me.

Most of the students were interested in pursuing a career in international finance and commerce. The Japanese economy was booming and good language skills would give them an edge over their competition. Linda, another American, had already learned some Japanese while working at the Hiroike Institute in Washington D.C. and she had very ambitious plans for her future. Sandra, an African-American and the only black student in our class, was at Reitaku on a scholarship from a Japanese businessman who believed that blacks were treated poorly in his country. Cindy, a very serious student from Hong Kong, was often mistaken for a Japanese, which always made her feel self-conscious since her language skills were weak. She never missed a single class, a remarkable accomplishment considering how boring they were. Christina, a Filipina who had married a Japanese man, was also very keen on learning the language and never argued with the teachers. Moreover, she did not hesitate to tell the rest of us to shut up if we were talking too much. Outside of class, she was very nice and sometimes joined us for lunch at a local restaurant, giving us a lift in her Crown Royal Saloon station wagon.

Dinesh, a tall Sri Lankan, had the easiest time because the pronunciation of Sinhalese and Japanese are surprisingly similar. Lee-san, a Korean, had worked in the maintenance department at Hiroike Institute the previous year and was reasonably fluent. He believed that stronger language skills would give him a chance at a better paying job. Nabi was from Bangladesh and interested in developing business relationships with the Japanese. He even managed to get a part-time job and had his own apartment near the university. Two Germans, Christian and Peter, were opposites. Christian was quiet and reserved while Peter had an outgoing personality with a great sense of humour. Unlike some of the others who enjoyed Japan bashing, Peter always laughed about his experiences.

And then there was Randall, who had trouble getting organized for classes and skipped them from time to time, especially after a late night on the town. Randall was a very friendly and likeable fellow. Though we were an unlikely pair, Randall became a good friend and confidant. We often shared our frustrations with the restrictive policies of the school. Randall had his own problems coming to terms with an over-protective guarantor who practically had him under house arrest while he was visiting his home. When Randall moved into the high school residence, he managed to convince Nonaka-sensei and the rest of the staff that he should be entitled to extra privileges since he had already graduated from high school. Just the same, Kitasaka-san never got used to Randall's "late" arrivals at 7 a.m. because he had missed the last train from Tokyo at midnight.

We also attended a number of social functions for *gaijin,* even singing a duet of "Frère Jacques" at an international get-together. I'm sure we sounded terrible, but the applause was a typical and polite Japanese response, warm and encouraging. One day, Randall and I were asked along with a couple of other *hakujin* (white *gaijin*) students to pose for photos for a promotional magazine for the university. I managed to make the cover, but that's probably because my hair was a more respectable length than Randall's. Our efforts were rewarded with a generous honorarium that we spent on lunch in Kashiwa.

≈

Throughout the year, the *bekkasei* attended several social functions organized by various groups to promote international exchange and friendship in the community. Chiba Prefecture youth centres arranged overnight stays for young people between the ages of 12 and 22. These events were well organized and I always had a good time, especially with the girls. Other meetings, sponsored by UNESCO and the cultural departments of various cities, were held at community centres. They were usually well attended by both Japanese and *gaijin* who were studying or working in the region. The sponsors pretty well guaranteed the presence of plenty of *gaijin* at these functions by serving lots of food and sometimes paying us an honorarium of ¥4000 or ¥5000 to attend.

The welcoming speeches were always too long, but at least they were in English and exceptionally good English, I might add. As soon as the speeches were over, circle games were organized to help break the ice. I could hardly believe my ears when the first game was announced to a gymnasium full of adults. Nonetheless, the Japanese have adapted many Western children's games to suit their own needs. Duck-duck-goose, musical chairs and similar juvenile activities were popular exercises to loosen us up. Regardless of what anyone might think, we actually had a lot of fun playing *jan-ken-fon* (paper-scissors-rock) where the losers grabbed onto the winner's back, eventually forming conga lines with appropriate Latino music drifting over the speakers.

Refreshments were served when we mingled during "*furii taimu*" (free time). I was usually bombarded with the same polite questions, always in the same order, as if they had been carefully rehearsed prior to the event.

"Where are you from?" an inquisitive local always asked.

"Canada."

"Where?"

"Near Toronto."

"Are you a high school student?"

"Yes."

"Where do you go to school?"

"Reitaku."

"Really? I know someone who has a daughter at Reitaku."

"Really."

"Do you like Japan?"

"Yes."

"Really? Do you like Japanese girls?"

"Yes."

"What are your hobbies?"

"Music, travel, *kendô*."

Most of the Japanese were satisfied with the answers to their questions and moved on to the next *gaijin*. I suspected that many of them were very limited in their ability to carry on a conversation in English. On the other hand, some of them had an exceptionally good command of English and we chatted for some time. Most of the Japanese attending these social functions were probably English teachers from local schools, as well as their friends and their children who were looking for an opportunity to meet "native speakers" and learn more about Western ways.

≈

Thanks to the generosity of an anonymous donor, the *bekkasei* received complimentary passes for Tokyo Disneyland on a school holiday. We met early in the morning and took the train to Maihama station on the outskirts of Tokyo, built specifically to accommodate visitors to Disneyland. Theme parks in Japan attract the same school crowds as the country's cultural treasures and the trains were packed with junior high school students neatly dressed in their uniforms. At least, I had managed to escape Reitaku wearing my jeans and a T-shirt. The dress code was one of the few rules I ignored whenever I thought I could get away with it.

Tokyo Disneyland was built to strict Disney standards. Although Walt Disney wanted to add other attractions, such as Samurai Land and a show based on "Little Peach Boy," a popular Japanese children's story, the Tokyo-based Oriental Land Company insisted on duplicating the original theme park in Anaheim, California. The park had to be as authentic as possible so that the Japanese people would feel as if they had taken a foreign trip.

However, some alterations to the original design were still necessary. Main Street U.S.A. was transformed into the World Bazaar, an indoor shopping arcade to protect the crowds from sudden showers during *tsuyu*. The park is also much larger to correspond with the Japanese perception that America is a spacious country. Sleeping Beauty's Castle has been replaced by Cinderella's Castle since her rags-to-riches story reflects Japan's post-war economic boom. Naturally, all of the principal characters are played by Caucasians.

When the park opened on April 15, 1983, Mickey-san was on hand to greet his first visitors with a vigorous handshake and a pleasant *konnichiwa*. Since then, Disneyland has been an enormous success. Needless to say, all of the popular rides had long line-ups. We waited forever for Star Tours, a George Lucas-Disney creation, which was a lot of fun and we braved other line-ups for our share of thrills on Space Mountain and Big Thunder Mountain.

Originally, all of the food on the site was Western, but people complained about the absence of traditional Japanese cuisine. Now, the Hokusai Restaurant on Main Street serves tempura and sushi and the Hungry Bear Restaurant in Westernland (Frontierland) serves curried rice. We ate hamburgers instead, which were terrible, but they were cheap and no one seemed to mind.

≈

Summer arrives early in Japan and by the middle of May, the weather was hot and sticky. The electric fans in our classrooms provided little relief from the oppressive heat. Some of the students were showing up to class wearing shorts and sandals, but I had to wait until June 1, the first official day of the summer season before I could change into my summer uniform. At least, I didn't have to wear a tie with my white short-sleeved shirt and light grey flannels.

Throughout the month of June, everyone in Japan carries an umbrella. Despite the hot, sunny weather, torrential storms have a tendency to strike unexpectedly during *tsuyu*. I never ventured outside without my umbrella during this period of erratic weather. Even when I travelled, I always packed it in my overnight bag.

Umbrellas have a tendency to disappear mysteriously in a country where theft is extremely rare. I managed to hold onto one umbrella for 11 months, possibly a record for a *gaijin*. Unfortunately, I left it unattended for a few minutes in a department store washroom and that was too much temptation for someone else. Around Reitaku, we used the communal umbrellas for staff and students, which could be left at the entrance of any building.

By early July, we packed away our umbrellas, but the heat was almost unbearable. Many of us questioned the wisdom of an educational system that forced students to study in summer. At least, the exams were held in the air-conditioned relief of the Moralogy studies building.

Traditionally, Japanese students visit a shrine prior to exams and write prayers on small pieces of paper or on wooden plaques, especially when they are studying for university entrance exams. As far as I know, none of the *bekkasei* shared their prayers with the Shinto gods. However, I might have benefitted from a visit to the local shrine.

The exams were tough because there was so much material to memorize. Somehow, I managed to pass the conversational part of the program where I usually talked about my trips to Tokyo. But I failed all of the written exams. Like so many others who have attempted to learn the Japanese language, I was faced with the humble realization that it was going to be much tougher than I expected.

Sneaking Off to Tokyo

Ours is the most dynamic town, twice as giddy as New York, thrice as raucous as Chicago.

Don Briggs
Tokyo (1971)

How happy I was in Town Number Six! From there I could plunge into the whirlpool of Tokyo as if into my own swimming pool and sport in the absurd and stimulating confusion of its streets, shops, theatres, bars, temples, libraries, restaurants, markets, universities, Turkish baths, department stores and museums. And when tired or satiated, I could drift back to Town Number Six as to a hermit village - to talk with friends, listen to music, write or just sit quietly thinking.

Fosco Maroni
Tokyo, Time-Life International

For centuries, Edo (river gate) was nothing more than an insignificant fishing village until 1457, when a noble lord, the *daimyô* Dôkan Ôta built a small castle on a hill overlooking the mosquito-ridden swamp below. In 1590, Ieyasu Tokugawa took possession of Edo-jô (Edo Castle) and expanded the fortifications of his new headquarters. When he was proclaimed "Sei-i-taishôgun" (Great General against the Barbarians) in 1603, Ieyasu began an ambitious landfill program to reclaim the swamps from the sea in order to accommodate the growing population of Edo.

Edo-jô became the largest castle in the world and the symbol of the shogun's power throughout Japan. The buildings and watchtowers at the base of the castle were protected by a complex system of inner and outer moats. The local *daimyô* and samurai aristocracy settled with their families into hundreds of little villages surrounding the castle. Streets were laid out in irregular zigzag patterns with unexpected dead-ends to confuse the enemy. By 1700, Edo had more than one million residents.

When the shogunate collapsed in 1867, the samurai and feudal lords fled back to the provinces. The young Emperor Meiji took control of his country, moving the imperial seat from Kyoto to Edo and renaming the city *Tôkyô*, Eastern Capital. His period of rule, from 1868 to 1912, became known as the Meiji Restoration and was nothing short of amazing.

Over the centuries, Edo suffered greatly from devastating typhoons, floods, earthquakes and more than 500 fires, all of which threatened to destroy the city. But each time, the people stoically reconstructed their traditional collection of densely populated villages. Even fires which swept through the city were dismissed as "*Edo no hana*," (The Flowers of Edo).

In 1923, the capital lay in ruins once again. The Great Kanto Earthquake had destroyed half of Tokyo and killed an estimated 140,000 people. The rubble was shoveled into the bay in an effort to reclaim additional land and the city was quickly rebuilt with modern steel and concrete buildings. During World War II, Tokyo was flattened by the Allied bombing raids. After the war, major roads were widened, but there was no attempt to change the existing layout of the streets. Beyond the main thoroughfares and elevated expressways, Tokyo is still a city of winding streets and hidden lanes with no names. Many of the narrow, crooked alleyways date back to the 1600s.

With the economic recovery of the 1950s, a massive rebuilding program assured the future prosperity of the capital. But the ever-present danger of earthquakes put severe limits on the number of storeys until the early 1970s, when new construction methods overcame these concerns. However, the height of buildings in the Marunouchi and Kasumigaseki financial districts continues to be restricted because Emperor Meiji issued a royal edict forbidding any building to overlook the Imperial Palace. The height of buildings is also restricted in the lower parts of Tokyo, where the lands have been reclaimed from the sea over the centuries. This area is more likely to suffer significant damage if a major earthquake strikes again. Today, Shinjuku, a modern shopping and business district, is the only area with a large concentration of skyscrapers.

Except for the spacious palace grounds in the middle of the city and a handful of parks, gardens, temple grounds and tree-lined avenues, Tokyo is not famous for its green spaces. Much of the landscape is dominated by an endless sea of drab grey and beige houses with clusters of stores and office buildings near the railway stations. There is little evidence of urban planning anywhere. Tokyo is still made up of thousands of small neighbourhoods, each with its own character and its own soul.

≈

By May, I was starting to feel like a prisoner of the school. I had been in Japan for six weeks without leaving Kashiwa and I was tired of boring Sundays with nothing to do in the dorm. Tokyo was so close and there was so much to explore. However, only third-year students were permitted to go to Tokyo by themselves. First and second-year students were only allowed to visit relatives, with permission, of course. Some rules were simply a pain.

Just the same, I spent some time weighing my options. Nonaka-sensei, my advisor and chairman of the Exchange Committee, took his responsibilities very seriously. I was expected to get permission whenever I left the school grounds. Usually, I complied with the rules, but not always. After all, I was in Japan for an adventure. And I was determined to see and experience as much as possible during my year in this wonderful, intriguing country.

Finally, I decided to take a chance and go on my own. I didn't dare tell anyone except Randall. Even if I was lucky enough to get permission from Kitasaka-san or the teacher on duty, they would insist that I wear my Reitaku uniform. Imagine exploring Tokyo on a warm Sunday afternoon in a crested blazer, a tie and grey flannel trousers. As a *gaijin*, I was visible enough. No point looking like a geek as well. And I couldn't be bothered changing in the railway station. Carrying around an extra set of clothes in a sports bag would only be a nuisance.

I had already skipped the 7:30 a.m. Sunday breakfast in the cafeteria. The hot dogs served with a mild wasabi mustard were almost an incentive to get up early, but I usually slept in. After breakfast, the first-year students brought up the lunch crates and left them outside the dorm. I picked up my *yakisoba* submarine (a bun stuffed with stir-fried soba noodles), a carton of sour-tasting milk and a melon-flavoured cream puff. A strange combination if ever there was one, but this was Japan. I ate quickly in my room.

I decided to borrow one of the bikes and check to see if there were any teachers or third-year students wandering around the school grounds. But it was quiet. I returned the bike and then casually walked off the campus dressed in jeans and a T-shirt. I have to admit that I felt a little nervous about taking off on my own. I just had to make sure that I made it back in time to change for evening assembly at 7:10 p.m. Hopefully, I wasn't going to get lost.

I only had a vague idea of where I was going so I checked out a large book, record and video store near Minami-Kashiwa train station for a copy of the popular *Tokyo City Guide*, written by Judith Connor and Mayumi Yukida. Unfortunately, even with Sinead O'Connor playing in the background, the local store only carried Japanese publications, which was hardly surprising considering very few foreigners lived in Kashiwa. I also checked an 1100-page volume of rail, bus and airfares and timetables for all parts of the country to determine the fare to Tokyo. But it was an impossible task trying to decipher pages and pages of tables in Japanese.

I didn't anticipate major problems because Tokyo has an excellent public transportation system. The names of the stations are written in *romaji*, *kanji* and *hiragana* and the ten different subway lines crisscrossing underneath the city are colour-coded. All of the subways and railways run frequently, on time, and operate daily from 5 a.m. to midnight. I didn't have to worry about missing the last train and being at the mercy of taxis, which charge extra after midnight. Besides, *gaijin* are often ignored by cab drivers who prefer to pick up drunken *sarariman* holding up two fingers, indicating their desperation to pay double the fare.

During rush hours, the trains are crammed with people, with everyone, especially old ladies, pushing and shoving to get on and off. Some of the busier Tokyo stations, such as Shinjuku, employ white-gloved "people pushers" to force as many passengers as possible onto the trains. If you have an itch somewhere, forget it.

But my first trip to Tokyo was on a Sunday afternoon and there were no great crowds at Minami-Kashiwa station. I bought a ¥440 ticket for Shin-Ochanomizu from a machine which issued fares ranging in price from ¥120 to ¥1640, based on the distance travelled. All of the information was in *kanji*, but I managed to figure out the fare to Tokyo using a map posted above the machines. Maps had never intimidated me before, but it did take time to decipher the foreign characters.

Everyone is on his honour to purchase the correct ticket and these tickets are turned in when you exit. There are attendants at most stations, but even so, cheating on train fares has become a very common practice in Japan. When automatic fare-checking machines were installed at some stations, the money collected increased by a whopping 73 percent. So much for honesty.

The train was fairly crowded as we raced along a surface track past two-storey stucco houses, some green fields beside a river, a nine-hole golf course and the unattractive downtown and industrial areas of the communities on the outskirts of Tokyo. After Ayase station, the train left the Japan Railway tracks and slowly headed underground, rumbling along the route.

When the Disneyland crowd exited at Shin-Matsudo station, I sat down beside a man in his fifties who smiled at me in a friendly sort of way.

"Where are you from?" he asked in reasonably fluent English.

I wasn't accustomed to strangers starting a conversation with me on a subway. But this was Japan and I didn't want to be rude.

"Canada."

"Really? Do you like Japan?"

"Yes."

"Do you like Japanese girls?"

"Yes. Of course."

"Do you like to do sex with Japanese girls?"

"Uh?"

Here I was, carrying on a polite conversation with a stranger on the train and all of a sudden, he broke away from the typical phrasebook script. By now, I was beginning to feel awkward. I was the only foreigner on the train and people were staring at us. How many of them understood English?

The stranger was edging closer to me, whispering more intimate questions.

"*Wakarimasen*," I responded, indicating that I didn't know because I didn't really understand the question.

After a while, the stranger gave up on my personal life and started asking questions about my parents.

"Do your papa like whisky? Do your mama like whisky?"

Reluctantly, I continued to respond to his questions as politely as possible. He was grinning like the Cheshire Cat while I was trapped in this bizarre situation.

After an agonizing 40-minute ride, I finally escaped at Shin-Ochanomizu station.

"*Sumimasen ga*," I apologized, "*watakushi no eki desu*." (Excuse me, but this is my station.)

The stranger smiled again, saying "*sayônara*" as I got off. So much for the reputation that the Japanese people are polite and reserved. Obviously, there are exceptions to every rule.

A Japanese woman who was also on the train approached me on the platform.

"That man was very strange, wasn't he?" she remarked, without a trace of an accent. I nodded. I was somewhat surprised that she bothered to comment on the incident, but at least she understood how embarrassing the ordeal was for me.

I walked through the extensive cream-coloured labyrinth of the subway station for about ten minutes trying to find my way out. After climbing several sets of stairs, I found myself standing on a deserted street in the heart of Tokyo, surrounded by glass and steel office buildings. In a city of 12 million people, there wasn't a soul in sight. But I had finally made it on my own.

Tokyo can be intoxicating with all of its sights and sounds. But I chose the district of Kanda for my first visit because of the concentration of bookstores in a neighbourhood dominated by universities. I walked toward a busy street, and found myself on Yasukuni-dôri, which was crowded with Sunday shoppers. There were numerous sporting goods stores, more than 200 in the neighbourhood, ranging from a hole-in-the-wall to five-storey superstores, catering to the students who spend more time playing tennis and driving golf balls than studying. But I didn't see any bookstores.

As I was walking along the street, I heard someone yell, "*Gaijin-da!*" (It's a foreigner!) I turned around and saw a small boy pointing at me as if I was a creature from another planet, an alien, bearing little resemblance to the human race.

For a moment, I felt ill at ease again. The encounter on the train was bad enough. I had never expected to feel unwelcome in a city as modern and sophisticated as Tokyo. And I had never been singled out in a crowd before. But then, the Japanese are never really sure of how they feel about us. I don't blame some of them for being contemptuous. Westerners have not always been gracious guests in a city dominated by customs and traditions that still influence every aspect of daily living. No wonder the number of foreigners working and studying in Japan is strictly controlled. Even though the numbers have increased substantially in recent years, they are still small when compared with other major cities around the world.

I escaped down one of the unnamed side streets with dozens of record and music stores located in tall, narrow buildings. Many were five storeys high, with separate floors set aside for Western pop music and heavy metal, "J-Pop" (Japanese popular music), classical music and jazz.

I wandered briefly onto Hakusan-dôri, which specialized in used pornographic books and magazines in small, crowded shops. But I had no interest in *ero-hon* (erotic books) and made my way back to Yasukuni-dôri, still looking for bookstores. Suddenly, I was staring at a familiar face.

"Hello!" greeted Christian.

I had just escaped Kashiwa for the first time and already, I was bumping into a Reitaku student from my Japanese language class. Christian proudly showed me a bilingual street atlas of Tokyo he had just bought and directed me across the street. I had been wandering along the wrong side of a wide avenue without realizing that the bookstores were on the other side.

With dozens to choose from, I hardly knew where to begin. Finally, I discovered Sanseidô, which carried an incredible variety of English books on the fifth floor, including the *Tokyo City Guide* for ¥2600. It was difficult to restrain myself as I checked out two Japanese slang phrasebooks, *Making Out in Japanese* and *More Making Out in Japanese,* a movie script for *Back to the Future II* and the *Billboard Book of Top Ten Charts*. I could just see my parents trying to scrutinize the Visa bill back home for ¥16,000, the equivalent of three months of allowance at Trinity. Reluctantly, I put them all back except for the *Tokyo City Guide*.

Tokyo bookstores are always packed with people of all ages. The Japanese are avid readers and many of them spend a lot of time browsing before buying at least a short novel or magazine. Teenagers are just as likely to be in a bookstore as a record store, whereas most Western teens wouldn't be caught dead in a bookstore. But then, not all Japanese teens are buying books. Instead, many of them are looking for a new edition of their favourite *manga* or sports magazine.

From early times, the Japanese have had a passion for books. Many attended the temple schools where Buddhist monks stressed the importance of reading. Today, their appetite for knowledge is just as strong, creating an enormous interest in books on all subjects. Bookstores sell an astounding variety of reference books covering every conceivable subject as well as encyclopedias. Most Japanese homes have several reference books, a world atlas and at least one encyclopedia set.

There were plenty of other foreign students and English teachers rummaging through the shelves and I no longer felt out of place. Browsing in bookstores has always been one of my favourite pastimes, but in Tokyo, the sheer volume of books on any city block was mind-boggling. As much as I enjoyed Japan, I devoured English-language publications in an attempt to escape the overwhelming presence of the Japanese around me. By the time I had left the country, I had spent a small fortune on books, including a number of British music publications that I had never seen before.

Near Jimbôchô intersection, the used bookstores were just as crowded. In one building, 11 specialty shops covered subject matter ranging from medicine to pornography. I never ceased to be amazed by the sheer quantity of pornographic books catering to the more lascivious nature of the Japanese male. Rape and other forms of sexual violence are common themes and yet, Japanese customs officials censor all foreign publications entering the country. Soft porn magazines such as *Playboy* and *Penthouse* are popular targets because many photographs of nude women display pubic hair, which is strictly forbidden in Japan. Even foreign art books are closely scrutinized for photographs of offensive paintings.

Strolling among the crowds along the narrow streets, I noticed that everyone was smartly dressed in fashionable clothes. Absolutely no one was walking around in torn jeans or ragged shorts that were so popular back home. There were no homeless people either, wandering aimlessly about begging for yen or sleeping in doorways of buildings. Occasionally, newspapers reported that the number of "floating drifting ones," who slept in subway corridors and underground pedestrian walkways, were on the rise. Many of the homeless, who are usually alcoholics or mentally ill, live in working class neighbourhoods so I never saw them. Despite the country's highly structured society with low unemployment, some people fail to find a place for themselves and fall through the cracks.

I passed numerous small restaurants with glass showcases displaying plates of very realistic-looking plastic replicas of food. These imitation meals ranged from squid and octopus specials to spaghetti with meat sauce.

There are more than 45,000 restaurants in Tokyo, serving everything from classic French (and very expensive), Italian, Indian, Korean and Chinese to more obscure African and Arabic cuisine. There are also 10,000 sushi bars, which are moderately expensive, at least from a student's point of view. Restaurants specializing in Japanese food range from cheap *soba* shops, selling a bowl of noodles for ¥300 to *ryôtei* offering elaborate dinners complete with traditional geisha entertainment costing ¥40,000 and more, per person.

I was fascinated by the variety of restaurants, but I kept my eye out for the golden arches. I have never been fond of McDonald's, but I was suffering from junk food withdrawal and desperate for a Big Mac. I hadn't had a burger in two months and I was curious if the Japanese version was the same as back home. Finally, I found McDonald's on a side street, along with other local competitors, Love Burger and Lotteria. The restaurant was familiar in a comforting sort of way.

The menu at McDonald's in Japan is basically the same as everywhere else, except for the "corn potage soup." Also, coffee and tea are served either hot or cold. During late afternoon, the restaurant wasn't busy and I had to wait five minutes for my Big Mac, *furai potehto* (French fries) and chocolate shake. When I opened the styrene clamshell, my Big Mac was huge, like the ones advertised on TV. As I bit into it, the bun scrunched up and I figured out the mystery of Big Macs. The bun was full of hot air. But everything tasted exactly the same as I had remembered and I was satisfied. Lunch cost ¥750, which was somewhat pricier than the same meal back home in Elliot Lake.

Makudonarudo Hambahgah, as McDonald's burgers are called, are extremely popular in Japan and some people actually believe that the restaurant chain is a homegrown invention. More than 20 years ago, a junior high school student returned from a Boy Scout Jamboree in the United States and exclaimed, "Even in America, they have McDonald's." Likewise, the Japanese always seemed to be impressed when they learned that my hometown in Northern Ontario, with a population of less than 14,000 residents, supports a *Makudonarudo*.

When I finished my meal, the sun had sunk behind the buildings and it was time to head back to Reitaku. I was reasonably pleased with myself as I retraced my steps to the subway station and found the right train to Kashiwa. I made it back to school without a mishap and no one mentioned my absence. I was present for evening assembly and that's what mattered.

≈

While I was a student at Reitaku, I made 22 trips to Tokyo. Most of them were during the first term, when I had a room of my own and experienced a certain amount of freedom. Almost everyone, including Kitasaka-san, assumed that I was spending the day at the university campus with my friends from the Japanese language class. However, once I moved into the dorm room after the summer holidays, I lost all of my special privileges. My activities were restricted and I was required to let my dorm leader, Takebe-san, know of my whereabouts at all times. Besides, additional *kendô* practices were scheduled on Sundays, starting at 10:30 a.m. and lasting two-and-a-half hours. By then, it was too late to go anywhere.

I was always grateful that no one ever snitched on me. Some of the boys were certainly aware that I was sneaking off the campus, especially when I returned with shopping bags displaying prominent logos of stores in Tokyo. If anything, they were surprised that I enjoyed exploring the city on my own. The group mentality was so ingrained at Reitaku that none of them would have considered going to Tokyo by themselves. Often, I wondered if some of the staff members suspected anything. Just the same, I was always very careful and never got caught. Though, I felt somewhat cheated because I never had a chance to experience the excitement of Roppongi at night.

Roppongi is described as the "playground of the rich, the beautiful, and hordes of lecherous off-duty English teachers" in Lonely Planet's *Tokyo City Guide*. This popular American businessman's ghetto has plenty of gourmet restaurants, throbbing discos, flashy nightclubs, including a number of clubs catering to jazz aficionados.

Instead of catching the excitement at night, I was forced to explore Roppongi on a Sunday afternoon. The air was sticky and hot but plenty of people were wandering along the streets. Although a few women were wearing shorts, they were modestly dressed. Short-shorts and halter-tops were non-existent, despite the sweltering heat. Japanese women choose their fashions very discreetly. Men are even more conservative about their dress. None of them wore shorts in the city.

Walking from the subway station, I saw some reassuring signs of Western civilization, such as Wendy's, Arby's and McDonald's, and some not so reassuring signs, including a 50-foot high poster advertising the New Kids on the Block, who were hardly a favourite of mine. Then, there was Wave, a jet-black five-storey record store, one of the largest in the world, which also featured expensive modern Japanese art. There were other art and bookstores in the area, including ABC Bookstore, with a fabulous collection of coffee table books. I also checked out the famous Almond, a garish pink and white, four-storey coffee shop, notable for serving some of the worst coffee and cake in the city. But I wasn't tempted to try them out. Coffee served at a café is a real luxury in Japan, costing between ¥300 and ¥500 for a small cup. No refills either. I had seen enough and headed along Roppongi-dôri on my way to Ginza, about five kilometres away.

Most of Roppongi-dôri lies underneath a busy, elevated expressway. I walked through some pretty shabby areas sandwiched in between the foreign embassies of

Toranomon on one side and the expensive hotels and *ryôtei* restaurants of Akasaka on the other. There wasn't much to see, except for office buildings, a few garages and neighbourhood restaurants. For the most part, the street was deserted.

In any other city, I would have been reluctant to hike over to Ginza along such a desolate route. But Japan is still one of the safest countries in the world for foreigners to visit. It is probably the only country where women can feel free to walk the streets, day and night, including the narrow alleys of Kabukichô in Shinjuku, the infamous red light district, without worrying about being assaulted. Chances of getting mugged or raped are zilch. No drive-by shootings to worry about either. Crime committed by individuals is very rare and organized criminal activity is usually not directed at foreigners.

Japan's gun control laws are among the toughest in the world. The right to bear arms ceased more than 400 years ago when Hideyoshi Toyotomi organized a sword hunt to remove weapons from everyone except the samurai. At the beginning of the Meiji Restoration, the samurai were also stripped of their swords. Only the police are allowed to carry guns while on duty. At all other times, their ammunition is kept locked in a safe at the station.

A very efficient and well-respected police system also helps keep the crime rate low. *Kôban* (police boxes) are usually located every few hundred metres in busy areas of Tokyo but there were none along the Roppongi-dôri. The police, known as *omawari-san* (Mr. Walking Around), patrol their beat on foot and bicycle. They are responsible for a specific neighbourhood and usually know most of the shopkeepers and many of the residents. Twice a year, they conduct surveys of all the businesses and homes, keeping a file of names, occupations and driving licences of all the residents. The *omawari-san,* who are very friendly and helpful, spend much of their time providing directions since most the streets have no names and homes do not have consecutive numbers.

I turned onto Sotobori-dôri and walked to the southern end of Ginza at Shimbashi. Ginza was originally a swamp, but the land, like so much of Tokyo, was reclaimed from the sea in the early 1600s. In the 1870s, Ginza was one of the first modern districts of Tokyo with Western-style brick buildings and wide tree-lined avenues. Today, this chic, sophisticated district also commands the highest real estate prices in Japan. The main street, Chûô-dôri (Central Avenue), the Fifth Avenue of Tokyo, becomes a pedestrian walkway on Sundays, crowded with shoppers searching out the latest in fashion and design. In 1990, the Japanese were unaware that their bubble economy was about to burst.

Nearly every major department store has its flagship store on Chûô-dôri and most companies have their showrooms in the Ginza as well. I checked out the Sony showroom, but it didn't match the fascinating discount electronics stores in Akihabara, a few miles up Chûô-dôri.

Ginza is not for bargain hunters. Just the same, you can't beat Chûô-dôri for window-shopping or snob appeal. At Matsuya, like all of the classy department stores, clerks are on hand to greet customers as they enter the store.

"*Irasshaimase!*" (Welcome!)

I was not accustomed to a clerk bowing to me as if I was someone important. Hey, I was only 16 years old. Back home, I was usually ignored by the department store staff. Even when I wanted to purchase something, it was difficult getting service sometimes. But in Japan, the word for customer is *okyakusama*, a combination of honourable guest and lord. Customers don't abuse their privileges either. There are no security tags on any of the merchandise, an indication that shoplifting is not a concern. The packaging of all goods is very elaborate and everything is carefully wrapped before being placed in a distinctive shopping bag.

All of the elevators have young female attendants who greet everyone at each floor and list all of the features of the store in high-pitched service voices, a full octave above the normal speaking voice. An older woman waited until I got on the elevator. But the custom of men always boarding the elevators first is changing. None of the younger women bothered to step aside for me.

The eight-storey department store has beautiful interiors, including an atrium in the middle. I was always in awe of the lavish and extravagant displays throughout the store. On one visit, I was impressed with a Canadian wilderness display, complete with a log cabin and canoe, set among birch trees. The store was promoting a new line of expensive, outdoorsy clothing. All of the mannequins were tall and thin with Caucasian features.

Tokyo's most expensive restaurants and watering holes are also located in Ginza. The top clubs are the haunts of Japan's major corporations where drinks and snacks, known as "charm," along with hostess fees and table charges can easily cost the company ¥100,000 per person. That's quite a tab on anyone's expense account. Even the sushi bars and tempura restaurants were way beyond my means. Chikuyôtei (bamboo leaf cuisine), a restaurant specializing in eel dishes was tempting, until I saw the ¥10,000 charge for a full course meal. Once again, I settled for an affordable Big Mac at *Makudonarudo* before catching the train back to Kashiwa.

≈

Shibuya is one of the more interesting districts to visit and the streets are always teeming with young people. They often meet at Hachikô Square in front of Shibuya station beside a bronze statue of a dog, named Hachikô. The famous landmark commemorates the loyalty of Hachikô, who walked with his master, a professor at Tokyo University, to the station everyday and also met him on his way home. According to legend, the professor suffered a stroke one day and never returned home. For seven years, Hachikô returned to the station every evening to wait for his master. The dog was admired for his uncompromising loyalty and the statue was erected in 1934. When Hachikô died, he was given a grand funeral and placed in the National Museum of Science.

Many of the trendy shops, including Seibu Seed and One-Oh-Nine, are located in Shibuya, as well as plenty of record stores, theatres and discotheques. I was fascinated with the 25-level "Creative Life Store" called Tôkyû Hands, which specializes in do-it-yourself (DIY) projects on a much larger scale than the hardware and automotive stores back home. Tôkyû Hands sells everything, including the kitchen sink. The English-language brochure advertises a number of DIY clinics at Hands Labo as well as interior refurbishing at Hands Reform. The store also sells sporting goods but I wasn't about to ask how much a custom-made bicycle cost. Just before Christmas, Tôkyû Hands is the ideal place to find plastic Santas, reindeer, and even manger sets complete with baby Jesus.

At Tower Records, new CD releases were a bargain at ¥2100 and there was a special deal for the *Village Voice,* which cost less than in New York. Tower Records also carried *The New York Times, The Los Angeles Times* and *Rolling Stone* at two to four times the American cover price.

Lunch at Pizza Hut on Kôen-dôri (Park Avenue) was rather extravagant considering the small *pahsonaru* (personal) pizza cost ¥1000 and the Pepsi set me back another ¥300. But it was the best pizza in Japan, even if it took 30 minutes to arrive. Like McDonald's and other Western franchises, the ingredients, preparation and service were the same as back home. Unless of course, you order their Idaho Special (potato chunks, bacon, onion, corn, parsley, olives, mayonnaise and double cheese) or Sea Food Special (squid, shrimp, tuna, broccoli, onion, mayonnaise and double cheese). I was tempted, but they cost ¥1800 each. There is no shortage of strange and exotic toppings for pizza in Japan. Other choices, depending on the restaurant, include corn, asparagus, egg yolk, cod roe, eel, flaked tuna, scallops, raisins and entire chicken breasts.

After lunch, I walked over to Harajuku where trendy shops cater to pampered young people with expensive tastes. Many of them are located on Omotesandô, often called the Champs-Elysées of Tokyo because it is one of the city's few tree-lined avenues.

Harajuku's other claim to fame is Yoyogi Park, the site of the 1964 Summer Olympic Games. Sunday afternoon concerts on the boulevard have been popular as long as anyone can remember. More than anything else, Yoyogi Park reflects the obsession of Japanese teens with Western culture since the late 1950s when television broadcasts introduced them to lifestyles on the other side of the globe.

Dozens of groups were set up side by side, with their sound equipment and generators, playing everything from 1950s rock "n" roll to heavy metal and reggae. Each group had an audience even if their sound or style was lousy. And believe me, some of it was dreadful. The band members and the street dancers were all trying to be cool. Every fashion statement since the rock "n" roll era was represented, including dancing girls with pony-tails, wearing flared skirts, ankle socks and saddle shoes and guys with the greased-back look wearing tight black leather pants and jackets. The more extreme elements showed up as well, with their Mohawk haircuts and orange dye jobs.

Anything goes and everyone can participate. The lead singer for one of the groups was strumming on a cheap trash heap acoustic guitar while the drummer was banging on a padded tissue box. The singer was awful. But he, too, had an audience. Most of the music was Western pop but the lyrics were usually in Japanese. A handful of performers were actually decent but it was strictly amateur hour at Yoyogi Park.

The outrageous outfits seen only in Harajuku could be found in the hundreds of cheap clothing shops and boutiques along Takeshita-dôri. Unlike similar shops catering to the alternative element in many Western countries, there was no drug paraphernalia for sale in any of the shops on the narrow side streets. The rebelliousness and decadence of most of the kids performing in Yoyogi Park is only skin deep. They are back at school the following day, dressed in their uniforms.

Juveniles who venture over the edge and become involved with criminal activity are usually caught. In prison, they are forced to sit perfectly still in lotus position for long periods of time and meditate over their "sins" as well as work for eight hours each day in one of the prison shops. The punishment may be harsh by our standards, but most of them manage to leave prison with a trade certificate and are integrated back into society. There are few repeat offenders.

≈

The Hibiya subway line was constructed prior to the 1964 Olympics and has never been renovated. The stations are grungy and the ceiling fans are next to useless when the sweltering heat suffocates Tokyo in the summer. I would not have bothered with the Hibiya line except that it was the most convenient train to Akihabara, the largest discount centre in Tokyo for home appliances, audio and video equipment, cameras, computers and other electronic items. Climbing out of the hellhole of the subway station, I wandered past dozens of small shops and stalls, brightly decorated with neon signs and playing Japanese rock.

I was intrigued by the pocketsize electronic English-Japanese-*kanji* dictionaries as well as the portable CD-ROM players that were ideal to take along to a baseball game to check out a player's stats. The Japanese love electronic gadgets and the variety of products was awesome. New inventions are test-marketed here for a year or more before they are sold outside of Japan. If they fail, these products will never be shipped overseas.

I purchased a Japanese word processor, which operated on four D-cell batteries, for ¥27,000. But first, I was sent to another floor for a duty-free form to avoid paying sales tax. The process can be a real hassle, but each clerk was very courteous and helpful. The sales clerk, however, carefully scrutinized my signature on the Visa card. I presume he wasn't too familiar with a Western scrawl.

The computer era has freed Japan from the tedious task of writing everything by hand. With so many *kanji* characters, there was no such thing as a conventional Japanese typewriter. But the computer chip offers endless possibilities when there are several alphabets to deal with. Still, using a computer in Japan is a complicated process. First, the phonetic *hiragana* equivalent of the *kanji* is typed into the computer. When the space bar is pressed, the computer hunts for the correct *kanji* equivalent. If the word is not in the memory, each character has to be worked out separately. For someone like me, writing anything in Japanese takes some time, even with a word processor. If I knew all of the correct characters, it would actually be easier to write it out by hand. But at least, the final product from a computer is much neater.

My trip to Akihabara was brief since I had to rush back to school in time for practice at 2:30 p.m. No one said anything about my packages on the shelf just inside the doorway of the *kendô* hall.

≈

One Sunday, I transferred to the Hibiya line on my way to Hiro-o. When an elderly woman got on, I offered her my seat, a customary practice back home.

"*Dôzo*," I said, pointing to the seat.

She looked at me puzzled. In Japan, men never offer their seats to women. Etiquette actually dictates that men and boys have first rights to a seat on a train even though no one bothers about etiquette when travelling on the subway.

"*Dôzo*," I repeated. Finally, she sat down, thanking me quietly by responding with "*Dômo arigatô gozaimasu*."

When she got up at her station, she bowed gracefully. "*Dômo arigatô gozaimashita*," she said once again, in such a soft voice that I wondered if I had somehow caused her to feel embarrassed by singling her out.

The Hiro-o station was a steam bath and I hurried through the underground labyrinth. When I resurfaced, my first impression was that I was back on the other side of the world. Hiro-o has the dubious distinction as the *gaijin* ghetto of Tokyo. Almost all the foreign executives and their families live in subsidized company apartment buildings in this district. Two large Western-style supermarkets cater to expatriates who are not fond of Japanese food. The National Azabu Supermarket was filled with American, British and Australian shoppers. Everything was considerably more expensive than back home.

I felt comfortable in Hiro-o and enjoyed the sense of freedom, just being able to walk around unnoticed by the crowds. All of the signs on the stores and restaurants were familiar. Even the Japanese kids hanging outside Baskin-Robbins were speaking in English.

The *Tokyo City Guide* recommended Homeworks for an authentic charcoal-broiled burger. As much as I enjoyed Japanese food, I missed red meat, and steaks were out of the question. When I entered the restaurant, I was greeted with the customary "*Irasshaimase*" and directed to the counter. The Japanese formalities ended there. The menu had many tempting choices and I ordered an avocado burger with fries and onion rings for ¥1150 along with a black cherry soda for ¥400. Lunch was an extravagant indulgence, but well worth it. Homeworks was a place where I was able to forget about *kanji* and even Japan for a while.

≈

One Saturday, shortly before final exams at the university, Nonaka-sensei decided that I could go to Tokyo on a shopping excursion by myself. I'm sure he was curious about my culinary skills when I offered to prepare my father's award-winning Eggplant Parmigiana for him, Merwyn and Itoh-sensei. Not about to turn down an Italian meal, Nonaka-sensei generously gave me ¥5000 for my shopping expedition and provided some directions to the Olympia Market, which specialized in Western foods. Even though I assured him that I could find the shop without too much difficulty, Nonaka-sensei still worried that I might get lost (me, lost?) since this was my "first" trip to Tokyo. Was he wrong!

After morning assembly, I decided to "play hooky" by skipping classes. Just as I was heading out of the dorm, I was stopped by Nagahara-san, a third-year *kendô* teammate with an ugly Stalin moustache. I always wondered about such a break from convention. Even at Trinity, we were expected to be clean-shaven.

"*Zubon*," he said sternly, pointing to my pants. The summer dress code was grey flannels and a short-sleeved white shirt. Instead, I was wearing a comfortable pair of grey cords. Under my white shirt with its Reitaku insignia,

I had on my Bob Marley "Be Happy" T-shirt. Like Kabuki actors, I was planning to go through an onstage costume change known as *hikinuki* (pulling out the threads) as soon as I got to the train station.

"*Gomen nasai*," I apologized. Then I just shrugged my shoulders and walked past him.

Once at Hibiya station, I spent 25 minutes trying to find my way out of the underground maze. With more than a dozen exits, I was having difficulty finding the one closest to the Tourist Information Center (TIC). Me lost in Tokyo? Yeah, right. Think again. But I wanted some pamphlets to plan my summer vacation and the TIC was only open on weekdays and Saturday mornings.

I made several other detours before looking for the shop recommended by Nonaka-sensei. I checked out Maruzen, a fairly good bookstore, which is also closed on Sundays. I wandered into Ochanomizu, a district famous for its universities including *Tôdai*, or Tokyo University, Japan's most prestigious academic institution. I had lunch at Shakey's, where I devoured 15 (small) slices of pizza, two plates of spaghetti and an iced tea for ¥800. In Ikebukuro, I got lost in Seibu, the world's largest department store. Finally, I made it to the recommended Olympia Market in Harajuku, but it turned out to be a hole-in-the-wall. Except for its extensive wine selection, there were better stores in Kashiwa.

Heading across to the Ginza, I found Meidiya, Japan's oldest imported food store, where I bought olive oil, mozzarella cheese, Hokkaido butter (so good, you can eat it by itself), spaghetti, as well as the essential herbs, basil and oregano. The tab was already over ¥6000 and I still had several other ingredients to purchase.

Next, I checked out Takashimaya (which literally translates as "expensive island store") and looked for expensive eggplant, expensive tomato sauce and expensive tomato paste. After an exhaustive search by two sales clerks who first thought I was looking for ketchup, I settled for Kagome tomato puree instead of Hunt's tomato sauce. It was almost 8 p.m. by the time I left Takashimaya. But not before blowing another ¥4000!

Fortunately, the subway entrance was right by the store so I did not have to shell out another ¥1000 for a cab to the nearest station. The walk through the station was painful enough since I was carrying enough groceries to necessitate a hip operation. And I still had to transfer at Ôtemachi station. When there wasn't a bus waiting at Minami-Kashiwa station, I started walking back to school. I wasn't sure how I was going to manage when, miraculously, the right bus did come along. My problems were hardly over. I wasn't familiar with the bus stops since I had always walked the mile from the train station and I ended up getting off one stop early by mistake.

As I struggled along the street with all my bags, I spotted a first-year student. Yes, a porter to help me carry some of the groceries. What a stroke of luck! He didn't hesitate to give a hand and I was most grateful for his assistance.

At the dormitory, I unpacked all of the groceries, surprised that none of the bottles were broken and the eggplant wasn't bruised beyond recognition. Somehow, I managed to find space in the refrigerators shared by the students in the dormitory, hoping that no one would steal my goods. I had already lost a couple of bottles of Coke. I clearly wrote "JON" on my groceries and hoped that preparing the meal itself would not be as difficult as the shopping excursion.

I spent the following Sunday afternoon in the Nonakas' tiny kitchen. There was no shortage of pots and pans as I cooked the sauce, fried the sliced eggplant and boiled the pasta. The convection oven was on the small side, but I managed to bake the eggplant dish without any problems. At least, they had an oven, which is rare in Japan. Dinner was a big hit though I cringed when Itoh-sensei liberally sprinkled Tabasco sauce on his portion. If only my father could see him.

≈

In July, Nonaka-sensei arranged for Yuki Minoru and his father to take me on a tour of Tokyo. Yuki was in his third year and had been the first exchange student at Trinity in 1988, so his English skills were pretty good.

Yuki arrived at my room, promptly at 9 a.m. on a Sunday morning, neatly dressed in his summer Reitaku uniform. I was wearing a T-shirt and jeans, my usual garb for prowling around Tokyo. As a senior student, Yuki could have insisted that I dress appropriately but he didn't say anything. It's just as well since I had no intention of changing.

At Tokyo station, we met his father, brother and a woman who was considerably younger than Mr. Minoru and very pretty. Yuki politely acknowledged her presence but later whispered in my ear, "She is not my mother."

We joined a Japanese bus tour, courtesy of Mr. Minoru, at ¥4000 per person. Our first stop was the immense grounds of the Imperial Palace in the heart of Tokyo, where the emperor has lived since 1868. Many of the ancient wooden buildings on the site were destroyed during the bombing raids of World War II. Reconstruction of the palace was postponed until Tokyo was completely rebuilt since scarce building supplies were urgently needed to provide housing for millions of people left homeless after the war. The new ferroconcrete Imperial Palace was finally completed in 1968, 100 years after Emperor Meiji took possession of Edo-jô. Except for New Year's Day and the Emperor's birthday on December 23, the grounds are restricted to tour groups and parties of two or more individuals with special permission from the Imperial Household Agency.

We followed our tour hostess with her yellow flag, walking through the beautiful gardens beside the wide moat surrounding the palace until we finally reached Nijûbashi, the bridge connecting the outer world to the inner palace. Like thousands of tour groups before us, we posed together in front of Nijûbashi, reportedly the most photographed spot in Japan. Hatô Bus Tours had their own photographer and he was not going to let this record fall. I was surprised when a large number of the people on our tour ordered a souvenir photo for ¥1200. As if we were close friends! Surely they weren't buying because there was a *gaijin* in their midst. Or were they? Stranger things have happened. Neither Yuki nor I bothered with such an extravagance. Instead, in the true Japanese tradition, we took photos of each other at the famous bridge with the turrets of the palace showing between the trees.

At Yasukuni Jinja (Peaceful Country Shrine), we passed through the enormous *torii* gates, constructed from steel and bronze, to view the Shinto shrine dedicated to 2.5 million Japanese war dead since it was built in 1869. The cremated ashes of soldiers have been brought here whenever practical. Otherwise, the spirits have made the trek on their own. Prior to World War II, Yasukuni was the most important Shinto shrine in Tokyo. In more recent years, however, it has had been the centre of controversy since several war criminals were enshrined here in 1979. Nevertheless, Yasukuni Jinja continues to be a popular tourist attraction.

Our tour bus took us along the Metropolitan Expressway, a series of toll roads that weave their way around the city, over canals, between buildings and even under the Imperial Palace. We were certainly travelling fast enough for a tour bus, going at about 80 kilometres (50 miles) per hour along the narrow road. The speed limit was 60 kilometres per hour, not 60 miles per hour. When the expressways opened in the late 1960s, the Japanese were just beginning to benefit from the economic boost of expanding export markets and could finally afford to buy their own cars. The low speed limit reflected the lack of experience more than anything else. Back then, there were more casualties on the expressways in Tokyo each day than from the fighting in Vietnam. Although the highway death toll has dropped considerably during the past three decades, there has been a tremendous reluctance on the part of government to change the speed limits on the city expressways. It hardly seems to matter. No one pays attention anyway.

As we passed through the various districts, the hostess gave a brief description of each of the areas and Yuki translated the highlights. He obviously had no idea that I was already familiar with the city from my previous visits to Tokyo.

Finally, we parked beside dozens of other tour buses at the bright red and white Tokyo Tower, rising 333 metres

(1,092 feet) above the city. When television broadcasts began in Japan in the mid-1950s, every major city in the country rushed to build an observation tower near the centre of each city as a symbol of postwar progress. Built in 1958 to transmit the city's eight television networks, the whimsical copy of the Eiffel Tower in Paris attracted thousands of visitors each day. Even today, the Tokyo Tower is the tallest structure in the city, and has good views, as long as the skies are reasonably clear from fog, smog and haze.

After a *bentô* lunch in a vast dining hall for tour groups, which was included in the tour price, we took an elevator to the Grand Observation Platform, only 150 metres (492 feet) high. Although it was a hazy day, we could still see a vague outline of Mount Fuji in the distance. The most fascinating aspect of the Tokyo Tower was the perspective of a miniature world as we watched the cars and people on the streets below us through the glass tiles in the floor of the balcony.

At the end of our tour, the bus dropped us off at Tokyo station and we took the Ginza subway line to Asakusa, a district famous for its *ryotei* restaurants with geisha entertainment. But most of the tourists flock to Asakusa to visit Sensôji, the oldest temple in the city. According to legend, the temple enshrines a small golden statue of Kannon, which was fished out of the nearby Sumida River by local fishermen in AD 628. There are several temples in Japan dedicated to the Buddhist goddess Kannon, who is revered for her compassion for human weakness and suffering, and Sensôji is the most famous of them all.

During the Edo Period (1600 to 1868), the temple attracted thousands of pilgrims seeking favours from

Kannon. The surrounding area was crowded with shops and theatres, giving the place a carnival atmosphere. Although most of the buildings have been ravaged by fires, floods, earthquakes and war over the years, Sensôji was always rebuilt, most recently in 1958, according to original plans saved from the Edo Period.

At the entrance, Kaminari-mon (Thunder Gate), we posed for obligatory snapshots under the huge red paper lantern. The crowds of people wandering along the wide boulevard, or more accurately, midway, were something else. Hundreds of colourful stalls and shops, peddling souvenirs and food, have changed little since Edo became the capital of the shogunate in 1603. All of the fun cliché "Japanesey" gifts can be found here, everything from good luck charms to silk boxer shorts, kabuki make-up and cheap toys. You can spend a bundle on more exotic gifts such as tortoise-shell hair combs, wigs and hand-carved wooden masks.

Buddhist monks still gather in the Main Hall to chant the Sutra at the altar three times each day. After cleansing ourselves with the heavily scented purple smoke rising from a large bronze urn, we made a small donation for good luck and headed over to Kappabashi.

This wholesale district caters to restaurants, supplying them with everything from ovens to the fake food displayed in their windows. The manufacturing of plastic food replicas is an art and the items are very expensive. A small piece of sushi cost ¥750, a Coke around ¥3000 and a complete entrée can set you back ¥7000.

The Asakusa area has always been the home of merchants and craftsmen. The cabinets in one of the shops along Asakusa-dôri were beautifully made and very expensive. In the Edo Period, merchants and tradesmen were regarded as lower classes, as opposed to their highly regarded counterparts in medieval Europe.

At Tawaramachi station, Yuki and I took the train back to Reitaku, switching at Ueno. We stood all of the way to Kashiwa. Then we waited quite a while at Kashiwa station before catching a train for Minami-Kashiwa station. I didn't bother to mention that the Chiyoda subway line from Nishi-Nippori would have been much faster. Yuki and many of the students who lived in Tokyo believed that the express trains to Kashiwa were faster, in spite of the long wait.

≈

On November 17, which is also Labour Day in Japan, the entire school participated in the *Daijôsai*, the Emperor's Thanksgiving Rite, or Coronation Parade, although the actual coronation took place a week later. Some of the teachers were concerned that left-wing extremists might set bombs along the parade route. A number of incidents had already occurred at train stations in Tokyo but no one had been killed or even injured. I wondered if the radical opponents of the emperor were just trying to get their point across rather than endangering lives.

Controversy over the role of the emperor in Japan has existed since the end of World War II. Japan's imperial line is the oldest hereditary monarchy in the world and can be traced back to the fifth century AD through Chinese literature, and even further back to 660 BC through Japanese folklore to Jimmu Tennô, a direct descendant of Amaterasu-ômikami, the Sun Goddess. Throughout the centuries, all of the emperors as well as empresses were worshipped as Shinto deities. Even when Japan was first governed by an elected parliament called the Imperial Diet in 1889, the emperor, or *Tennô*, was still revered as a leader with divine power.

After Japan was defeated in 1945, the Supreme Commander of the Allied Occupation Forces, American General Douglas MacArthur kept Emperor Hirohito as "a symbol of the State and of the unity of the people" for practical reasons. He was worried that the Japanese might revolt, or even worse, turn to communism. Hirohito, however, was forced to denounce his claim to divinity.

When Hirohito died in 1989, people throughout Japan debated the future of the figurehead of state. Many wanted to abolish the role of the emperor altogether, while others were anxious to give him a greater governing role. But nothing changed. The Japanese clung to their customs and Hirohito's eldest son, Akihito, the 125th emperor of Japan, succeeded his father to preserve the country's traditions and values. And I was fortunate to be in Japan to witness such a momentous occasion.

Soon after I had arrived at Reitaku, Nonaka-sensei and I were returning to the high school from the university when a helicopter flew extremely low over our heads and one of the men on board was shouting at us through a megaphone. I asked about the unusual incident, but Nonaka-sensei only said, "Don't worry about it." I found it rather strange that he was avoiding the question, as if he was ashamed of the incident. Later, I learned that it was probably a hard-line nationalist shouting revolutionary slogans. The ultra right-wing nationalists, known as *uyoku*, are a small minority but very zealous in their efforts to defend the Chrysanthemum Throne and reinstate the emperor's political powers. During my trips to Tokyo, I occasionally saw trucks with loudspeakers mounted on them, blaring nationalistic music and slogans as they drove through the streets. According to rumour, the *uyoku* are well financed by the *yakuza* gangs.

On the day of the parade, we met in front of the Social Education Building where we were given instructions and assigned our buses. The buses were new and very luxurious in comparison to my experiences on Greyhound coaches in Canada. Just as the Japanese made use of space by turning an empty *tatami* room into a bedroom at night, these buses had another row of seats that folded down into the aisle, increasing their capacity. The seats were comfortable and the TV hanging from the ceiling in the front of the bus featured a soccer game.

We joined the rest of the students from Reitaku at Ueno Kôen, Tokyo's largest and most popular public park, famous for *hanami* (cherry blossom viewing) in the spring. After we assembled as a group, we walked through the park past a number of museums, galleries and a zoo. Remarkably, the Tôshô-gû Shrine built in the memory of Ieyasu Tokugawa in 1651 still stands, considering all the disasters that have befallen Tokyo over the centuries.

After reaching Chûô-dôri, we waited for more than an hour for the parade to begin along with thousands of other students dressed in their school uniforms and *sararimen* dressed in dark business suits. Each of us carried a fragile paper lantern with a large red sun imprinted on it. Promptly at 4 p.m., we started walking along Chûô-dôri and occasionally, we would cry out "*Tennô!*" as a salute to the new emperor. I stayed with Matsuda-sensei, an English teacher who kept fretting about the chance of a bomb going off along the parade route. I wasn't sure I needed the added excitement, and hoped that Matsuda-sensei's fears were unfounded.

The sun had already set by the time we reached the uter Garden of the Imperial Palace. We lit our lanterns and the sight of thousands of golden paper lanterns glowing in the dark was truly awe-inspiring. Huge Sony Jumbotrons had been installed throughout the grounds so that all of us could actually see the activities on the stage. An *enka* singer, in her sixties with an exceptionally good voice, led the crowds in the singing of a song saluting the new emperor. For a brief moment, Emperor Akihito and Empress Michiko greeted us from Nijûbashi and the crowds roared, shouting "*Banzai! Banzai! Banzai!*" (Ten thousand years!)

As soon as the ceremonies were over, we walked back to the buses, with most of us stopping at the dozens of portable toilets along the way. There was a careful check of the students when we boarded the bus, although I couldn't imagine anyone straying from our carefully organized groups.

≈

As my year at Reitaku drew to a close, I think Nonaka-sensei felt somewhat badly that I had seen so little of Tokyo. At least, that's what he thought. One day, he suggested that I might want to consider doing some sightseeing on Thursdays because I only had a math class first thing in the morning. Needless to say, I was delighted that he was actually sanctioning my expeditions.

The only downside was Kitasaka-san. She insisted that I must be properly dressed in my Reitaku uniform if I was going anywhere. That Thursday, I took the train to Yokohama neatly dressed in my blazer, grey flannels, white shirt and tie.

After stopping in the Tourist Information Center for a comprehensive brochure on the city, I headed out on the Hibiya line that connected with the Tôkyû Tôyoko line to Sakuragi-chô station. I transferred to the Japan Railways Negishi line and got off at Ishikawa-chô station where an elaborate and very colourful gate greets visitors to Chûkagai (Chinatown). Yokohama is probably the only truly cosmopolitan city in Japan, with a large Chinese population as well as a fair number of Europeans and Americans. When Commodore Perry sailed his fleet of black ships into the harbour, Yokohama was a village with hardly more than 100 houses built in the mud flats southwest of Tokyo. After the treaties were signed, Yokohama became a thriving port with a large concentration of foreigners.

Chûkagai is famous for its restaurants and I checked the display cases of fake food but couldn't find any lunch specials. A complete meal for less than ¥2000 didn't seem to exist. So, I ventured into a back alley and found a hole-in-the-wall with affordable appetizing dishes. I couldn't read the *kanji* on the menu posted in the window so I asked someone inside to accompany me to the display case, where I pointed to a bowl of noodles. The *ramen* was exceptionally good but the food was not necessarily Chinese since I could hear the cooks in the back chatting in Japanese.

The tourist brochure enthusiastically describes Yokohama as "one of Japan's most enticing cities with its fresh seaside and mountain scenery, its friendly people and some of Japan's most enjoyable shopping...A first-time visitor to Yokohama will take an instant liking to the city for its sophisticated, cosmopolitan atmosphere." In an effort to upgrade its reputation, Yokohama was undergoing a facelift with major development projects planned for the future. When I visited the city, dark clouds blocked the view of Mount Fuji in the distance and emphasized the dreariness of its dull landscape. The harbour front was disappointing so I headed up Motomachi, famous for its pedestrian shopping mall with clothing stores, record stores and coffee shops. While browsing in Tower Records, I felt self-conscious in my Reitaku uniform checking out the CDs, but there were plenty of foreign English teachers dressed in conservative business suits in the store as well.

After exploring the shops, I managed to find a city bus to Sankei-en Garden, a beautifully landscaped park built by a wealthy Yokohama silk merchant. In 1906, when the city was shunned by others because of its "unclean" foreign settlements and honky-tonk bars, Tomitarô Hara began to transform a large tract of land in the centre of Yokohama into paradise. He moved many historical buildings, including a teahouse, farmhouse, a three-storey pagoda and other wooden structures, dating from the 15th to 18th centuries, into the secluded valley with its large pond and beautiful gardens surrounded by densely wooded hills. Walking along the quiet trails, I could hardly believe that I was still in the heart of Japan's second largest city, only a short distance from Tokyo.

≈

My last trip to Tokyo was filled with mixed emotions. I had never expected Japan to take such a hold of me, but it did. Just as I was getting used to the Japanese way of living, and acquiring reasonably good language skills, I was about to leave it all behind.

By the end of the year, I had explored most of the districts in Tokyo in spite of the confusing layout of a city where only major thoroughfares have names. I had also mastered the subway system. I no longer got lost at Shinjuku station, with its extensive underground plaza and more than 60 exits to the streets. I had become familiar with most of the lines and transferred from one to another with the ease of a *sarariman*, even when it meant a 15-minute hike in the underground labyrinth between Ogawamachi and Shin-Ochanomizu stations to catch the Chiyoda line back to school. Early on, I learned to carefully calculate the time I needed to get around, including train transfers, so that I would never be late for evening assembly.

In spite of the wonderful variety of restaurants in Tokyo, I usually ate at a familiar spot such as *Makudonarudo* ordering a burger and fries. As much as I enjoyed Japanese food, I needed an authentic fast-food fix from time to time. Unlike other restaurants advertising Western food, there were no surprises at *Makudonarudo*.

Once I bought a milkshake and made the mistake of heading out the door with it. Of course, it never occurred to me that eating or drinking while walking around was poor manners until I tried to find a garbage can. There were none to be found. By then, I felt rather embarrassed strolling down the street with an empty milkshake container in my hands.

I had seen most of the sights promoted in tourist guides and then some. One day, I took the elevator up to the observation deck of the 52-storey Sumitomo Building in Shinjuku when I discovered there was no charge. The skies were hazy and I couldn't be sure if the speck in the distance was Mt. Fuji. More than anything else, I enjoyed exploring the back streets of Shinjuku with all of the shops selling records and music videos. And I never tired of browsing in the bookstores.

Merwyn joined me on my last trip to the city. I wanted to pick up a few CDs including the B-52's and the Rolling Stones. I had been away for a year and didn't realize that they were actually much cheaper back home. No longer craving a Big Mac, we opted for a *soba* lunch in Ueno. Then we walked through the Ginza once more, and ended up in Shibuya, land of Tower Records and Tôkyû Hands.

Merwyn was surprised that I knew the city so well. But then again, Tokyo requires a certain amount of patience to get around and patience was one of the many lessons I learned while at Reitaku.

Shifting Gears

In a Japanese village, the most striking type of misfit is an individualist.

Anthropologist John Embree, 1930s

Alone we are weak, together we are strong. We shall work together as a family in a mutual trust and responsibility.

Words from the company creed at Matsushita, a giant in the electronics industry, selling its products worldwide under familiar labels such as Panasonic, Technics, Pioneer and National.

The cherry is a king among flowers, as the samurai is a king among men. But the blossom's life is short as is the samurai's.

Japanese Folk saying

A samurai was a military retainer of the *daimyô* and his primary duty was to give faithful service to his feudal lord. *Bushidô* (The Way of the Warrior) was the samurai code of conduct: "I will be dutiful to my parents, faithful to my brethren and loyal to my master until death."

This feudal warrior class virtually ruled Japan from the 12th century until the Meiji Restoration of 1868. During the late 15th century, the *daimyô* began building massive castles in the heart of their domains. Castle towns such as Osaka and Hiroshima became important urban centres and samurai, along with their families, were summoned from their villages in the countryside to live within the confines of these citadels where the *daimyô* could easily control them.

After centuries of bloody battles, the Tokugawa Shogunate (1603 to 1867) unified the country under a peaceful reign and enforced a system of four classes: samurai, farmer, artisan and merchant. The samurai, consisting of less than ten percent of the population, were the elite members of society. The merchant class was at the bottom of the social ladder.

Even among the samurai, there were different social levels according to their wealth and rank. And privileges were based on a ranking system with a broad distinction between the upper and lower classes of these warriors. An *ashigaru* (foot soldier) always had to prostrate himself on the ground in the presence of a samurai who rode on horseback. The children of an *ashigaru* were also obliged to use a more respectful form of address when speaking to the children of samurai families from a higher class.

Rules governed every imaginable aspect of daily life including which clothing, food and even sleeping positions were allowed for each class of society. The ordinary

Japanese had no choice but to learn the lessons of obedience and *jishuku* (self-discipline) during the harsh years of feudal rule. When common people did not show respect to their superiors, they were cut down on the spot by the swift sword of the samurai.

The samurai always carried two swords, one for his foe and one for himself. When defeated by the enemy, a sense of honour and duty required the samurai to take his own life rather than surrender. Even the wives of samurai were prepared to protect the family honour by committing *seppuku* (suicide by disembowelment). The most famous expression of loyalty occurred when Emperor Meiji died in 1912. General Nogi a hero of the Russo-Japanese War (1904-1905) and his wife, unable to face life without their beloved emperor, both committed *seppuku*.

Only the samurai were allowed to wear swords and assume a family surname. Commoners who lived in the villages and castle towns were identified simply by their occupation, such as farmer, carpenter or merchant. Even the headman, who was responsible for settling disputes, maintaining order, keeping records and collecting taxes, a position of prestige and status, was known only by his role in the village. The children were named according to their order of birth, such as oldest son or youngest daughter.

During the Meiji Restoration (1868-1912), everyone was made equal before the law and everyone had a right to a family name. By 1872, the samurai lost all of their special privileges, including the right to wear swords. Attempts were also made to abolish many of the old customs since Emperor Meiji was anxious to gain the approval of Western society. Just the same, many traditions survived. Social status, often defined by job seniority rather than occupation, continues to be reflected in the honorific language, with its different forms of politeness.

The samurai code of conduct still dominates Japanese society. The values of absolute loyalty, solidarity, self-discipline, physical courage and personal sacrifice are imbedded into everyone's psyche from an early age.

≈

I had no idea that adjusting to such a different culture from ours could be so difficult. Communication was a major problem. In spite of the language barrier, I was determined to fit in but it wasn't easy. In the dorm, I lost my *gaijin* identity. I was simply Jon, a second-year student in Dormitory 5. The pressure to conform to everyone's expectations was enormous. I had no choice but to adapt to their way of life or be miserable. Besides, I had an obligation to the group to comply with their code of conduct. In spite of my efforts to comply, I'm sure I committed enough social blunders during the early months to reinforce the Japanese belief that *gaijin* are basically barbarians.

The lives of the Japanese people continue to be governed by traditions that have remained unchanged for centuries. Sometimes, I felt as if I was living in a time warp. Despite all of the Western influenccs, and in particular, the pervasiveness of the pop culture in recent years, Japanese teens are still very different from you and me. They have not changed as radically as some people believe. There is no escape from their rigid and structured lifestyle. Order is essential and everyone knows exactly where he or she belongs. I quickly learned my place as well. I wanted to be part of the group even though the group mentality of the Japanese leaves little room for individual expression. Even the *shinjinrui,* a word coined in the 1980s to describe the new breed of Japanese youth who reject parental and traditional values, only represents a tiny minority of the teens. It is almost as if they do not exist. Certainly, rebellious Japanese teens are not a visible threat to society as a whole.

I could not have imagined that there were so many unwritten rules covering every aspect of school life. The Reitaku dorm was hardly boot camp, but it was close enough. Although I experienced a fair amount of freedom during the first term when I had a room of my own, life changed drastically when I shared a dorm room with other students. I was expected to let my room leader, Takebe-san, know where I was at all times. Even third-year students, who had the freedom to go to Tokyo on Sundays, had to report on their activities during evening assembly. These reports were rather vague ("I went to Shibuya to shop"), but they satisfied Takahashi-san, our dorm leader, who recorded all of the information in his notebook.

At Reitaku, students were expected to "act politely and extend their respect to both staff and peers alike." Everyone was either *sempai* (senior) or *kôhai* (junior) and we were always conscious of the distinction when addressing each other with the appropriate suffix: *sensei* for teachers; *san* for senior or equal students and support staff; and *kun* for juniors. I never saw a student being rude or obnoxious in front of a superior. Such behaviour was extremely rare, even among fellow students.

From outward appearances and first impressions, Reitaku and Trinity are very similar boarding schools. The philosophy governing both schools is almost identical and the goals that the parents have set for their children are pretty much the same.

Trinity also promotes the precedence of duty over personal rights in its handbook, *Trinity Life*. "In every successful community, there is a high degree of surrender to common values. Indeed, it is these shared ideals which define the community. At Trinity, honourable conduct and consideration of others are not only the most treasured common values, but they are expected from every student every day."

In both countries, good schools almost guarantee respectable grades and the right connections. These are the "keys to the kingdom" that translate into *shusse*, or success in life. There are major differences, however, when it comes to the commitments made by the students. In Japan, students would never consider disgracing their parents by getting kicked out of school. Each and every school year is an important building block and has a direct effect on a student's future career and *shusse*. There is no room for screw-ups.

Still, even at Reitaku, there were exceptions to every rule. On one occasion, four second-year students were suspended when they were caught smoking and playing mah-jong at 2 a.m. in one of the dorm rooms. Suspensions are not taken lightly in a society where discipline is based on honour, mutual respect and concern for others. Before suspended students are allowed to return to the school, they are required to meet with the staff, not only to apologize but also promise that the incident will not occur again. Needless to say, such a confrontation is humiliating for everyone and is usually not repeated.

The second-year students were stunned by the suspensions and decided to show their support by boycotting breakfast that morning. Even though it was pouring rain outside, we gathered silently outside the classroom building. Such an organized protest was a sign of change in the students' traditional attitude toward blind acceptance of the decisions made by their superiors.

The show of solidarity had no impact on the staff. Instead, we were ordered to meet in the lobby of the classroom building for a special assembly, kneeling in *seiza* position on the hard blue carpet for at least half-an-hour. There wasn't the slightest movement in any of the orderly rows as Nonaka-sensei delivered a lengthy, forceful lecture. Although I didn't understand all of the words, there was no mistaking the anger in his voice. And there was no mistaking the message: insubordination will not be tolerated. Some of the students were clearly shaken up. That evening, I saw another side of Nonaka-sensei, stern and inflexible when enforcing discipline.

When the lecture was finally over, there was a loud, painful chorus of "oohs" and "ahs" as we stretched our legs and limped back to the dorm.

≈

Smoking on school property was a serious offence and I was hardly surprised by the strict disciplinary action. But I wasn't prepared for all the unwritten rules at Reitaku, especially the petty ones. I also had trouble adjusting to the restrictive dormitory lifestyle and the astounding ability of the third-year students to order everyone about.

The first Sunday afternoon after I had moved into a dorm room with four other students, I was sprawled out on the *tatami* mats in the sleeping quarters, reading *Cujo* by Stephen King. The sunlight was streaming through the windows and I had the place to myself, a real luxury at Reitaku. I had barely read a chapter when Takebe-san walked into the room and simply uttered, "*Bokusu.*"

I had no idea what he was talking about. What exactly was a "*bokusu*?" He ignored my look of surprise and said in English, "Go to your box," pointing the way to my *bokusu*. My study cubicle was the "box" in question. But I still didn't understand why I should have to sit in the dark, cramped space of my cubicle to read a novel, especially when no one else was around. Finally, Takebe-san explained that the bedroom was only for the use of the third-year students during the day. There were no exceptions and there was no argument either. As far as dormitory life was concerned, the third-year student was in charge. I felt that Takebe-san was being unfair. But then, only Western society is obsessed with fairness.

At Trinity, there were no such territorial rights in the dorm rooms. Two students, usually from the same grade, shared a room. In the highly structured life at Reitaku, however, hierarchy was imposed on us even in our dormitories. I was only a second-year student and obviously, my concerns were not an issue. Even the placement of our *bokusu* was based on hierarchy. The third-year students had the choice cubicles beside the window. The rest of us had no view, and our only source of light was the harsh glare from the fluorescent fixtures overhead.

≈

There are plenty of studies on the social aspects of collective bathing in Japanese culture. The friendly relations developed while bathing together at the public bath or a hot springs resort is called *hadaka no otsukiai* (naked bonding). Even at Reitaku, there was a relaxed attitude in the *ofuro* as we unwound in the hot tub before hitting the books.

And yet, the rules of hierarchy were strictly followed whenever the bathing room was crowded. Naturally, the senior students had the best spots along the wall with convenient showerheads for washing themselves and rinsing away the soapy lather. The first-year students were forced to use the row of taps set up in the middle of the room. The set-up was rather primitive since they had to fill small basins with water in order to wash and rinse off properly. The senior students also had the choice positions for soaking in the tub while the junior students huddled together in the middle.

≈

One Saturday night, I missed evening curfew. I had been visiting Randall's friend, who was a maintenance worker on campus and lived in a nearby dorm. At some point, while we were watching *The Abyss*, I realized that it was getting pretty late. If I stayed until the movie was over, I was going to miss the 9:50 p.m. roll call when a first-year student yelled out, "*TENKO*!" But I really didn't think it would be a big deal if I was a few minutes late.

Machigatta! (What a mistake!)

Takebe-san, Takahashi-san, Yamamoto-san (the assistant dorm leader) and Hiro-san (Takebe-san's friend), were all waiting for me when I got back to the dorm.

"Where have you been?" Takebe-san asked in English.

"Workers' dorm...video," I said, failing to come up with the appropriate Japanese vocabulary.

"Tokyo Dome?" Hiro-san asked, mistaking dorm for dome.

"*Iie*, workers' dorm," I responded, almost wishing I'd been to Tokyo. By now, it was common knowledge among the third-year students that I had been sneaking off to Tokyo on Sundays during first term. At least, they would understand words like Shibuya and Shinjuku. Instead, they sent a first-year student to summon Seijiro, who had been to Trinity as an exchange student the previous year. Seijiro acted as an interpreter and kindly but sternly explained that my dorm mates, who were responsible for me, had been very worried when I did not show up for roll call. The fact that I was only ten minutes late was inexcusable. Missing *tenko* was a very serious breach of school rules. There were no threats but they certainly knew how to rub it in. I had never experienced such a guilt trip before.

"*Gomen nasai*," I apologized humbly.

After that unpleasant encounter, I knew better than to test the system. I was never late for curfew again. But I continued to be frustrated because I didn't know I had broken a rule until a senior student stopped me with a curt "*Damé!*" which means, "It is useless to do that," rather than simply saying, "No."

And I always apologized. In Japanese society, apologies are expected to be a sincere sign of repentance as well as a promise that the "crime" will not be committed again. During my year at Reitaku, lecturing the students was still an effective means of discipline. Serious offences resulted in suspensions, and very rarely, expulsions. But almost always, the students followed the rules.

At Trinity, we also had rules so that students could "lead a happy and productive existence." When rules were broken, which was often enough, a prefect (a senior-year disciplinarian and advisor), housemaster or the headmaster lectured the culprits either during chapel, at a house meeting, or behind closed doors for more serious offences. But the scolding had little effect on many of the problems that occurred on a regular basis, such as late night rowdiness, yelling in the hallways and golfing on the cricket pitch.

Ironically, many of the rules at Trinity are stricter today than they were 25 years ago. And yet, there is a far more relaxed attitude about discipline. Nobody is getting caned or whipped anymore. Just the same, other measures have been adopted to keep us in line. Over the years, an elaborate and very complicated system of punishment was implemented at Trinity, which ranged from a few demerits, called "quarters," for minor indiscretions and expulsion for serious offences.

Quarters were handed out for a "whole host of sins" including skipping chapel or classes or being rude to prefects or teachers. When a student accumulated 13 quarters, he was "gated" and confined to the school grounds for a week. For students who were accustomed to the freedom of going almost wherever they wished, especially on the weekend, gating was an unpopular form of punishment. Every year though, at least one student managed to accumulate the maximum number of seven gatings and was finally expelled from the school because of his reluctance to obey the rules.

In the past, prefects whacked the boys' backsides with a thick wooden paddle for many of the same "sins" that are now punished by handing out "quarters." The names of the culprits were written on these paddles, which had names such as "Excalibur" and "I Hear a Rhapsody." The headmaster, however, used a cane to discipline unruly students until the mid-1970s. The principals of public schools usually used a broad leather strap to keep the kids in line. Most North American schools have abolished corporal punishment for two reasons: a more humane attitude toward disciplinary action and the growing fear of lawsuits.

Taibatsu (corporal punishment) is illegal in Japan but incidents continue to be reported in the media, especially when the punishment causes serious injury or accidental death.

Reitaku was no different than Trinity when the school's reputation was on the line. Embarrassing incidents were avoided at all cost. And when they occurred, they were kept as quiet as possible.

The teachers at Reitaku were always concerned about the conduct of the students, especially when they were off the school property. One of their worst fears was petty theft. I was shocked to learn that a disturbing number of first-year students had been caught stealing candy from local convenience stores. No wonder the teachers were sensitive about the school's reputation in the community.

≈

There were other indiscretions at Reitaku. Alcohol consumption by students was more common than I expected. In spite of the strict rules and regulations imposed by the school, not to mention the high moral standards we were expected to follow, "illegal" drinking events were organized on a regular basis. And it was easy enough to get away with it. Teachers rarely made the rounds to check up on us in our rooms. After all, the third-year students were in charge of the dormitories. We didn't have to worry about Kitasaka-san either. She never left the dorm office, where her apartment was conveniently located.

Takebe-san organized a secret drinking *paati* once a month, which was usually held around 1 a.m. on a Saturday night, after the teacher on duty had gone home. "The party is secret," our room leader emphasized as only the pale light of a desk lamp illuminated us, sitting around on the *tatami* mats in our sleeping quarters. Morishita-san, a second year student, passed around the *biiru*. He had been delegated to sneak out after midnight to the local convenience store and buy the beer for each party. Takebe-san also kept a bottle of sake for special occasions. He usually cooked *oden*, a stew made from fish and vegetables, on a hot plate he kept hidden in his futon closet. There was plenty of good-natured joking but we didn't dare play any music. We also limited ourselves to one pint of beer, so these parties never got out of hand. Getting caught meant a week's suspension. However, there was a strong sense of loyalty within the group and everyone always participated. Of course, no one dared tell anyone, including fellow students, about the *paati*. I have to admit that I was somewhat nervous about the whole affair. But I felt an obligation to comply since I was part of the group. Besides, these were not typical "rebellious" teens who were blatantly abusing the system. In any case, I wasn't about to turn down a beer.

At the end of second term, Takahashi-san let us bring *biiru* to the dorm party. When Itoh-sensei dropped in for a brief visit, we simply slipped our Budweisers under the table. A major *paati* was also organized on our last night at Reitaku in mid-March. But it didn't begin until 3 a.m.

after the teacher on duty had finally gone home. Toyota-san, my room leader during the third term woke me up at 5 a.m. and asked if I wanted to join the group. Spaced out as I was at this hour, I declined his invitation and went back to sleep. Besides, I had to give a *sayônara* speech in front of 600 people during closing ceremonies. Some of my classmates were quite hung over the following morning, but everyone showed up on schedule.

Trinity's policy on drinking was just as strict as Reitaku's and most of the students complied with the rules. We never knew when teachers or prefects were making the rounds of our dorms, so there was a certain amount of risk involved with drinking in the rooms. There were logistical problems as well. Access to alcohol was much more difficult in Port Hope than in Kashiwa. Only two stores sold beer and both of them would have asked for I.D. We didn't have the convenience of vending machines where we could buy cold beer without any questions being asked.

Notices were occasionally posted on the discipline bulletin board, revealing the names of anyone caught drinking or bringing alcohol onto school property. The disciplinary action was suspension for the first offence and expulsion for the second. The year after I graduated, girls were also expelled from Trinity for drug and alcohol use.

Although not as serious as alcohol use, smoking is another disciplinary problem facing both schools. I was always amazed by the number of smokers at Reitaku. Yet, cigarettes were cheap and at least one-third of the boys smoked. But I never saw a girl light up a cigarette. In most Asian countries, it is socially unacceptable for women to smoke.

Smoking was banned only recently at Trinity. For years, students were allowed to smoke in designated common rooms if they were at least 16 years of age and had their parents' written consent. The practice was slowly phased out while I was still at the school. Unlike Reitaku, the ban on smoking at Trinity also included the teachers. Today, the anti-smoking sentiment is so strong that students tell others to "butt out" if they catch them smoking in a washroom. Hardly anyone risks smoking indoors anymore even though the punishment is not very severe, a week's gating and eight quarters. Instead, they find refuge in the nearby apple orchards or "dip" chewing tobacco to ease their nicotine dependency.

As far as illegal drugs were concerned, they simply did not exist at Reitaku. In spite of all the Western influences, the drug culture is not one of them. While I was in Japan, I never heard a serious discussion about the subject. Sure, there was the odd joke from time to time. Once I was acting silly and my roommates asked if I had been snorting cocaine. Still, I couldn't help wondering if some of the young people might be tempted to experiment with drugs if they were available. Lack of cash certainly wasn't a problem. All of the students at Reitaku had plenty of spending money.

But the drug laws in Japan have always been very harsh. In the past, the death penalty was not uncommon for anyone caught smuggling opium into the country. Today, most of the illicit traffic in heroin is controlled by the *yakuza*, commonly called the Japanese mafia. And yet, these white-collar gangsters with elaborate tattoos covering their bodies follow a strict code of honour. Their illegal activities, which also include gambling, extortion, loan-sharking and prostitution, are not at the expense of young people.

For centuries, marijuana was grown in Japan for making colourful cloth. However, *marifana* was banned during the Allied Occupation after World War II when American soldiers were caught smoking the weed. Today, marijuana is smuggled into the country in small quantities from Hanoi.

In Japan, the major drug problem is the abuse of *hiropon* (amphetamines). Invented in 1887, amphetamine was promoted as a miracle drug supplying unlimited energy. During World War II, amphetamines were distributed to soldiers to keep them ready for combat at all times. By 1954, Japan found itself with more than half-a-million addicts on its hands and consequently passed tough anti-amphetamine laws. Although the penalty for selling the drug is life imprisonment, the demand on the street is great and thousands of arrests are made each year. Tokyo has not lost its notoriety as the "speed capital of the world."

In Canada and the United States, drug abuse has been a constant threat to the integrity of schools, both public and private. Marijuana and LSD are popular and readily available in Toronto, less than 60 miles away from Trinity. Despite all of the efforts to eliminate underground trafficking on campus, incidents keep cropping up with alarming frequency. Getting caught is grounds for immediate expulsion, but hardly a deterrent.

During my senior years, the use of illicit drugs by high school students was a very painful subject at Trinity. A survey at our school revealed that 1 out of every 16 students "regularly used illegal drugs," slightly less than the national average of 1 out of 12 high school students across the country. Another private school, Upper Canada College in Toronto, expressed its concerns to the parents in the school brochure: "We continue to believe that there is more casual use of soft drugs among our boys than we care to admit. The anguish which occurs for a boy and his parents when an offender is caught, is enormous."

When I was in Grade 12, a well-publicized drug bust occurred at the school's formal, held on board the cruise ship *Captain Matthew Flinders* in Toronto. A senior student was caught with a significant amount of LSD and a shopping list with a dozen potential buyers at the dance. However, he hadn't had a chance to distribute the drug before he was caught so there were no other charges. In a letter to all parents, Mr. Wright referred to the school's "very visible loss of good standing in the community" and his "deep disappointment in all those involved." Mr. Wright concluded the letter by saying, "This incident has shaken our whole community. The students, I think, realize that this has brought shame to the school and hurt us all."

Shame is an emotion the Japanese understand very well. And it is a sense of shame, rather than guilt, that deters most students from committing an offence. Nonetheless, the most shameful incident occurring in Japanese schools is *ijime* (bullying).

Ijime is a group activity where a number of boys or girls gang up on a single individual. Such adolescent behaviour is usually more prevalent in the junior, rather than senior schools. Often, it is just petty, cruel behaviour such as teasing or name-calling by fellow students. The tormented victims are usually loners who feel isolated from the group because they are different somehow. Even when they are beaten by their classmates, they are not likely to complain. Everyone hates snitches, particularly in

Japan, where harmony plays such a major role with group dynamics.

Reitaku was not immune to the practice of *ijime*. A major incident occurred late in the year when a second-year student, suspected of stealing a CD player from a roommate, was beaten up. Such actions were not tolerated by the staff at Reitaku and the five culprits were suspended for a week. Once again, the boys' residence was ordered to suffer through another lengthy, gruelling lecture in *seiza* position in the lobby of the classroom building.

Despite what Western critics say, *ijime* is hardly an indication that the Japanese educational system is in trouble. Many North American children fear for their lives when going to school. That's not surprising when teenagers, even youngsters, are bringing guns to school and killing their classmates. At many schools, security guards regularly frisk students for weapons, knives and drugs. Some school entrances are reminiscent of airports, where students pass through security gates and dogs sniff the backpacks of students for illegal drugs.

Canada is not facing the same crisis. We have much tougher gun control laws in our country and lethal weapons, such as handguns and sawed off shotguns, are out of reach for most people, especially teenagers. However, knives are carried by a disturbing number of kids in tough neighbourhoods across the country for "protection."

Bullying is not the only inhumane activity practiced in Western high schools and colleges. Often, new students are harassed and humiliated in a number of ways as a means of gaining acceptance into the group, particularly when joining sports teams and college fraternities. Most of the pranks are harmless. Tragically, some initiation rites, such as drinking binges, have gone too far and students have died.

We had our own initiation rites at Trinity. For many years, the defining moment of acceptance occurred at the New Boy's Picnic, a rather cute name in the calendar of school events for a sinister Sunday activity held at the Presqu'ile Provincial Park. The rite of passage was an obstacle course where we were required to crawl through a pit of weeds, mud, urine and a dead seagull thrown in for good measure. Meanwhile, the headmaster took photos for posterity. Not appreciative of the importance of such an initiation into the ranks at Trinity, I hid out Rambo-like in the woods. When I was finally spotted by two senior students, they promptly dragged me through a stagnant pond. An odd baptismal rite indeed!

Another popular prank for many, many years was called "gitching," where a student, or a whole gang of them, grabbed a new boy's underwear from the back and pulled at it until it tore. Such crude behaviour was typical for an all-boys' school. The practice was finally banned in 1991, when Trinity became a coed school.

≈

Soon after I arrived at Reitaku, I decided to take the train to downtown Kashiwa on a Friday afternoon to look for a pocket-size English-Japanese dictionary. I hadn't bothered to ask for permission since I was only going to be gone for a short time. While I was checking out the floor guide of the Sogo Department Store, I heard someone say, "Hello."

I turned around and a woman in her late thirties was smiling at me.

"Are you busy right now?" she asked pleasantly.

"No," I responded, wondering what I was getting into.

"Good," the stranger continued. "Please allow me to introduce myself. I am Yuka Kitano, a high school English teacher. What is your name?"

Not feeling threatened, at least, not yet, I obliged her.

"I'm Jonathan Buchanan."

"Where are you from?"

"Canada."

"Are you a high school student?"

"Yes, at Reitaku."

"Really? I have a friend who teaches there. I'm busy now," she continued, "but would you like to meet on Saturday? I have a daughter about your age. I'm sure she would like to meet you. Are you free?"

This was the first time I had managed to leave the campus on my own and already, it seemed as if I was being set up for *omiai* (an arranged meeting possibly leading to marriage). Oh well, I wasn't about to pass up the opportunity, especially since *kendô* class was cancelled that afternoon.

"Yes, I'm free," I replied. "When would you like to meet?"

"Two o'clock. We'll meet back here."

When I informed Nonaka-sensei that I was going to visit a friend in Kashiwa on Saturday afternoon, he was curious about the relationship since I had only been in Japan for a few weeks. So I came up with this incredible story that Mrs. Kitano was actually a friend of my mother's. When he asked where they had met, I explained that they had met many years ago in New York. Nonaka-sensei accepted my story at face value but I suddenly felt uncomfortable because I was being dishonest. After all, Nonaka-sensei was responsible for my welfare and I certainly did not want to put him on the spot. And yet, I was afraid to admit that Mrs. Kitano was just a casual acquaintance, someone I had met at a department store. To make matters worse, I had gone to Kashiwa without asking for permission.

On Saturday, Mrs. Kitano was already waiting for me beside the elevator. In a move I would never dare make in North America, I followed Mrs. Kitano to her car. But I had learned to trust the Japanese people so there was no hesitation whatsoever when she invited me to her home.

Mrs. Kitano's teenage daughter was waiting for us.

"Hi, I'm Keiko," she said. "Pleased to meet you."

"Hi, I'm Jon. Pleased to meet you."

We sat at a low table in the *tatami* room where Mrs. Kitano served green tea and *sembei*. She explained that her family was visiting the west coast of Canada and the United States in the summer. We talked about Canada while Keiko excused herself. Within minutes, she returned with a splendid strawberry shortcake.

"*Dôzo*," Keiko said, offering me a piece.

"*Oishii*!" I exclaimed, after the first bite. The shortcake was delicious. The strawberries were enormous and sweet, probably costing a fortune.

"Thank you," said Keiko politely. "I learned to make it from a cookbook I bought." She showed me the Japanese cookbook with an English title, *Recipes from Avonlea: an Anne of Green Gables Cookbook*.

Back then, I didn't realize the tremendous interest in "Anne of the Red Hair" written by Canadian author Lucy Maud Montgomery. Set in rural Prince Edward Island during the early 1900s, Anne is portrayed as a feisty, independent girl with great ambitions for the future.

"Have you read *Anne of Green Gables?*" Keiko asked.

"Yes," I answered. "We also performed a play based on the book when I was in elementary school."

"I like Anne very much," Keiko confided. "I would like to visit Prince Edward Island some day."

During the afternoon, one of Mrs. Kitano's friends dropped by for a brief visit. I was introduced to Kakei-sensei who was a part-time calligraphy teacher at Reitaku. She didn't seem at all surprised to meet me. Of course, she would have assumed that the school knew exactly where I was.

Before I knew it, it was five o'clock and Mrs. Kitano invited me to stay for dinner. I phoned my dorm and informed Takahashi-san that I was having dinner at a friend's house. Although he seemed somewhat puzzled that I had been invited out for dinner, Takahashi-san didn't object when I assured him that I would be back for *tenko*.

We ate dinner at a dining table. I was amused that we were eating bite-size morsels of chicken teriyaki with a knife and fork instead of chopsticks. The meal was delicious and a welcome break from cafeteria fare.

"*Dôzo, dôzo*," repeated Mrs. Kitano, offering me more food. No one commented on Mr. Kitano's absence but he was probably still at work or socializing with his colleagues.

After dinner, Keiko had to rush off to her *juku* class.

"Most *juku* are simply cram schools," explained Mrs. Kitano, "but Keiko is learning study habits so it is different."

Different maybe, but sacrificing a Saturday evening for a class had to be tough. I could just imagine the comments from my friends back home. "Classes Saturday night? Are they stupid or something?"

Mrs. Kitano was more concerned about her 12-year-old son's addiction to Nintendo and she strictly limited the number of hours he was allowed to play. I assured her that it was not just an affliction of young Japanese boys. Western kids were also big Nintendo fans. When Mrs. Kitano drove me back to Reitaku, I thanked her again for the lovely afternoon and wonderful dinner.

My little "white lie" to Nonaka-sensei came back to haunt me the following term when I joined Kakei-sensei's calligraphy class. She reminded me that we had already met at Mrs. Kitano's home.

≈

Although my Japanese friends faced rather severe restrictions as far as personal freedom was concerned, I certainly didn't feel sorry for them. They were spared many of the growing pains that Western teens experience. As strange as it may sound, they didn't seem to suffer from raging hormones either. And no one worried about contracting AIDS even though there were full-colour posters on the bulletin board outside Reitaku's health office warning students of the dangers and symptoms of sexually transmitted diseases. None of my classmates expressed any concerns about relationships with the opposite sex. Even the seniors didn't experience the same pressures as Western teens to have a steady date. They were also spared the anxieties of prom night. In fact, the dances at Reitaku were pretty tame affairs. But they were lots of fun, just the same.

Naturally, attendance was compulsory. However, they were so popular that everyone would have shown up anyway. Of course, there was a specific dress code since the dance was an organized school function. The boys were required to wear their grey flannels and the girls, their grey skirts. At least, we could choose our own shirts and most of us showed up in colourful T-shirts.

The first dance, under the glare of the sodium lamps of the gym, was a mixer to the tune of "Turkey in the Straw," played four to five times in a row. We danced in circles, constantly switching partners. It was reminiscent of square dancing in elementary school phys ed classes.

After the warm-up, the lights were dimmed and the curtains opened up on the stage, revealing a rock band with brightly dyed orange hair, the same shade popular with the punks in Yoyogi Park in Tokyo. As soon as the music blasted over the loudspeakers, the girls began to scream. Many of them hung around the stage throughout the evening, presenting band members with bouquets of fresh red roses in between sets. Girls weren't the only ones who got carried away. Some of the first-year boys occasionally stormed the set and danced on the stage.

I was amazed by the transformation in the gym but I was even more surprised when I discovered that the band members were Reitaku students. I could have sworn they were a hot rock group brought in from Tokyo. The band had a terrific sound and an extensive repertoire of Japanese numbers. I'm not sure when they found the time to get together and practice but they put on a great show while we stood around and watched them perform.

Between sets, a student DJ played both Western and Japanese rock music. Almost everyone danced, whether or not they had specific partners. There were no slow dances, so there was no physical contact between the girls and boys. The dances ended promptly at 10 p.m. and we headed straight back to our separate residences.

Most of the dances at Trinity were also held in the school gym but they were much flashier affairs. Often, we had strobe and laser lighting effects as well as a large screen for music videos. Each year, one of our dances featured a professional rock band, and one group, the Northern Pikes, headed straight out of our gym onto both the Canadian and American pop charts. Except for the semi-formal, the dress code was casual, jeans and shirts. Music ranged from heavy metal to reggae with a fair number of slow songs toward the end. Although most students danced in small groups, we always had a large number of wallflowers who watched from the sidelines. Before Trinity became a coed school, girls from other private schools were invited to our dances, arriving in chartered buses. Before the dances, there was time to socialize and get to know some of the girls. But our contact with them was usually fleeting and casual.

≈

Even though Reitaku was a coed school, we didn't have much of an opportunity to spend time with members of the opposite sex. For one thing, there was little free time in a daily schedule that carefully accounted for almost every minute of our day. And the 9:50 p.m. curfew on Saturday nights was pretty restrictive. Only some of the third-year students, who had the freedom to go to Tokyo on Sundays, went to the big city on their *deito* (date). But they always left the school in uniform, usually carrying their casual clothes in a knapsack and changing in the washrooms of the train station. And they were back in time for *tenko*.

In Western society, dating often begins at an early age. But life at an all boys' boarding school was very different.

We weren't faced with the same pressures as our friends in the public school system. Even after Trinity became coed, there weren't enough girls to go around. Not surprisingly, some of the students became involved with serious relationships. The rumour mill was always pretty steamy at Trinity so we were kept well informed of the various affairs on campus.

The concerns among staff members about students making out on school premises were probably justified. Almost everyone seems to take for granted that Western teens will participate in sexual activities. Whether or not the assumption is true, sex education already starts in elementary school. When I entered Trinity, the AIDS scare was full-blown and the emphasis in our physical education and health classes, especially in grades 7 and 8, was on safe sex. We were not spared any of the anatomical details of the reproductive organs, but I wonder if any of us really cared where the female fallopian tubes were located.

Despite the vigilance of our housemasters at Trinity, students still managed to venture into the dormitories of the opposite sex for a secret rendezvous. In the first two years, however, only one couple was caught in a compromising position. The two students, who were already on disciplinary probation, were expelled.

Trinity also discouraged "PDAs" (public displays of affection), but walking hand-in-hand on campus or even in the hallway was common practice. No one, not even the staff, paid much attention to such indiscretions even though the consequences were outlined quite specifically in the school handbook.

> It is expected that students will conduct themselves with the utmost propriety concerning public displays of affection while in the School's charge. Initially, any problems in this area would be handled by talking to the people involved. Further transgressions of the "PDA rule" could result in disciplinary sanctions being applied.

At Reitaku, however, it was unthinkable for students to walk around holding hands. And a *seppun* (kiss) in public was out of the question. Before the Allied Occupation, a *seppun* on the street was a statutory offence punishable by a fine. Even the smooching scenes in foreign films were censored. Today, the Japanese prefer to use the word *kisu* because of the stigma still attached to a *seppun*.

Trinity had more to worry about than students sneaking a *kisu* in the school corridor. Condom machines were located in "discreet places within the washroom of all residences," including the girls' dormitories. In Bickle House, where I resided, the machine was hidden away in the second stall of the second floor washroom. But the presence of condom machines didn't mean that most of the students were promiscuous. The availability of condoms has become a hotly debated issue in most Western schools. Some have placed condom machines in school washrooms while others are vehemently opposed to the practice, believing that it leads to promiscuity. And yet, many of the girls in these schools become pregnant just the same.

The use of condoms has been popular in Japan ever since the Allied Occupation, when Americans sent regular shipments identified as "rubber sanitary goods." Needless to say, the Roman Catholic Church was not amused.

Today, condoms are still sold discreetly door-to-door by saleswomen who make regular rounds to housewives in the neighbourhood. In Japan, there is not a wide choice of contraceptive products for women. The birth control pill was finally legalized in 1991, but it is only prescribed in high dosages to women with menstrual problems. So much for advances in science and technology.

Sexual liaisons between the students at Reitaku did not exist. Or if they did, none of us knew about it. Surveys indicate that Japanese teens are having intercourse by the age of 16 but it is still a very small percentage when compared with American, Canadian and British statistics. In Japan, girls are expected to remain virgins until they marry, even though the Japanese do not have religious taboos against premarital or even extramarital sexual relations. In a country where there are no social support systems for unwed mothers, teenage pregnancies are practically non-existent. If a girl becomes pregnant, abortions are readily available. No self-respecting girl would ever consider disgracing her parents by dropping out of school, or taking time off, since continuing classes while pregnant is out of the question.

Still, Reitaku did not take any chances. The girls' dormitories were strictly off limits to the boys. The message was clear enough with a barbed wire fence surrounding the residence compound to discourage unwelcome visitors. One morning, though, the mood in the English office was sombre and some of the teachers were visibly quite upset. When I inquired, I found out that a first-year student had been caught trying to sneak into the one of the girls' dormitories. He was sent home permanently and the incident was kept quiet.

Far from being shy and reserved, the girls at Reitaku were surprisingly friendly and outgoing. They were certainly not timid about approaching me in small groups of three or four and starting up a conversation. Almost always, the leading question was, "Do you like the Beatles?" Sometimes, they asked if I liked the popular Japanese rock groups, Dreams Come True and the Southern All Stars (which, despite their names, usually sang in Japanese). A group of them even invited me to a rock concert in Tokyo on New Year's Eve. Were they really interested in my opinions about the music scene? Or did they simply want to practice their English with me? Of course, they always wanted to know if I liked Japanese girls. Did they also wonder, like my dorm mates, if I was still a virgin?

≈

The Japanese concept of *amae* defines the nurturing, caring and even indulgent relationship between the child and his family and teachers. When young people head off to the workforce, Japanese companies take on the same role, caring for, as well as controlling the lives of their employees. It's hardly surprising when employees develop the same dependency on corporations as they experienced with their mothers and teachers.

There is no direct English translation for this phenomenon because we don't experience a similar dependency on others outside of our families. If anything, we are encouraged to become more independent as we grow up.

Nothing prepared me for the degree of intrusiveness into my personal life by Nonaka-sensei, other teachers and in particular, students who were always looking out for each other. Kitasaka-san also had a tendency to be overprotective, just like a mother. When the boys were ill, she was their nursemaid, always around to comfort them when they needed her. Even I learned to appreciate her attentiveness when I was sick. Kitasaka-san didn't speak a word of English but she was always concerned about my welfare.

Just as winter set in, I developed a hacking cough and a fever. Instead of handing me some Tylenol and ordering me to bed, Kitasaka-san insisted that I see a doctor. For her, a *gaijin* with a common cold was a medical emergency. Clearly, the staff at Reitaku were not about to take any chances and Nonaka-sensei drove me to a local physician, Ito-sensei (doctors are also honoured with the suffix *sensei*). Like many Japanese doctors, he had his own clinic on the first floor and a small private hospital upstairs.

When the nurse handed me a thermometer, I naturally started to put it under my tongue.

"*Damé! Damé!*" the nurse exclaimed with a horrified look. She grabbed the thermometer and placed it in my armpit. Fortunately, I wasn't in Korea. Lee-san, from my university language classes, enlightened us one day with the tidbit of information that the thermometer was usually inserted rectally for adults as well as children in his country.

After examining me, Ito-sensei prescribed *kampô*, Chinese herbal medicine, which he dispensed from his office. He also inquired if I was taking any other medication. When I mentioned that I used an asthma inhaler only occasionally, he promptly advised me that it was hazardous to my health. There was no point arguing with him. In Japan, doctors are never challenged by their patients. Getting a second opinion from another physician is unheard of, regardless of the diagnosis. Obviously, Ito-sensei had more faith in ancient remedies than modern medicine. Western physicians often scoff at traditional Chinese herbal solutions, which may include ground up organs and bones of exotic animals too numerous to name, but they haven't found a cure for the common cold either.

I was confined to the dormitory's infirmary and suffered through my worst experience while I was in Japan. I felt terrible. The room was bare except for ten beds and it was unbearably stuffy. There was nothing to do but sleep. I had no visitors, except for Kitasaka-san, who checked up on me regularly. At meal times, I was served weak tea and rice porridge garnished with a pickled plum to help cure my illness. The medicine from Ito-sensei was ghastly. If I was given a choice, I would not have taken it at all. But I didn't have the heart to give Kitasaka-san a hard time. My cough disappeared within a few days and I was released from the infirmary.

There is nothing worse than having a cold in Japan. Blowing your nose into a tissue or handkerchief is unacceptable behaviour in public. Sometimes, we had several snivellers at our dining room table, trying to be as discreet as possible, resorting to a quick wipe with a tissue only when absolutely necessary. Ever since I returned from Japan, I have been uncomfortable about blowing my nose in public. Instead, I have become a sniveler, which is probably just as rude in our society.

There is a strange inconsistency in the rules of conduct in Japan. While something as innocuous as blowing one's nose is considered disgusting, spitting on the street is acceptable, as long as it's not directed at anyone. I presume these rules have something to do with the spreading of germs. Perhaps that is why drunken *sararimen,* urinating in dark alleyways, are tolerated as well.

≈

Without a doubt, Japanese teenagers are under tremendous pressure to succeed in school. They are constantly reminded of their obligations to family, school and society. Indeed, their whole life is focused on getting a good education. As long as they work hard, their parents pamper them with substantial allowances. Boys, in particular, are spoiled to the hilt to encourage them to do well in school.

On Parents' Day, Mr. Takada drove from Suwa (a three-hour trip each way) just to visit me. I was surprised to see him, since I hardly expected him to take Friday off work. I was also overwhelmed by all of the junk food he brought along, enough to last the rest of the year. My parents never indulged me with care packages.

Although Trinity has often been considered to be an elitist private school, nothing could be further from the truth. Certainly, many of the students came from affluent homes, but only a few of them had expensive stereos, a car and a closet full of designer clothes. A large number of us relied on the generous bursaries and scholarships offered by the school and survived on modest weekly allowances from our parents. Borrowing money from friends was a common practice, although some of them took their time paying back debts.

At Reitaku, nobody ever complained about being broke. As far as I know, none of the students ever borrowed from each other. I don't even recall any discussions about personal finances or about money, for that matter. Such a conversation would have been poor manners for the Japanese. In any case, everyone seemed to have plenty of pocket money. Consequently, business had never been better, especially in the music industry. Japanese teens bought expensive compact disc players, CDs and anything else that is *shinhatsubai* (newly on sale). They were also obsessed with expensive, trendy clothes. Most of my friends at Reitaku were very conscious of designer labels such as Ralph Lauren, Calvin Klein and Levi's for the *shibui* (cool, sophisticated) look. Nobody cared if they dressed like slobs in the dormitory. "The baggier the better" was the unofficial dress code in residence, though there was still a certain neatness about my dorm mates since they always tucked their T-shirts into their sweat pants. But even the slobs dressed appropriately when they went out in public.

The fashion statement at Trinity was similar to that of Reitaku. Since we attended classes dressed in a jacket and tie, we wanted to be as comfortable as possible in the evening. Many of us wore T-shirts and sweatpants on campus. Whenever we went anywhere, we usually wore jeans. During my first year at Trinity, we were still supposed to dress in our Sunday uniforms when travelling to and from the school in chartered buses. But the rule was broken by so many of the boys that the practice was abandoned altogether.

While at Reitaku, I basically got away with murder as far as the dress code was concerned. Even when I was biking around Kashiwa, I rarely wore my uniform. The staff members never said anything when I signed for the bike at the dorm office because they presumed I was going to the university campus to visit my *bekkasei* friends. One afternoon, when I was returning the key for the bike lock, the teacher on duty noticed that I was carrying a bag from a convenience store in a nearby shopping area. It wasn't the first time that I was reminded to wear my uniform whenever I left the campus.

"*Hai, wakarimasu,*" I replied. (Yes, I understand.)

And then I apologized, but who was he kidding? I didn't mind obeying most of the rules, but some were a nuisance. And others seemed senseless.

Paper Cranes

Never in all history did a nation take such a stride as Japan did... she completely dispelled the persuasion that Asia was in some irrevocable way hopelessly behind Europe. She made all European progress seem sluggish and tentative by comparison.

H.G. Wells

I will sing the praises
Of this exalted peak
As long as I have breath.

Yamabe no Akahito,
8th century

Greet the peace happily,
but don't sleep and
forget the war.

Paul Theroux

The Japanese have had a love affair with train travel ever since Commodore Perry presented a miniature railroad set as one of many gifts during treaty negotiations at Kanagawa in 1854. The Japanese are said to have had "great fun riding up and down" in their new toy. Other American gifts included rifles, pistols, a telegraph apparatus and 100 gallons of bourbon whisky. In return, Perry received silks, gold lacquer ware, porcelain and a "box of obscene paintings of naked men and women, another proof of the lewdness of this exclusive people."

When Japan isolated itself from the rest of the world from the 17th to the mid-19th century, the introduction of new technologies ground to a halt. During the Meiji Restoration (1868-1912), however, the Japanese quickly made up for lost time as Emperor Meiji pushed for reform. In 1872, with the help of British engineers, the first railway opened along the seashore between Tokyo and Yokohama, a distance of less than 29 kilometres (18 miles). The passengers, however, must have had mixed feelings about the trip. They were shocked when their shoes were not waiting for them at their destination. Back then, the Japanese were accustomed to leaving their shoes outside the door of all buildings, even shops and restaurants. Naturally, they left their shoes on the platform before boarding the train in Tokyo and expected them to magically reappear at Yokohama station.

Before long, railroad lines and railway-operated ferries linked the four main islands of the country and Japan became famous for its efficient transportation system. The bullet trains of the *shinkansen* (new express lines) are among the fastest in the world, travelling at speeds of up to 320 kilometres (200 miles) per hour between major Japanese cities. The first branch of the "super-express" lines connected Osaka with Tokyo and opened in 1964, in time for the Olympic Games. Today, more than 300 bullet trains run each day in the heavily travelled corridor between the two major cities. The most popular line runs between Tokyo and Fukuoka on the southern island of Kyushu and stops include Nagoya, Kyoto, Osaka and Hiroshima. The route is 1180 kilometres (730 miles) long and the trip takes only five hours.

The *shinkansen* has an excellent safety record and its operations are controlled from a computerized station in Tokyo, which monitors the location of each train. There are never any delays and you can set your watch by their arrival and departure times. The odd delay in typhoon season is front-page news in all of the newspapers.

≈

I spent my summer vacation visiting a number of cities in the southwestern region of Honshu Island, including Hiroshima on the 45th anniversary of the explosion of the first atomic bomb. At first, I had wanted to see all of Japan but Nonaka-sensei discouraged such an ambitious undertaking. After all, summer holidays only lasted six weeks. Instead, he suggested that I pick out a region and he arranged for me to stay with a number of families, most of whom had an association with the Hiroike Institute.

I had no apprehension about visiting strangers despite the obvious cultural differences and language difficulties. I was grateful for the opportunity to learn more about Japanese customs and traditions and I was aware that such an invitation was very special. The Japanese regard their home as a haven from the outside world and it is seldom open to strangers. Not even neighbours are invited in for tea or a casual drink.

On August 2, the sun was shining as I boarded the bullet train for Fukuyama. I enjoyed train travel in Japan, especially on the *shinkansen*, with its reclining seats and lots of legroom for all travellers, including lanky *gaijin* such as myself. The *shinkansen* cost considerably more than regular trains but their speed and efficiency are essential for the pace of Japanese life.

As the train left Tokyo station, a list of stops was read out over the public address system, both in Japanese and English. The same cities were also displayed on an electronic signboard at the front of each car. The rest of the announcements were in Japanese only, explaining how and when to change trains, on which side the doors opened, and the location of the dining car, the bathrooms and the telephones. Every now and then, an announcement came across the loudspeaker, such as, "Toyota Motor's Ishi-san, please go to the telephone in the buffet car for a call."

Despite all of the technological advances of the Japanese railways, half of the toilets on the bullet trains were the squat-style facilities. Not surprisingly, there was usually a queue outside the preferred Western-style johns. By comparison, the facilities on the old *tokkyû* (express) trains were still antiquated and a careful aim was necessary as the train rattled down the track.

As the train raced past the congestion of offices, apartment buildings, shops, homes and factories, a female attendant walked down the aisle pushing a cart containing a variety of refreshments. In a high-pitched voice, she sang out the list: *bentô* (box lunch), *hotto kôhii* (hot coffee), *aisu kôhii* (iced coffee), *aisu tii* (iced tea), *aisu kuriimu* (ice cream) and *biiru* (beer). Many travellers bought their *bentô* before boarding at a small shop on the station platform. But forget the photos in travel magazines or coffee table books of beautifully packaged *bentô* containing sushi and other delicacies. Most *bentô* are about as appealing and tasty as airline food, particularly the ones featuring tiny portions of cold *soba* noodles and *onigiri* (rice balls) with pickled plums. Introduced in 1885 specifically for train passengers, the first box lunch consisted of a couple of rice balls wrapped in bamboo leaves. Today, an estimated 12 million *bentô* are sold daily in Japan.

Beyond the urban sprawl of Tokyo and Yokohama, we passed Mount Ashitaka, an expensive resort area with numerous golf courses. As the train travelled around a bend, everyone automatically turned to look out the windows on the right-hand side. Within minutes, the view was dominated by Fuji-san, Japan's highest mountain, towering over the flat fertile green fields 97 kilometres (60 miles) southwest of Tokyo.

"*Subarashii!*" The view of the majestic and perfectly shaped volcano on a clear day was indeed spectacular and the highlight of my travels on the *shinkansen*. For the first time, I understood why Fuji-san inspires such awe and reverence in everyone who has seen the sacred mountain rising 3776 metres (12,388 feet) above the Fuji plain. Many Western books refer to Mount Fuji as Fujiyama, which is an insult. The suffix *yama* is used with ordinary mountains but the honorific suffix *san* shows respect and is reserved for a mountain with special status.

Fuji-san is the home of Shinto deities as well as an abode for the souls of the dead. Until the Meiji Restoration, women were not allowed to approach its sacred slopes in fear of upsetting the female resident deities. Now, they join people from all over the world as well as devout Japanese pilgrims who climb to the top of the famous landmark during July and August.

The dormant volcano has been silent since its last eruption in 1707 when it covered Tokyo with 15 centimetres (6 inches) of ash. In 1985, the tranquility of Fuji-san was interrupted once again when a jumbo jet crashed into the side of the mountain. In an instant, the souls of 520 passengers and crew on board joined the resident *kami* spirits.

Within minutes, the train entered a series of tunnels and Fuji-san disappeared from view. As the train approached each city, the number of kilometres to the station appeared on the electronic signboard, counting down from 20...19...18 and so on. We arrived at Fukuyama, nearly 800 kilometres (500 miles) southwest of Tokyo, in 4 hours and 45 minutes.

I was met at the station by Mrs. Okano, and her son Akio, a former Reitaku student. They had no problem picking me out of the crowds since I was the only *gaijin* on the platform. Fukuyama is an industrial city of little interest to foreigners.

"Hello, Mr. Jon," said Mrs. Okano, greeting me politely and extending her hand. The Japanese always meet their friends and family at the train station and they are there as well to see them off, even though each person is required to pay ¥140 for a special platform pass.

"Hello," I said, shaking her hand. I thanked her for meeting me at the station and explained that it was not necessary to call me "Mister."

The Okanos live in a very attractive, Western-style home with a decorative white wrought iron patio set in the middle of the gravel front yard. Western-style homes are fashionable in Japan, but not everyone can afford such expensive tastes.

"This is bigger than my house!" I exclaimed when I was given a tour.

"*Hontô?*" (Really?) Mrs. Okano wondered, not believing that a Japanese house could be larger than one in a vast country like Canada. Until now, I didn't believe a Japanese house could be bigger either. Except for one *tatami* room, the house had beautiful hardwood floors and all of their furniture was very modern.

While visiting the Okanos and other families, I usually slept in the *tatami* room on a futon. Almost 80 percent of the Japanese still sleep on futons because they live in tiny houses or cramped apartments. Futons are also used in *tatami* rooms since they do not damage the woven mats. During the day, they are stored in *oshiire* (large closets with sliding doors). I was usually given a *makura*, a tiny pillow made from buckwheat chaff, which was quite hard but I was always too tired to notice.

Like everyone else, I left my shoes in the *genkan* (vestibule), always pointed outward, and walked around the house in my socks. The Japanese are always horrified when they discover that North Americans wear street shoes in the house. The Japanese usually wear slippers in the home, but even these are taken off before entering a *tatami* room. When using the toilet room, I put on the blue plastic slippers left outside the door. The Japanese never wear their house slippers in the john and I didn't dare imagine their reaction if I walked in there with stocking feet!

Shutting the door behind me, I couldn't believe my eyes. Instead of an ordinary Western toilet, the Okanos

: of the new computerized models, which had ' been introduced in Japan. The high-tech toilet was originally designed for people in wheelchairs, but they quickly became popular as every trend-conscious household rushed out to buy one. I had never seen one before and all of the buttons with *kanji* symbols were confusing. I had difficulty figuring out which one was for flushing but I wasn't about to ask for instructions, not after I had already used the facilities. So I took my chances, stepped aside and pushed one of the buttons.

"*Iya da!*" (No!) I watched hopelessly as water sprayed on the door, just missing my shirt. That must be the bidet button, I concluded. The next time, I was lucky. The toilet flushed. These sophisticated toilets have numerous features, including a choice of music or a flushing sound to drown out any embarrassing noises. The seat warmer is a nice feature in winter since most homes in Japan don't have central heating. Soichira Honda, the founder of one of Japan's largest car and motorcycle manufacturers, was absolutely right when he said, "Technology is a tool to serve mankind." Leave it to the Japanese to find more and more useful ways to use the computer chip. Most of the Western-style toilets also have a basin for washing hands on top of the water tank, as a conservation measure.

Many homes still have the traditional squat facilities though I was always surprised to see them in modern homes. But I wasn't prepared for the primitive facilities at Hiroyuki's home, which I visited a few years later, when I was cycling through Japan during the summer holidays.

Hiroyuki lived on the outskirts of Osaka in an older, very traditional house. But there was a mini-satellite dish on the roof and we watched music videos on MTV and *Larry King Live* on CNN. So, I was shocked to see an outhouse attached to the house. Neither the urinal nor the squat toilet had a flush mode and the familiar smells were quite powerful. I held my breath and spent as little time as possible in there. These pit toilets are still quite common throughout Japan and they are emptied out on a regular basis by private sanitation trucking firms.

The Japanese always separate the toilet room and the *ofuro*. At the Okano's home, the bathing room was typically Japanese, with tiled walls and a drainage hole in the middle of the floor. I sat on a small stool and scrubbed myself thoroughly, rinsing off the soap suds with a handheld showerhead. There are many stories of Japanese tourists attempting the same bathing procedure in American hotel bathrooms, realizing too late that there isn't a drainage hole in the floor and then trying to mop the floor with towels. Guidebooks now inform the Japanese how to take a bath in Western countries, just as guidebooks inform Westerners how to take a bath in Japan.

The deep tub, large enough for me to stretch out my legs, was already full of scalding hot water. Most tubs in private homes were much smaller and almost square in shape, where I sat with my knees huddled up against my chest. As the honoured guest of the Okano household, I was the first one to bathe and relax in the hot tub before dinner. Traditionally, the most important members of the family bathe first, starting with the grandparents but today, people bathe in the most practical order. The water remains unchanged throughout the evening so it is essential to be squeaky clean before stepping into the tub. While Westerners have a bath to get clean, the Japanese get clean to have a bath. I can't imagine bathing like a Westerner anymore, sitting in a tubful of dirty water. Of all the

Japanese customs, I enjoyed the bathing ritual the most. After soaking for ten minutes or so, I carefully replaced the mat on top of the tub to keep the water as hot as possible for the next person.

While Mrs. Okano prepared dinner in a large, modern kitchen, her ten-year-old daughter, Naomi, diligently practiced her piano lessons on a Yamaha keyboard in the corner. Dining at the Okano's was almost like having dinner at home. We sat around a table in the kitchen, eating our meal with knives and forks off regular size plates and drinking Australian Chardonnay. Instead of grace, we all said "*Itadakimasu*" when the food was placed in front of us and "*Gochisô sama deshita*" at the end of the meal.

Mr. Okano, however, was not home for dinner. In Japanese society, most men put in long hours at work and then go drinking with their colleagues in the evening. The group at the office comes before family, although most *sarariman* have indicated that they would prefer to spend more time at home. Socializing after work with colleagues has become an important escape from the pressures of the job and the rigid structure of their lives. And getting drunk together is an extension of the group activity. *Sarariman* use the opportunity for frank and boisterous discussion of ideas otherwise frowned upon in the office setting.

Even though a wife may prefer to have her husband spend more time at home, she is not anxious to see him on the doorstep right after work. The neighbours would assume that he was nothing more than a failure. Just the same, the long hours, six days a week, take their toll, with 50 percent of Japanese *sarariman* claiming to suffer from a chronic shortage of sleep. *Karôshi* (death from overwork) is not uncommon and some widows have even tried to sue the companies for compensation.

I met Mr. Okano the following day when I was taken on a tour of his factory. Even though he was the owner, Mr. Okano shared a large administrative office with other staff members. The modern office was well equipped with a number of computers, but an older employee was still using an abacus for all his calculations. The abacus was introduced to Japan in AD 600 by Buddhist monks from China. There are still plenty of die-hards who insist that they can add and subtract much faster on an abacus than a calculator. All six-year-old children are still taught how to master the *soroban*. In 1993, an editorial in *The New York Times* suggested that Asian students excelled in mathematics because they were taught how to use an abacus at an early age. There are several theories to support such a statement, and there are skeptics as well. But the fact remains undisputed; Japanese students perform better on math tests than Western students.

After our tour, Mrs. Okano took us sightseeing. Driving in Japan is a real challenge. Except for the expressways, the lanes of all roads, including national highways, are very narrow, barely wide enough to accommodate a small car. Meeting up with a bus or a transport truck usually requires someone to pull over on the shoulder. The speed limit on highways is an unrealistic 60 kilometres (37 miles) per hour. But then, the roads in and around all major urban areas are always congested with traffic. The sheer number of cars on the road has created conditions that would not be tolerated in North America. Traffic, particularly in the larger cities, can be absolutely insane. Still, the Japanese have lots of *nintai* (patience) and have managed to put up with it for years.

Whenever possible, people use expressways, despite the expense of ¥23 per kilometre, roughly ¥37 per mile. Such high tolls reflect the tremendous cost of carving expressways out of Japan's mountainous terrain, as well as bolstering them to withstand frequent tremors whenever the great catfish stirs.

The Japanese love high speeds and the flow of traffic usually moves considerably faster than the posted limit of 80 kilometres (50 miles) per hour on the expressway. Mrs. Okano managed to maintain a steady 140 kilometres (88 miles) per hour along the winding expressway. Radar detectors are legal and with many of them on the road, traffic slows down whenever police are in the vicinity. Cars are also equipped with an annoying *beep-beep* warning sound from the speedometer when they exceed 100 kilometres (63 miles) per hour. But Mrs. Okano wasn't paying any attention to the *beep-beep* sound and we made the 50-kilometre (31-mile) trip to Kurashiki in no time at all.

Kurashiki is a charming historical town, which was very prosperous during feudal times. The old canal, lined with storehouses for rice shipments from nearby farms, gives the city a European atmosphere. We checked out some of the shops before heading east to the coast.

The views of the Inland Sea from Mount Washû-zan were very impressive. The sweeping length of the giant Seto Ôhashi (Inland Sea Great Bridge) stretched out in front of us, linking the island of Shikoku to Honshu. The toll charge for the longest bridge system in Japan, crossing five islands and spanning 19 kilometres (12 miles), was a whopping ¥6490 for a passenger car, so we didn't bother with the sights in Shikoku.

Instead, Akio and I spent most of the hot sunny afternoon at a crowded public beach on the Inland Sea. During the 1970s, many of the ocean beaches were closed when Japan's aggressive industrial growth caused extensive pollution of its water resources. While we were at the beach, the water was murky and not very inviting. But everyone else was having a good time so I decided to go swimming as well. Many people rented large inner tubes, but we took out a rowboat instead. As we passed the swimming buoys, I noticed hundreds of large jellyfish floating on the water among the flotsam.

On our way back to Fukuyama, we stopped for gas. Fuel is very expensive since Japan has limited natural resources. At ¥140 per litre (¥635 per gallon), a fill-up could run close to $100 for a mid-size vehicle. (The price has dropped somewhat, in recent years.) All gas stations are full service and the attendants are impeccably dressed in uniform. We were served by two attendants who filled the tank, checked the oil, washed the windshield and emptied the ashtray. As we pulled away from the gas pumps, the two of them stood side by side and bowed in unison.

After dinner, we walked a short distance to Akio's grandparents' farm, where they grew watermelon on a small plot of land beside the Ashida River. On the other side, the pink neon lights of a *rabu hoteru* (love hotel) were glowing in the dusk. The love hotel is a Japanese institution, providing rooms by the hour or night, mainly for young couples who have nowhere else to be alone together or for married couples who share their house with the husband's parents. A sign in the lobby indicates that guests must be over 18 years of age. A lighted display board allows the guests to choose from a variety of fantasy theme rooms, from medieval to modern, with beds shaped like a heart, a 1950s Cadillac, a gondola, even a space shuttle. One businessman bought the US Virgin Islands bobsled to provide an authentic Olympic experience for one of his hotels. After a button is pushed to select the desired room, a voice from the wall requests payment. The couple pays through a slot on the counter, but the hotel manager remains hidden from view. The voice from the wall thanks the couple and directs them to their room. There are thousands of these hotels throughout Japan, some more plush than others, but always outlandish with their décor.

Inside the farmhouse, we sat on cushions on the floor of a *tatami* room around a low table, eating fresh yellow watermelon and drinking Asahi Super Dry Beer. Like everyone else, the grandparents asked me if I liked Japan and sushi. By now, I knew enough Japanese to respond to these simple questions. The Japanese love their country. Every mountain, lake and river is sacred to them. Needless to say, everyone always smiled approvingly when I told them I liked Japan very much and that sushi was my favourite food.

The following morning, after a generous breakfast of bacon and eggs with a garnish of tomatoes and raw cabbage along with toast and milk, Mrs. Okano was satisfied that I was ready for the next leg of my journey.

≈

August 4 was a hot, sunny day as the *shinkansen* approached Hiroshima. The city, whose name means "broad islands," is located on a collection of six islands in a wide delta of the Ota River with lush green hills on both sides and the Chûgoku Mountains in the distance. During World War II, the city was an important naval base and military communications centre.

Hiroshima was practically obliterated by the atomic bomb dropped by the United States Air Force on August 6, 1945. Nearly 200,000 people were killed and injured by the blast. Although Hiroshima's population was officially recorded at 380,000, more than 100,000 people had already been evacuated.

After the war, the industrial city was quickly rebuilt. As we approached the downtown area, I strained my eyes to see the skeleton remains of the Industrial Promotion Hall, gutted by the blast with its dome stripped to its steel frame. These ruins, supported with new steel girders so that the structure won't collapse, stand as a reminder of the bomb's destructive force.

The entire Abe family greeted me at the train station, holding a large colourful sign with a drawing of a Canadian flag beside "Welcome Jonathan Buchanan." Apparently, Mr. Abe was an old school friend of Nonaka-sensei. I had assumed Nonaka-sensei meant university and that my host spoke English fluently. But they were friends from high school days and Mr. Abe remembered very little English.

As we drove to the Abe home, I was struck by the irony that the Japanese rebuilt the residential areas with Western-style homes. The Abe's home was a prime example. There wasn't the slightest resemblance to a traditional Japanese home except for one *tatami* room. Despite the obvious affluence of many of the families I visited, none of them had a guestroom. Once again, I was assigned to the *tatami* room where I slept on a futon. But I didn't mind. Futons were comfortable and I was grateful that there was a portable air conditioner in the room.

The two children, a five-year old girl and an eight-year-old son, played Nintendo continuously. Mrs. Abe fretted about her kids being hooked on video games and asked if Western kids were the same. "Yes," I assured her. The children also had lots of stuffed animals, books and toys in their rooms, which were tiny by Western standards. And I always thought my room back home was small. As prosperity increased for the Japanese, the toy industry took off like a rocket and all homes with small children are crammed with playthings. But then again, no one has ever claimed that young Japanese children are not spoiled.

The vast majority of young children, however, do not have a room of their own. Most of them sleep with their parents until they are at least ten years old. Beds are not very common and cribs are almost non-existent. Instead, babies sleep beside their mothers on their own futons.

Motherhood is still an honourable profession and the overwhelming majority of Japanese women stay home to raise their children. With their husbands working six days a week and carousing late into the evenings, the women take on the burden of raising and disciplining the children as well as looking after the household and managing the finances. But they are very discreet about the sacrifices they make for their families. There appears to be little discontent and divorce is rare.

Dinner was served in a conventional Western-style dining room. Instead of saying, "*Itadakimasu*," when the meal was served, the Abe's son said grace. "God is good; God is great; let us thank Him for our food. Amen." In Japanese, of course. Like all mothers in the homes I visited, Mrs. Abe kept offering me more food. "*Dôzo, dôzo*," she said repeatedly, inviting me to please eat some more. I never dared to leave a morsel of food on a plate while dining as a guest in a home or restaurant. The Japanese are easily offended by Westerners who do not appreciate their cuisine.

Afterward, we relaxed in the living room, sitting on comfortable couches which are rarely found in Japanese homes. Mr. Abe handed me a large atlas and asked me to point out the precise location of my hometown in Northern Ontario. Many Japanese are familiar with most major cities as well as Niagara Falls, the Canadian Rockies and Prince Edward Island, the home of *Anne of Green Gables*. I was always amazed that the Japanese knew so much more about us than we knew about them.

Mr. Abe and I got along very well. We were on an equal footing as far as the knowledge of each other's language. Amazingly enough, the combination of his English and my Japanese was sufficient to carry on a conversation. Both of us had visited San Francisco, New York and Boston, so we talked about our travels in the United States. Mr. Abe showed me a picture book, titled *Big City ABC* that he bought for his daughter during a business trip to Boston. The Big City, coincidentally enough, was Toronto and Mr. Abe was very interested in learning more about Canada's largest city as I described the location of the paintings, such as "B is for Beach."

On the following day, we went to a beach on the Japan Sea with another family. The trip to the other side of the mountains was a three-hour drive along narrow, winding roads with Mrs. Abe navigating the route. We listened to the Carpenters on a cassette tape, which played over and over again. Arriving at the coast with "Close To You" still ringing in my ears, I noticed that the parking lot was filthy, with all kinds of garbage lying around. Even the beach, which was packed with people, had a lot of debris strewn about the sand and I wondered if the maintenance people were on holiday. Fortunately, we were able to find a clean spot near the ocean where we settled down on our towels. I was caught off guard by the fact that there were no facilities but Mr. Abe arranged with another family for me to use their tent so I could change into my swimsuit. Though the Japanese can be quite rude to each other on the subways, they are always very helpful and friendly while on holiday.

The water was warm and much cleaner than the Inland Sea. I had a great time swimming in the waves and chasing the children in the sand. But nobody had brought any sunscreen and by the end of the day, I was compared to a lobster by the Abes and their friends.

That evening, the Abes had arranged a small dinner party for their friends. Everyone drank plenty of beer except for me and the kids. We were served Coke instead. I suspected that Nonaka-sensei had given strict instructions to Mr. Abe not to serve me any alcoholic beverages. When someone offered me a beer, Mr. Abe interrupted, saying, "*Kôkôsei darô!*" (He's a high school student!) Another friend agreed, saying "*Mada kodomo da!*" (He's still a child!) By the end of the evening, though, we were all acting a little silly. I must have been a little light-headed as well, after spending the day in the hot sun. Otherwise, surely, I would not have had the crazy idea to ask them to pose for a group photo with cherry tomatoes in their mouths. The Japanese, who do not want to offend foreigners by denying small requests, were happy to oblige. Every time I look at their photo, each with a tiny tomato in their mouth, I am reminded of their graciousness and my craziness.

After dinner, I read a special supplement in English of the *Mainichi Shimbun* (one of Japan's most popular Japanese-language newspapers) about the upcoming 45th anniversary of the bombing of Hiroshima. The supplement included detailed reports of the atomic blast and the anguish of the people who were burned to death. Others suffered from radiation sickness and died several days, weeks, months and even years later. The victims who survived and their children are known as the *hibakusha* (explosion affected persons). They are still discriminated against because of the fear of genetic mutations affecting them for years to come, even though there is no medical evidence supporting such a preposterous theory. Nevertheless, the *hibakusha* have become second-class citizens who often have trouble finding marriage partners.

The Japanese have steadfastly whitewashed their aggressive military policies during World War II. While I was in Japan, high school textbooks had a few references to an "outbreak of war" between Japan and other countries including China, the United States and Great Britain, but there was no mention of atrocities, prison camps or war crimes. Even today, Japanese young people know very little about the role their country played during World War II and they don't understand why the Americans felt it was necessary to use atomic weapons against them. While textbooks may mention the "rape of Nanking" when the Japanese established their puppet regime in China in 1937, there is still a great deal of controversy over the number of actual deaths that occurred. Censors continue to peruse all history, geography and even home economics texts for delicate matter.

Over the years, the people of Hiroshima have lobbied passionately against further testing of nuclear weapons. Japan has always maintained a strong stand against the stockpiling of nuclear arsenals. The newspaper supplement also criticized France for its nuclear tests in the Pacific.

Every year, a memorial service, attracting thousands of Japanese and foreign tourists, is held at Peace Park. Enormous crowds were expected on the 45th anniversary, so Mr. Abe made arrangements for the son of a friend to take me on a sightseeing tour in the afternoon instead.

On the morning of August 6, I slept right through the siren that wails at 8:15 a.m. through a network of speakers connecting every neighbourhood to the city hall. When I finally awoke in the cool comfort of the Abe's air-conditioned home, the skies were clear and it was blistering hot outside, just like the day when the *genshi bakudaon* (atomic bomb) destroyed Hiroshima.

Tadayoshi and I took a bus to downtown Hiroshima where the Atomic Dome and the ruins of the Industrial Promotion Hall are located. The surrounding area has been transformed into the Peace Park, with numerous memorials where flowers and incense had been left by the family and friends of the thousands of people whose lives were lost when the United States retaliated against the Japanese military.

The Peace Memorial Museum, a long black building supported by concrete pillars, was crowded with both Japanese and foreign visitors. All of the walls were painted black to enhance the sombre atmosphere and the relics were a grim reminder of the true horrors of nuclear war. The exhibits and countless photographs depicted the agony of thousands of people when a "flash brighter than a thousand suns" cut across the sky. A few of the photos were enhanced in colour to show raw flesh burns and lacerations.

The *genshi bakudan* has been described as an "inhumane bomb" as if all other bombs in the history of war were somehow more humane. Before Hiroshima was destroyed, the death toll in Japan from massive fire bombings had already exceeded 500,000 and another 13 million people had been left homeless. Will world leaders ever learn that war is not a solution? Unfortunately, I don't think so, even though there were a number of photos of presidents from many countries, the Pope and celebrities who have visited the museum over the years and no doubt, felt just as moved as I was by the exhibit.

In the middle of the park, the Flame of Peace, held in sculpted outstretched hands, continues to burn with the hope that someday, nuclear weapons will be abolished. There is also a memorial to 51,000 children who were killed by the atomic bomb. A life-size statue of a young girl holding a golden crane stands on top of an arch housing a bronze bell. The bell was cast from coins contributed by children from all over the world. The monument was inspired by Sadako, who believed she could be cured of leukemia if she folded 1,000 origami paper cranes. Tragically, she died after finishing her 964th crane. Today, every Japanese child knows how to make these intricate paper cranes symbolizing long life and happiness. Countless colourful chains of *sembazuru*, each made from 1,000 cranes strung together, sent from all over the world, were laid at the foot of the statue by the children of Hiroshima as their wish for eternal peace.

Despite the sweltering heat, we decided to walk from Peace Park to Hiro-jô, a replica of the famous castle built by the Mori clan in 1593. The original castle, which was destroyed by the atomic bomb, was rebuilt in 1958 with a well-designed museum covering the history of Hiroshima.

Castles were the symbols of the pride and power of the *daimyô* and their samurai. Hiroshima Castle, with a wide moat surrounding the fortifications, is typical of the style built during the intensified power struggles of the Keichô Era from 1596 to 1614. The exhibits show the defences during the feudal period. The top floor of the five-storey castle is a mesh-protected observation deck, with vending machines selling cameras, film and ¥300 soft drinks.

That evening, the Abes took us out to dinner at a popular family restaurant which served both Western and Japanese cuisine. They were rather surprised when I started to order from the Japanese menu and made it clear that they wished me to enjoy some of the Western food. Of course, they didn't realize that Western food in Japan is usually mediocre except at expensive restaurants catering almost exclusively to foreigners. Besides, I preferred local Japanese fare. Just the same, I did not want to offend my hosts. They smiled as I ordered a hamburger patty and fried egg to accompany the *unagi* (eel). I could have lived without the bland beef and egg combo, but the *unagi* was delicious.

The following morning, we boarded a crowded ferry for a short crossing to Miyajima (Shrine Island) where Mount Misen is the ancient home of the mountain god and five fairy princesses. The enormous "floating" red *torii,* rising out of the water and guarding the Itsukushima Shrine since 1875, is one of Japan's most famous landmarks. During low tide, people walk through the *torii,* which purifies the soul before entering the grounds of the famous island. Miyajima has been one of the most sacred places throughout Japanese history and the Shinto shrine itself honours several female deities who are believed to have appeared on the site in AD 592. And yet, women were not permitted to visit the island before the Allied Occupation. Other deities inhabiting the island protect sailors and fishermen.

Miyajima is as pretty as a picture postcard with tame deer wandering around the walkways and monkeys swinging through the virgin forest hilltops, often snatching visitors' lunches. The natural beauty of Miyajima is evident throughout the year, with its cherry blossoms in the spring and red maple leaves in autumn. The opportunity to take advantage of the thousands of tourists who visit every day is not lost by local entrepreneurs and there is no shortage of gift shops and souvenir stalls. The crass commercialism in Japan never ceased to astonish me. As far as I was concerned, there was something irreverent about selling Nintendo game cartridges at one of Japan's most sacred sites.

After returning to Hiroshima by ferry, we had a quick *soba* lunch in one of the restaurants at the train station before I said goodbye to the Abes and boarded the *shinkansen* to my next destination.

≈

The two-hour train trip to Osaka was boring since we spent most of the time travelling through dark tunnels, 55 in all, with the longest almost 15 kilometres (9 miles) in length. Osaka is relatively flat since much of the city has been built on landfill in the tidal flats of Osaka Bay. In the seventh and eighth centuries, the city was an important port for trade with China. Although Osaka was destroyed during World War II, the city was quickly rebuilt. Today,

Osaka is the third largest city in Japan and a major financial and industrial centre with nearly three million residents.

Unfortunately, Osaka is still called the "City of Smoke" or "Manchester of the East" even though these descriptions are outdated. In recent years, Japan has passed some of the world's toughest anti-pollution laws and there were no obvious signs of heavy smog in any of the cities I visited, except for Kitakyushu, where black smoke still belched from the stacks of its steel mills. The smog in most Japanese cities was certainly easier to take than Los Angeles. Besides, there are no "beaters" running around in the city since nearly all of the cars in the streets were less than five years old. So I was always surprised to see people still wearing surgical masks in major cities, including Tokyo and Osaka. I'm not sure whether they were hypochondriacs or just people with a cold who didn't want to spread their germs to others.

Mr. Shinmei and his 18-year-old daughter, Megumi, a senior student at Reitaku, met me at the train station. With hardly any *gaijin* on the platform, Megumi easily recognized me in the crowd.

"Hello, Jon."

"*Konnichiwa*, Shinmei-san," I responded.

Although Megumi greeted me by my first name, which is the Western way, I never called Megumi by her given name. The honorific system of addressing people is very specific. In Japan, the surname is always written first and also used in conversations. Even Megumi's father did not use her given name. Instead, he called her "*Onée-san*" (older sister). Consequently, I did not know the given names of most of the students at Reitaku or other teenagers I met during my travels. However, everyone knew that

Westerners called their friends by their given names. Besides, "Buchanan" was too difficult for the Japanese to pronounce.

Mr. Shinmei drove us to the Sakamotos, who were putting me up for three days since they lived in a large farmhouse on the outskirts of Osaka. The farm had been in the family for several generations. When Osaka expanded quickly in the 1960s, the farmland was sold to developers.

The house was very traditional with several *tatami* rooms. We sat on cushions on the floor in one of the large rooms around a low table, drinking lemonade and eating cookies. This room, which was used during the day for dining and entertaining, also served as the grandparents' bedroom, with their futons tucked behind the sliding doors of the *oshiire*. I slept in another, smaller *tatami* room next door.

As usual, I was asked numerous questions about my impressions of Japan. I tried to answer as much as I could in Japanese, using English only when I was at a loss for the right word or expression. The Sakamotos' daughter was an interpreter for a major corporation and translated when necessary for the rest of the family and guests. All of them appeared to be very interested in my comments and pleased that I was enjoying Japan so much. They were surprised, however, that I didn't mind travelling by myself, and that I was able to get around on my own, especially in a strange country. The Japanese almost always travel in a group, whether it is with their family, classmates or an organized tour.

Mrs. Sakamoto also asked if I had any homework.

"*Nai*," I said. Loosely translated, it means, "No way."

"*Hontô?*" (Really?)

"*Natsu ni shukudai ga zenzen arimasen,*" I responded, explaining that I never had any homework during the summer. I even showed her my bag, which didn't contain any books.

Everyone was shocked to learn that Western students are not given assignments to complete during their holidays. All Japanese students are expected to do some studying while on vacation. Enough to ruin the summer, I'm sure.

Many tourists avoid Osaka, because it's such an ugly city. But then again, most of Japan's major cities are eyesores. Osaka is actually a lot of fun and Minami-ku is even flashier than Tokyo's shopping areas, with larger billboards and brighter lights, especially along the Dôtomburi Canal.

The following afternoon, Miss Sakamoto and I took the train downtown. Dozens of huge movie billboards on the walls of buildings were advertising everything from *Gremlins 2* to the latest samurai flick. The Western influence was very obvious everywhere. One of the arcades contained three McDonald's restaurants, all within view of each other. Even a side street was named Amemura (America Town), featuring a number of clothing stores, Western restaurants and an English bookstore for the benefit of the large number of Americans and American-wannabes in Osaka.

And yet, I always appreciated the opportunity to dine at authentic Japanese establishments, such as the large *okonomiyaki* restaurant, where we sat on cushions around a low table in a private booth. *Okonomiyaki* (cook what you like) is one of my favourite foods and we grilled our own pancakes filled with crab and a variety of vegetables, including cabbage, over a hibachi at our table.

The best (if you can call it that) view of Osaka, sprawling in all directions, is from Osaka-jô, once the mightiest fortress in Japan. Built on a strategic hilltop in 1583 by Hideyoshi Toyotomi, the warlord who helped unify Japan, Osaka-jô was destroyed and rebuilt several times, most recently in 1931 as a museum. I knew I wasn't in the original castle when we stepped into an elevator to go up to the observation deck on the roof.

We also visited Expo 90, the International Garden and Greenery Exposition, in the evening to avoid the crowds. The Japanese have a passion for gardens, not to mention midways, and the grounds were still packed with people. The variety of pavilions and exhibits was very impressive, considering this was not a major World's Fair, like the one held in Osaka in 1970. Even Canada had an attractive pavilion, a log cabin in a forest setting, but it closed early.

When we arrived back at the farmhouse after 9 p.m., dinner was waiting for us. The kitchen was very large by Japanese standards, with eight of us sitting at the table. Mrs. Sakamoto served *sukiyaki*, a stew consisting of thinly sliced beef, tofu, leeks, shiitake mushrooms and transparent noodles, with rice as a side dish. *Sukiyaki* is a communal meal cooked in a large pan over a hot plate in the middle of the table. *Warashita*, a sauce made from soy sauce, *mirin* (sweet rice wine) and sugar, is poured over the ingredients while they are cooking. I was given disposable chopsticks while everyone else ate with their own pair of ceramic *hashi*. We also had a special pair of extra-long chopsticks for cooking and removing the individual morsels of food, which we dipped into a small bowl of raw egg before transferring them to our plates. I had some trouble keeping the two different sets of chopsticks from getting mixed up as we cooked and ate at the same time. As tempted as I was to spear the morsel of beef or vegetable when it slipped into the bowl of raw egg, I didn't. Instead, I carefully fished it out with my *hashi*. By now, I was pretty adept at using chopsticks.

The next day, Miss Sakamoto suggested that I might want to get a haircut. No doubt, she took pity on me since my hair was hanging over my eyes. Actually, I wanted to let my hair grow long like Randall's, but I wasn't about to offend her. We found a barbershop near the train station with an elegant sign advertising the following in Japanese, "Butchering is our specialty. Glue at no extra charge."

Miss Sakamoto instructed the barber to give me the full treatment. First, the barber cut my *gaijin* hair as expertly as anyone back home. Then, he proceeded to give me a shave with a razor blade at least 30 centimeters (12 inches) long and sharp as a samurai sword. I almost freaked out when I saw the blade flash before my eyes. But I was paralyzed with fear, unable to move or say a word. Finally, the ordeal was over and the barber eased the tension in my neck and shoulder muscles by giving me a gentle five-minute massage before setting me free. Miss Sakamoto insisted on picking up the tab for ¥3000.

≈

The local train to Nara was packed with people travelling to their ancestral roots to celebrate *Obon*. The Buddhist festival of the dead is one of Japan's most important religious holidays and many people return to their hometown to visit family and relatives.

The ancient capital is an important historical city with a strong Buddhist influence dating back to the seventh century when the imperial court in Nara patronized

Buddhism as a means of unifying the country. Prince Shôtoku issued an imperial edict in AD 594 promoting the new religion. During his leadership, the Seven Great Temples were built in Nara and the new religion coexisted comfortably with the Japanese Shinto beliefs.

The Endos ran a successful wholesale business and lived in a modern two-storey Japanese home with hardwood floors and an enormous living room overlooking a rice field. So I was surprised to discover that they only had an Asian-style squat toilet. I had been dreading the moment. Squatting is a very awkward position for a *gaijin*.

I shared a tiny room with Yoshifumi, a first-year student at Reitaku, even though there was barely enough room for two futons. To make matters worse, the Japanese have a tendency to roll over the nearest body, as if they were still youngsters sleeping with their parents. But I wasn't accustomed to someone cuddling up to me in the middle of the night. Eventually, I put my travel bag in between the two of us.

The following morning, Mrs. Endo asked me to pack an overnight bag since Yoshifumi and I were going on a two-day Moralogy retreat. I could hardly believe my ears. First, I was asked by the Sakamotos about homework. And the next thing I know, I'm off on an outing organized by the Hiroike Institute. At the very least, I hoped to escape sermons while on vacation, especially when I didn't understand what was going on most of the time. Of course, it never occurred to Mrs. Endo to ask me if I was interested in tagging along with Yoshifumi. Still, she generously covered my expenses, so I shouldn't be too hard on her.

Ishihara-san, a family friend who was a seminar leader, drove us to a posh resort where we met about 30 other teens. My mood improved as soon as I saw the girls. Perhaps we could have some fun after all.

Dinner was served in a large dining hall and later, everyone met at the swimming pool for some races. Races? I felt trapped, like in the barber's chair. This was hardly my idea of fun. I hadn't been in a swimming race in four years, and then I came last in my class. I felt even worse when I was asked to anchor a relay team. My teammates obviously had great expectations because I was so much taller than anyone else. How could they possibly know that Western teens are not necessarily good swimmers? My team was doomed.

After that humiliating exercise, we spent the rest of the evening roaming the halls from one room party to another, drinking pop and munching on chips. The girls had an 11 p.m. curfew and suddenly disappeared but the rest of us carried on until 2 a.m. I suspect that our late-night prowls were tolerated by the staff because it is part of the same social bonding process as our dorm room *paati,* creating a strong sense of solidarity within the group. Everyone was very friendly and I actually had a good time. No one mentioned a word about my pathetic performance in the swimming pool and I was grateful for their discretion.

By the time I grabbed my futon from the closet, I was beat. There was no mercy the following morning as we straggled out to the parking lot at 6:45 a.m. for assembly. Within minutes, everyone was accounted for and we began our calisthenics and stretches. Nothing strenuous except for the jog to the top of the hill.

After breakfast, we met in a large conference room. I had a hard time following the seminar but I knew the gist of what was going on. When we were asked what we wanted out of life, most students responded by suggesting *heiwa* (peace), *shusse* (success) and *kazoku* (family). I complicated matters by adding a Ferrari to the list. All of the students laughed but not everyone seemed to appreciate a little humour. Instead, the moderator calmly suggested that my answer was not appropriate because it was self-indulgent. Of course, I should have known better by now. Moralogy followers strive to live by high moral principles and they believe that true happiness can be achieved by sacrificing self-interest for the good of the group.

On our way back to Nara, Ishihara-san drove as if his modest Nissan compact was a Ferrari, racing along the winding, narrow roads, even when passing around blind corners. I was terrified and pleaded with him to slow down.

"*Mô yukkuri kudasai*," I kept repeating. The death toll on the highways in Japan is staggering, with approximately 10,000 fatalities each year and I didn't want to be one of them. But he and Yoshifumi just laughed. Unbelievably, we arrived back in one piece. Even Mrs. Endo laughed at the Nara Indy story when Ishihara-san related details of the harrowing trip.

Mrs. Endo redeemed herself by offering to take Yoshifumi and me on a tour of Nara's historical sites the following day. Nara, like Kyoto and other cultural centres, were spared by the Americans during World War II. Instead, they targeted large industrial cities and important military bases. Unfortunately, we woke up to a heavy downpour. Yoshifumi and I amused ourselves by watching movies and playing Nintendo. By late afternoon, the rain finally stopped and we visited the Buddhist temples and Shinto shrines in Nara Kôen, the largest municipal park in Japan. Deer, considered to be sacred messengers of the gods, wander freely and are spoiled by tourists who feed them biscuits bought from vendors.

There were plenty of photo opportunities as Mrs. Endo took our pictures in front of famous landmarks. And she was always ready with ¥10 coins for us to throw into the bins in front of numerous altars. At Kasuga Taisha, a Shinto shrine dating back to the early eighth century, thousands of ancient stone lanterns lined the walks. Every year, they are lit during *Obon* to guide the spirits of the dead back to their former homes to visit loved ones. Tôdai-ji (East Great Temple) is an immense monastery compound with numerous interesting buildings, some of them dating back hundreds of years. We had wanted to see the world's largest bronze statue of Daibutsu (Great Buddha) but the buildings were already closed. It was just my luck -- once again arriving too late to see very much. Instead, we watched the brightly coloured orange and red *koi* (carp) swim in the surrounding ponds. These ornamental fish, which are common in garden ponds, are symbols of courage and strength, traditional male virtues in Japan.

Mrs. Endo treated us to dinner at the Nara Hotel, an elegant establishment built in 1909 with fashionable high ceilings and a lovely décor. The dining room overlooked the park and we had a wonderful view from our table beside the window. I ordered the New York steak rare from a bilingual Western menu. The food was exceptionally good, but this was a classy hotel catering to foreigners as well as Japanese visitors who were willing to spend ¥2800 for a prime cut of beef.

After dinner, we walked through Nara Machi, the old town from the Edo period on our way to Sarusawa (Monkey Marsh) Pond for the *Obon* rituals. A festive atmosphere filled the air as thousands of people milled about. Dozens of stalls lined the walkways, selling everything from religious mementos and cheap traditional toys as well as Nintendo game cartridges, disposable cameras and film. *Yakitori* stands, selling chicken kebobs, were just as popular with families crowding around to grab a quick bite to eat.

Scaffolding had been erected in the middle of the pond with a stage for *taiko* drummers to drive away evil spirits. The drummers were accompanied by several flutists as well as a singer. We joined a traditional circle dance already underway with hundreds of others, dancing around the pond under the warm and starry summer sky.

The next day, Mrs. Endo drove me to the train station and insisted on paying for my ¥12,000 ticket to my next destination, Suwa. After an unsuccessful attempt to refuse her offer, I thanked her profusely and boarded the train. The generosity of the Japanese toward a stranger never ceased to amaze me. Here I was, muttering under my breath about the squat toilet when Mrs. Endo not only accepted me as a guest in her home but also covered all of my expenses as if I was a member of the family.

≈

The scenery was breathtaking as the Nagano-bound *tokkyû* travelled through a lush green valley, with mountains rising above us. There were no major cities along the route after Nagoya. Instead, clusters of old wooden homes and a few concrete shops huddled around the train stations.

Suwa is located on Lake Suwa in the middle of the Japanese Alps. More than 200,000 residents live along its shores and the sprawling industrial areas are dominated by

Seiko Epson, manufacturer of watches, computers and electronic instruments, and Olympus Optics, a major manufacturer of cameras.

The *tokkyû* pulled into Shiojiri station, where I was supposed to catch another train to Kami-Suwa (Upper Suwa) to spend a week with the Takadas. The station was practically deserted and I could not find the other train listed on any of the timetables. After a few anxious moments trying to decide what to do next, I heard someone calling "Jonathan." I turned around and saw Kazuo's older brothers, Kenji and Masaru, waving to me from the gate.

Right from the outset, it was obvious that the Takadas were not a typical Japanese family. We drove the short distance to their home in an aging Volkswagen Jetta. German car manufacturers have dominated the import car market in Japan since their compact BMWs, Mercedes-Benzes and VWs are ideal for the narrow streets. But the VW was long past its prime, an unusual sight in Japan in 1990.

The Takadas lived in a nondescript, two-storey concrete building squeezed in between a major road and the railway. A yappy husky dog announced our arrival and the entire household came to the door to great me, including Mr. and Mrs. Takada, Noriko, their 13-year-old daughter, Mr. Takada's parents and his sister, along with her family, who were also visiting during *Obon*.

With so many people visiting at the same time, I couldn't imagine where everyone slept. I had been given Noriko's room, one of the three upstairs bedrooms. Her room was small, but I was comfortable. Noriko even had a computer on her desk, which was rather unusual back then. Surprising as it may seem, the Japanese did not begin to buy PCs until well into the 1990s. Both Noriko and her brothers had beds in their rooms even though the parents and grandparents still slept on futons. The traditional *tatami* room on the ground floor, used as the living and dining room during the day, was transformed into the grandparents' bedroom at night. In Japanese society, the grandparents often live with the oldest son. Many women refuse to marry the eldest, or only son in a family because of the duties expected from a *chônan's* wife, who must be willing to share her home with her in-laws. Besides looking after his parents, the *chônan* is also responsible for inviting the rest of the family to visit during *Obon*. No wonder the house was so crowded.

The endless generosity of the Takadas was put into action from the moment I arrived. We nibbled on broiled corn-on-the-cob and drank beer while Mr. Takada filled me in on Kazuo's summer activities in Canada. Mr. Takada spoke English quite well. A member of the Rotary Club, he was very active with several international programs and helped establish a Rotary exchange program between Nagano-ken (the area in which Suwa is located) and Florida. Mr. Takada also showed me the letters and pictures of Kazuo that my parents had sent while they were on vacation in Cape Cod. There was a photo of Kazuo grinning broadly as he sat behind the wheel of my mother's Toyota Supra. At 17 years of age, Kazuo was very proud of his Canadian driver's licence since Japanese teens have to wait until they are 18 years of age to drive a car.

After four or five small glasses of beer, I decided to call it quits. I probably had enough to drink because we got into a rather philosophical discussion and I blurted out, "*Minna wa ôbaka desu,*" which means, "Everyone is a great idiot." We all roared with laughter even though it is very insulting to call anyone an "idiot" in Japan. But then again, the Takadas were not a typical Japanese family.

The following morning, I was wide-awake by 9:30 a.m. because of the trucks roaring past on the road outside my room. Mrs. Takada served me the traditional breakfast of miso soup, rice, pickled vegetables and tea in the *tatami* room.

During the day, I helped barbecue *yakitori* on a large outdoor hibachi. The chicken kebobs were one of the specialty items sold by the Takada's catering company during *Obon*. Everyone pitched in including Kenji and Masaru who were busy delivering platters of fried chicken, shrimp and *yakitori* throughout the neighbourhood by van and scooter. Except at the Takada's home, I never noticed other children helping out with the chores, beyond clearing the dishes from the table after each meal.

Each day at 5 p.m., Mrs. Takada served a formal English-style tea with lemon and milk along with small cakes. All other meals were served in the traditional Japanese manner. Dinner was usually served at 7 p.m., just in time for the evening news. In many Japanese homes, all of the conversation is carried on prior to the meal. So we ate silently, with our eyes glued to the tube, helping ourselves from various dishes on the table with our own chopsticks and eating off tiny plates.

Television news broadcasts in Japan are very dramatic and explicit in content. None of the gory details are left out, especially if a cameraman is lucky enough to be present on the scene of an accident. Otherwise, Japanese television programming is poor by Western standards. A large TV aerial on the roof picked up the limited range of six local stations. I was shocked to learn that there was no cable television in most of Japan and that the industry was highly regulated by the government. Even in Tokyo, there were only eight channels to choose from. Not surprisingly, the forest of TV aerials on the rooftops is slowly being replaced by satellite dishes, which provide dozens of additional channels of BS (broadcast by satellite) Entertainment. Even cable television has finally spread to most cities.

Sometimes, we watched game shows, which have a tremendous following in Japan. These are big budget programs where most of the money is spent on production costs rather than prizes for the contestants. For one five-minute segment, the crew flew out to New York just to see how much it costs to bribe the man on the street into shaving his beard. The contestants in Tokyo try to guess the crew's cash outlay. Most of the game shows are downright silly, but I found myself laughing along with the others. Commercials are aired more frequently in Japan than North America, but they are always very entertaining. Cartoons are also popular with both adults and children. The *animé* are an extension of the country's addiction to *manga* and feature-length animated movies are usually in the top ten at the box office.

I usually spent the evening in Kenji's room, which was crammed with a bed, a stereo system, a television, two VCRs and an enormous video collection. Kenji was 22 years old and very fluent in English. Currently, he held two jobs, training as a cook in a local restaurant and selling Amway products. Masaru was 19 and in his second year at university. Like his brother, he had a great sense of humour and the three of us got along very well.

After watching everything from *Star Wars* to *Young Guns* with Kenji and Masaru, I'd head past the washing machine, dryer and stacks of Amway products to the *ofuro* for a bath in their shocking pink tub. With so many people staying at the Takadas, I always waited until everyone else had gone to bed so I could relax without feeling rushed.

On the evening of August 15, we watched the *hanabi* (fireworks) over Lake Suwa from a municipal park along the waterfront. The Japanese are crazy about fireworks and buckets are sold everywhere for ¥3000 during *Obon*. After each round, there was a lot of clapping accompanying the oohs and aahs. Commentary on the origin and nature of each display was carried across loudspeakers. The explosions of chrysanthemums, plum and cherry blossoms were spectacular as the 37 rounds of fireworks lasted for more than an hour.

While I was visiting Suwa, Mr. Takada wanted me to understand more about Buddhism and made arrangements for me to visit a temple near their home. Buddhism was introduced to Japan in the sixth century when priests from China crossed the treacherous seas from Korea to Japan. Today, there are thousands of Buddhist temples of various sizes and historical significance. But the number of monks who live in monasteries and practice Zen Buddhism is very small in comparison.

Many Westerners believe that the Japanese are not very religious because they do not attend regular "church" services. And yet, I found them to be quite the opposite. Most Japanese homes have a *butsudan* (Buddhist altar) where they honour their ancestors as well as a Shinto shrine to worship the local deity. Daily offerings of food, such as rice and fruit along with flowers and a small container of sake, are set on the altar and shrine. Some of the families I visited also placed a photo of Dr. Hiroike, the founder of Moralogy, on their Shinto shrine.

Buddhism dates back to 528 BC in Northern India and the Eastern religion introduces a mystical dimension that transcends the natural world. On the other hand, Shintoism celebrates nature and life here on earth and more than 40,000 gods, called *kami*, preside over the mountains and villages. Japanese funerals are usually conducted by Buddhist priests while Shinto priests bless newborn babies and perform most of the marriages in Japan.

The Japanese have also adopted the teachings of the Chinese philosopher Confucius. Confucianism is not a religious belief but a moral philosophy based on ethical principles. The basic concept of Confucianism is social harmony, which is achieved through the loyalty of the people to their ruler, obedience of inferiors to superiors as well as respect for one's parents and reverence for one's ancestors. Confucianism also emphasizes hard work and the importance of an education as well as the benefits of pulling together as a team and belonging to a group. The teachings of the Chinese philosopher continue to influence Japanese standards of behaviour.

Historically, the Japanese never accepted Christianity despite the efforts of many missionaries who tried to convert the Asian "pagans." The only large concentration of Christians remains in Nagasaki, where the Jesuits landed more than 450 years ago. However, Dr. Hiroike borrowed from the teachings of Christ, as well as Buddha, Confucius, Socrates and Mohammed when he developed the principles of Moralogy. I had certainly become very familiar with Dr. Hiroike's philosophy while at Reitaku so I was keen on exploring another dimension of religious beliefs while visiting Japan.

The Buddhist temple was built on the side of the mountain long before the electronics industry moved into the valley. The spacious wooded grounds, with thick carpets of moss and a large pond containing carp, were beautifully maintained. Kenji and I were invited into a *tatami* seminar room where a monk handed me an English-language brochure, which explained Zen Buddhism to pilgrims searching for the meaning of life, as well as proper conduct in the temple and the correct sitting position during meditation. An English video described daily life at a Zen monastery, where priests believe that the salvation of their souls can be achieved through self-sacrifice, self-discipline and meditation. Their day begins at 3 a.m. with meditation followed by endless chores, sweeping the steps of the temple, cleaning the floors, polishing all of the furniture and tending the garden without speaking to anyone all day long. Their meals, consisting of simple vegetarian dishes, are eaten in silence. The day ends, as it begins, with more meditation before they retire to bare, modest dormitories for six hours of sleep. Twice a week, their heads are shaved. Women have always been excluded from entering the monastery and, until recently, from entering many of the temples.

The rigorous training and stoic lifestyle did not appeal to me but I was willing to participate in a serious *zazen* meditation. By blanking out all thoughts I, too, might gain *satori* (enlightenment or the awakening of the True Self) like Buddha. I sat upright in a cross-legged lotus position with my hands on my lap, one resting on the other. A monk holding a wooden paddle stood beside me, ready to whack me across the back if I made the slightest movement. During 40 minutes of meditation, I didn't feel any different spiritually and I couldn't hear the sound of one hand clapping. Instead, my legs were numb and I was relieved when it was over. Once I had staggered to my feet, I bowed to the monk.

"*Dômo arigatô gozaimashita,*" I said, thanking him for his time and the experience. Even though *satori* was out of my reach that day, I gained a much better understanding of the character of the Japanese people and how self-discipline continues to play such an important role in their lives.

≈

One day, Mr. Takada, Noriko and I visited an outdoor art gallery at Utsukushigahara-kôgen. The small resort in the mountains was reached by a torturous, winding route with hairpin turns and sheer drops into the valley far below. Both Noriko and I felt like we were riding an endless rollercoaster with all the twists and turns in the road and we were relieved when it was over.

Japan has a number of very modern art parks throughout the country exhibiting unusual sculptures from all over the world. At first, I thought the gigantic thumb was an obscene sculpture. But on closer examination, it was just a massive replica of a thumb. Other sculptures were quite bizarre, like the nude diving from a board pointed upwards.

On our way back to Suwa, we stopped at a *ramen-ya* (bowl of noodles store). I assumed we were having dinner since it was already late in the afternoon. The portions were generous and I managed to fill myself up on *ramen* and *gyôza* (dumplings). That was a mistake. As soon as we arrived home, Mrs. Takada served an elaborate *sukiyaki* meal. While everyone was busy helping themselves, Mr. Takada must have noticed my puzzled expression as I delicately picked up a few morsels from one of the side dishes with my chopsticks. He quickly explained that they were baked locusts marinated in soy sauce. Hesitating, even for a moment, would have been impolite. Actually, the locusts were quite tasty, even if they were a bit chewy.

The following morning, plans for hiking in the mountains were cancelled when I injured my ankle. In many Japanese homes, the *genkan*, where we leave our shoes, is usually a foot lower than the rest of the house. I forgot about the step and slipped, bruising my ankle. Mr. Takada insisted on taking me to a local doctor, who had a small clinic down the street. The doctor bandaged my ankle and suggested I stay off my foot for a day or so. So I spent the rest of the day with Kenji, sightseeing around the Suwa area.

By the end of my week, I felt a special bond with my surrogate parents who treated me as if I was a member of the family, rather than a guest in their home. Everyone was exceptionally accommodating throughout my stay. Even Mrs. Takada was pleased (and undoubtedly relieved as well) that I was very fond of Japanese food and enjoyed her cooking.

I was sorry that summer was almost over. I had been able to escape the constraints of the school and even sleep in most of the mornings. All of the families went out of their way to make me feel welcome in their homes. At times, I even forgot that I was a *gaijin*.

≈

On August 20, I boarded the train for Sôka, a *beddotaun* (bed town) only 30 minutes from Tokyo. I was spending a couple of days with the Sasakis before heading back to school. Real estate within commuting distance of Tokyo is very expensive and a condominium in the heart of the city can cost as much as ¥100 million for a tiny bachelor apartment. Owning a new home so close to Tokyo is certainly beyond the means of most families.

The Sasakis lived in a very narrow four-storey modern house with three teenage children, including a son, Yohichi, who was a first-year student at Reitaku, and two daughters who attended local schools. As soon as I arrived, *Onée-san*, the oldest sister, was keen on practicing her English.

"Excuse me," she asked, ever so politely, "may I have English conversation with you?"

We spent most of our time playing Monopoly after I discovered the American version of the game at a local toy store. The kids lost no time at all learning the rules: buy, buy, buy. Even they knew the value of real estate.

While staying in Sôka, I was jolted awake one morning by another minor earthquake. At first, I thought I was dreaming. But reality set in soon enough when I realized that the entire house was shaking on its foundations. Thirty seconds later, it was all over.

Sacred Arrows

O friends, no more these sounds!
Let us sing more cheerful songs, more full of joy!

Joy, bright spark of divinity,
Daughter of Elysium,
Fire-inspired we tread
Thy sanctuary.
Thy magic power re-unites
All that custom has divided,
All men become brothers
Under the sway of gentle wings.

Friedrich von Schiller, 1785
"Ode to Joy"
Beethoven's Ninth Symphony

Traveller's heart
never settled long in one place
like a portable fire.

Basho

The feudal lord Sumitada Ômura opened Nagasaki on the southern island of Kyushu to Portuguese traders and Jesuit missionaries in 1571. The exotic foreign religion appealed to many Japanese people, including several important *daimyô* in Kyushu. By 1582, there were an estimated 200,000 converts in the thriving port city, which quickly became the centre of Western culture. However, many of the warlords were suspicious of the motives of the missionaries and believed that the new religion was a threat to their own political power. In 1587, Hideyoshi Toyotomi banned Christianity and kicked out the troublesome Portuguese "disturbers of national unity." Converts were forced to recant or they were persecuted. In February 1597, 26 European and Japanese Christians were arrested in Kyoto and Osaka on Hideyoshi's orders and marched to Nagasaki, where they were crucified at Nishizaka. A memorial wall with 26 bronze statues of the martyrs commemorates the crucifixion. The martyrs were canonized by Pope Pius in 1862 and a museum was built in their memory 100 years later.

After the death of Hideyoshi in 1598, Ieyasu Tokugawa took control and the persecution continued. Hundreds of Japanese Christians were tortured and killed. The influence of Christianity came to a tragic end in 1637 when 40,000 faithful converts were slaughtered during the bloody Shimabara Uprising in Kyushu. Within two years, Iemitsu Tokugawa, the third shogun, closed Japan to the outside world to prevent subversive foreign doctrines from challenging his authority. The Japanese people were forbidden to travel to foreign lands and anyone who was abroad at the time could not return home.

Nagasaki remained the only gateway to foreign trade. All of the Europeans had been expelled except for the

Dutch, who were confined to the closely watched, tiny, man-made island of Dejima in Nagasaki Bay. Trade also continued to be carried out with the Chinese and Koreans but under similar restrictions. For more than two centuries, Japan was virtually cut off from the rest of the world but the influence of the Jesuits remained strong. Some families continued to practice Christianity in secret. During the Meiji Restoration, the ban on Christianity was lifted and missionaries played a major role in education, creating new schools and influencing social change. Today, Nagasaki has a large Roman Catholic population, but the total number of Christians in Japan is only one million, approximately one percent of the population.

≈

I had no sooner returned to Reitaku after summer holidays when I started to think about the winter vacation. Adjusting to dorm life was much tougher than I expected and I missed all of the freedom I had experienced during the first term. By the time *fuyu yasumi* (winter holidays) arrived, I was ready to take off again.

Hayase-sensei, my geography teacher, was very interested in my plans and for a month, we had discussed various options. I decided to head south so I bought a *furii pasu* (free pass) at Minami-Kashiwa station which would allow me to travel around Japan's southern island of Kyushu for a week for only ¥25,000. Better yet, the winter skies were sunny, a sharp contrast to the sodden typhoon season that greeted me after summer vacation was over.

On December 17, I boarded the *shinkansen* with Muneomi, a first-year student at Reitaku, on our way to Tsuyama in Western Honshu. Dreary winter clouds hid

Mount Fuji from view so Muneomi and I spent most of the four-hour trip to Okayama sleeping. There, we transferred to an old diesel train with a milk run route through the mountains to Tsuyama, an industrial city of 90,000 people. In contrast with the high-speed bullet train, the 40-mile (65-kilometre) trip by *donkô* (local train in the country) took one hour and 34 minutes.

A Christian missionary from India was sitting across from us and started up a conversation. I was surprised to see another *gaijin* on a train going to nowhere but he was teaching English at a school in an isolated town called Yuge. Like all *nehtibu supiikaa* (native speakers of English), we were curious about each other's experiences in Japan. The English teacher had already lived in the country for several years and had adjusted to the customs and traditions. He indicated that he was quite fond of his pupils but I suspected that the town of Yuge was a lonely outpost, even if he was a missionary.

By the time we reached Tsuyama, the skies had darkened and there was a chill in the air. The Yamazakis met us at the train station and we drove a short distance to their home on the outskirts of the city. They lived in a typical two-storey stucco frame house but there was a lawn in their front yard, a very unusual sight in Japan. Later, I learned that the family was in the landscaping business.

Tsuyama is hardly a tourist destination, except for historians interested in the excavated site of a pit dwelling dating back 3000 years to the Yayoi period. Muneomi and I visited the ruins of an old castle, Tsuyama-jô, which was destroyed in 1873. During the early years of Emperor Meiji's rule, hundreds of historic castles were burnt to the ground. Many of the castles have been rebuilt in recent years but Tsuyama-jô remains in ruins. However, a park has been created on the site with thousands of cherry trees and a fabulous view of the city of Tsuyama, wedged in between the mountains.

≈

Two days later, I boarded the train to Beppu on the southern island of Kyushu, where I was spending the night at a youth hostel. Nonaka-sensei had felt that I should be able to manage on my own since my language skills had improved considerably during the second term at Reitaku.

Reservations are essential at all youth hostels in Japan. Although they prefer bookings by letter, a telephone reservation is acceptable, even if you are calling from across the street. Be prepared to let them know what time to expect you, and which meals you will be eating while at the hostel. The food isn't terrific, but it's a better deal than many local restaurants. The real benefit of dining at the hostel is meeting other travellers. And the price is right. Back in 1990, dinner cost about ¥600 and a bunk bed ranged from ¥1900 and ¥2300 for a night.

I didn't mind the dormitory sleeping arrangements, usually about six to a room, compared with 20 to 40 in a room at the ones I've stayed at in North America. In Japan, anyone can stay at a youth hostel. The only downside is the rather restrictive rules, such as the 10 p.m. curfew with lights out at 11 p.m. All hostels have a TV and a library of donated books and *manga* in the common room. The *ofuro* can usually handle four to six people at a time (a notice on the entrance specifies the hours for men and women) and the manager always checks with foreign guests to make sure that they understand the rules of Japanese bathing.

Beppu is a strikingly beautiful city famous for its hot springs resorts and public bathhouses which attract more than 12 million visitors each year. Volcanic heat rises as steam from cracks and fissures in the ground all over the city and creates an eerie sight, especially at night. Beppu has more than 3,000 hot springs, gurgling pools of steamy water released from the earth, which are rich in minerals, such as salt, iron, sulfur and even radium. Some of Beppu's hot springs are called *jigoku* (the hell pools), because the volcanic activity causes the water, along with the dissolved mud or red clay, to boil.

Hotels offer their patrons bubbling mud baths, hot sands or mineral-laden waters tumbling over manmade waterfalls in a fantasyland setting. The *onsen* (hot springs) are noted for healing the maladies of the *kokoro* (heart or spirit) as well as the body. One of the most popular tourist destinations, Suginoi Palace features a museum, nighttime entertainment, games, bowling and swimming in addition to the baths, but the entry fee was ¥1800, almost as expensive as a night in a youth hostel. One of Beppu's oldest public baths, the Bakegawa Bath House, was built in 1879 and it still draws visitors from all over the world.

Public bathing is a Japanese tradition. Prior to the 1960s, most people could not afford their own private baths, so they trekked over to the municipal *sentô* every evening. The *sentô* still exists in many cities and it continues to function as a neighbourhood social centre. All of the public baths have been segregated since the Meiji Restoration, when prudish Western influences had an enormous impact on Japanese social customs. Ordinances were posted prohibiting mixed bathing. "Although this is the general custom and it is not so despised among ourselves," officials explained to the bewildered people, "in foreign countries, this is looked on with great contempt. You should therefore consider it a great shame."

Today, only a small number of traditional *onsen* inns offer mixed bathing, either in an enclosed area or outside in a more natural setting, well protected from inquisitive eyes.

≈

The following day, I took the train to Kumamoto. Halfway there, the train stopped abruptly and we boarded a bus that was waiting for us. I was caught off guard by the interruption of the normal service caused by construction work along the railway. The three-hour detour before resuming our train travel was certainly an inconvenience, but no one complained. I was disappointed, however, since I would miss the opportunity to see much of Kumamoto, where one of Japan's finest reconstructed castles dominates the centre of the city.

Although I arrived much later than I had expected, I decided to walk to the Kumamoto-Shiritsu youth hostel. Youth hostels are often in inconvenient locations and Kumamoto-Shiritsu was no exception. I should have heeded the notation in the guidebook indicating that it "is more difficult to reach" than Suizenji hostel which was close to one of the train stations. But it was quite a bit more expensive and I was always very conscious of my budget while I was travelling.

The map I picked up from a tourist information kiosk wasn't much help except for identifying a few points of interest in Kumamoto. Without street names, I had no choice but to follow the streetcar as far as I could. After the streetcar line came to an end, I used my instincts. Somewhere along the route, I knew I was lost. To make matters worse, the sun had already set and darkness was quickly closing in. I wasn't too thrilled about walking through a strange neighbourhood identified as "delightfully seedy" in my guidebook. I knew I shouldn't have been apprehensive. After all, this was Japan. But I wasn't used to seeing groups of teenagers hanging around street corners, with their cigarettes glowing in the dark. I wasn't about to ask them for directions, especially if they belonged to any of the notorious gangs written about in the newspapers. Eventually, I found the main road again winding up the hill. Much to my relief, I arrived at the youth hostel shortly after 6 p.m.

The manager appeared rather annoyed with my late arrival since dinner had already been served. I apologized and explained that I didn't realize how far the hostel was from the train station. When I mentioned that I had lost my way, his manner softened and he led me into an empty dining room. I was served a tasty pot roast dinner and told not to worry about doing the dishes.

There were few travellers at the hostel during the holidays but everyone was very friendly. As I was getting ready for bed, Hiroaki, a young Japanese university student peered down from the top bunk and asked, "Do you have big penis?" I was well aware that the Japanese have a fascination about the size of the male organ but no one had dared to make direct inquiries before. Apparently, the Japanese believe that the prominent nose of a Western male is indicative of similar proportions of other appendages. I didn't want to disappoint Hiroaki, so I assured him that it was a "good size." Hiroaki appeared to be satisfied with my answer and settled back on the bed. Within minutes, he was sound asleep.

≈

The next morning, I boarded the express train to Nagasaki, an attractive city built into the hills rising from the harbour. Nagasaki was the unlucky victim of the second atomic bomb that was actually meant for Kokura, a major industrial city, now incorporated into Kitakyushu. But on August 9, 1945, the skies above Kyushu were cloudy and "Bock's Car," as the American B-29 bomber was called, headed for the secondary target, the Mitsubishi shipyard in Nagasaki. "Fat Man," almost twice as powerful as "Little Boy," the atomic bomb dropped on Hiroshima a few days earlier, missed its target by over a mile and landed on a residential area.

One-third of the city was reduced to ashes. Approximately 75,000 people were killed and another 75,000 people were injured by the blast. The Japanese viewed the Americans as the cruelest people in the world.

Nagasaki was completely rebuilt after the war though some ruined remnants of buildings have been allowed to stand so that we will never forget the devastation caused by nuclear weapons. Like Hiroshima, the atomic explosion has been commemorated in a Peace Park. An enormous bronze statue of a man was erected in 1955 appealing for world peace. The base of the statue houses memorial tablets for the dead and a sign explains the meaning of the sentiments of the people of Nagasaki, in spite of their suffering. "Divine omnipotence and love are embodied in the sturdy physique and gentle countenance of the statue, and a prayer for the repose of the souls of all war victims is expressed in the closed eyes."

Wandering through the museum overlooking the bombed area was just as sobering as visiting a similar collection of grim reminders in Hiroshima. Endless rooms contained photographs documenting the terrible aftermath of the fiery blast along with numerous exhibits of melted glass and scorched stones. On the fourth floor, the museum staff invited me to join them for a coffee. Not one to decline a free beverage, I sat down to chat with them. During our conversation, one of the gals opened up an atlas and asked me to show them my hometown. When I pointed to Elliot Lake, which had the characters for "uran" (uranium) written in red right beside it, there was an awkward silence. I quickly explained that the uranium for the atomic bombs which devastated Hiroshima and Nagasaki did not originate from Elliot Lake, even though my town played a major role in the stockpiling of nuclear weapons for Western defence in the late 1950s. A decade later, the uranium from Elliot Lake was designated for more peaceful purposes, including Japan's nuclear power plants.

One of the best-known landmarks of Nagasaki is the Glover Garden, on the top of a hill overlooking Nagasaki Harbour. A number of the original homes of former European residents have been reassembled as museums in this hillside garden. The most famous house was built in 1863 by Thomas Glover, an Englishman who supervised the construction of the railways, shipyards and the opening of the mines. Glover married a Japanese woman who has been romantically associated with Puccini's *Madame Butterfly*.

The skies were unusually clear and I took a gondola (called a "ropeway" in Japan) to the top of Mount Inasa, overlooking Nagasaki and the East China Sea. The view of the city, the surrounding green volcanic countryside and the sparkling blue ocean was magnificent.

I approached one of the Japanese tourists.

"*Sumimasen ga, chotto shashin wo totte kudasai?*" (Excuse me, but could you please take a photo?)

"*Hai*," the man nodded, taking my camera and snapping a picture of me with Nagasaki in the background.

"*Dômo sumimasen.*" (Thank you and excuse me again.)

The Japanese are always very obliging to tourists. Even though I wasn't fluent in Japanese, it hardly seemed to matter. And I didn't have to worry about anyone running off with my camera.

In the evening, I wandered through several arcades in Nagasaki listening to "Jingle Bells" and "Silent Night" blaring across the speakers in English. All of the stores were decked with lights, wreaths and boughs, just like the shopping malls at home. The overwhelming display of Christmas, as the ultimate Hallmark holiday in Japan, was hardly surprising in Nagasaki because of the early Christian influence in the port city.

≈

On Christmas Eve, I took the train to Kiyama, a small town on the outskirts of Fukuoka. Ken, my *bekka* classmate had invited me to join him for a few days at his future in-laws' home. He met me at the train station and we walked the short distance to the Inoue home.

Mrs. Inoue greeted us at the door and I handed her a *kasutera*. The small cake, beautifully packaged by the bakery, is a popular present to bring from Nagasaki.

"No, no," she said, blushing. "You should have it."

"*Ii desu yo*," I said, assuring her that it was all right to accept a gift from me. After all, it was Christmas Eve and I was not about to arrive empty-handed. Besides, it was only a small gesture, considering the generosity of the Inoues, who were accepting me as a guest in their home.

After a polite argument over the cake, Mrs. Inoue gave in graciously, thanking me.

"*Dômo arigatô gozaimasu.*"

The presentation of *omiyage* (gifts) is an important part of Japanese culture. Gift giving helps strengthen the relationships between community members as well as superiors at work and there are several occasions to give gifts. *Oseibo* are given at the end of the year to persons of higher social position, particularly at work, as well as doctors and teachers to express gratitude for their assistance. The rules of obligation are followed very closely for *oseibo*. The gifts must not be too lavish or expensive; otherwise the recipient feels an obligation to the giver. Usually there is a set value for each gift, depending on the status of the recipient. Each year, the average family spends about ¥70,000 for these gifts, which may range from boxes of soap and fancy teas to bottles of sake and premium whisky. All gifts are delivered to the home, appropriately wrapped.

Gift giving is also essential for carrying out business in Japan. Imported whisky, American cigarettes and golf balls are highly valued presents. I had brought a number of token gifts with me from Canada: small bottles of maple syrup, a few T-shirts and sweatshirts featuring a scene of a loon swimming on a lake in the wilderness and dozens of Canadian flag pins.

While I was walking around in Nagasaki, I bought a light lunch, milk and *onigiri* (a rice ball wrapped in seaweed), from a convenience store. I had just sat down in a small grassy area to eat my snack when a woman approached me and invited me into the warmth of her dry cleaning shop next door. Some Japanese have an insatiable curiosity about foreigners and there I was, practically at her doorstep. After chatting for a while, I thanked her for her hospitality and gave her a Canadian flag pin. Although I expected nothing in return, she immediately responded in Japanese fashion by presenting me with a gift of greater value, a promotional T-shirt. During our gift exchange, a regular customer walked in and after the shopkeeper introduced us, I gave her a pin as well. Much to my surprise, the older woman burst into tears. Apparently, such a small but unexpected gesture from a *gaijin* put her on the spot since she had nothing to give in return. When she finally regained her composure, she thanked me and put the pin on her coat.

I experienced a similar sense of helplessness when I was presented with a gift while visiting the Yamazakis in Tsuyama. After dinner one evening, the grandfather handed me a small envelope and asked me to open it. Inside, there were three ¥10,000 bills and a telephone calling card worth ¥6000. I was overwhelmed by his generosity. After all, I was not accustomed to receiving substantial cash gifts from a stranger.

"*Kekkô desu,*" I stammered, as I recovered from the shock. The rough translation was, "I can't possibly accept this gift."

But the grandfather insisted.

"*Ii desu yo*," he said, meaning, "It's all right to accept this."

There was no choice. I had been in Japan long enough to realize I would risk offending my host family if I did not accept the gift. I thanked the grandfather several times before slipping the envelope into my pocket.

≈

We celebrated Christmas Eve in the Inoue household with a chocolate cake decorated with a plastic Santa Claus holding a *Joyeux Noël* sign. As a guest, I was given the honour of cutting and serving the cake.

There was, however, another special significance to Christmas since Ken and his fiancée Minako were getting married the following morning at the Kiyama town hall. A formal Shinto wedding would follow in the spring and Christian nuptials in the summer on Long Island in New York. Ken was hoping to speed up the immigration process with the United States government by arranging an earlier civil ceremony in Japan.

Ken and Minako had met the previous year when Ken was working at the city hall in Fukuoka. *Ren-ai kekkon* (love marriages) are becoming more common although many couples still prefer an *omiai kekkon* (arranged meeting wedding), where they are suitably matched. A *nakôdo* (matchmaker) is usually called upon and she takes everything into consideration: social standing, education, occupation, hobbies and personalities. After an introductory meeting, the suitor can either have the *nakôdo* arrange further meetings or seek another mate. Some families hire private detectives to check out the family background to determine whether there is a history of mental illness. There are other concerns as well. A potential spouse can not be descended from the *hibakusha* or other minority groups such as the *burakumin* (sons of small villages) who are still outcasts and shunned by the rest of society. Many Japanese also frown on mixed marriages, but Minako's parents were very supportive of her decision to marry Ken. His parents, however, were having more difficulty coming to terms with an interracial marriage.

In Japan, there is considerable social pressure for a young woman to marry before she is 25 even though the average age for marriage has climbed to 28 for men and 26 for women. The Japanese even have a term to describe the plight of single women, *kurisumasu kehki* (Christmas cake). On the 23rd, a Christmas cake is fresh and worth buying. By the 24th, it is pretty close to the deadline and questionable. After the 25th, the cake is starting to get stale and no one wants it anymore. Not that Japanese men are always desirable. Many of them are "spoiled, self-centered, boorish and predictable," even "wimpy," according to news reports. Some Japanese women feel that a *gaijin* husband is a real catch since they have a better chance at an equal relationship. Otherwise, their role is still rooted in the Confucian tradition of service and obedience to father, husband and the first-born male.

Ken could not have been happier and we celebrated with a bachelor party at a local karaoke bar. Ken, Kevin (a friend from nearby Fukuoka), Kiyokazu (Minako's brother), Mr. Inoue and I sat around a low table feasting on fried chicken and drinking Kirin beer. Even though the legal drinking age is 20, no one ever bothered to inquire about my age. The general rule is "old enough to reach the counter." Back home, photo identification such as a driver's licence, is essential for any bar-hopper who looks under 25.

In Japan, there is no social stigma attached to drunkenness as long as no one is hurt. And it is no secret that the Japanese have a low tolerance for alcohol. They only need a couple of beers to let loose. Beer is always served ice cold and poured into small glasses. Even in a bar, we followed strict rules of etiquette, filling each other's glasses before they were empty, but never pouring our own.

Karaoke bars are a favourite watering hole. And singing badly is part of the entertainment. The first karaoke bar opened in Kobe in 1972 and it quickly caught on throughout the rest of East Asia. Mr. Inoue stuck to old favourites while Ken and I crooned together, singing a number of Christmas songs including "Santa Claus Is Coming To Town." Even *mama-san*, the female bar manager, joined us. By midnight, we were all feeling pretty good as we headed back to the house. But the party was hardly over. Ken, Kevin and I continued to celebrate, diluting our beers with Sprite.

No doubt, we passed out in the *tatami* room, which the three of us shared. I slept right through until 3 o'clock the next afternoon. My head felt like a basketball and I had forgotten it was Christmas Day.

"*Ohayô gozaimasu,*" said Mrs. Inoue.

Early indeed.

I also forgot to stoop when I was going through the low doorway and banged my head once again. If only I had brought along some Tylenol.

Crowds of people had already gathered outside to celebrate the construction of the nuptial home for Minako and Ken on a gravel patch next to the Inoue's home. Work on the frame house had begun that morning, incorporating the traditional Japanese post-and-beam method instead of nails. The bride and groom had returned from the town hall and were also on hand for the celebrations. Candies were thrown from the rafters for good luck. Though I was still slightly hung over, I managed to grab a few for myself. Yum, breakfast.

I spent the next few days sightseeing in the Fukuoka area with Ken and Minako visiting a number of shrines and temples. The evenings were chilly and I enjoyed relaxing in the soothing, almost scalding, water in the tub. The Inoues did not have running hot water in their home so all of the water for the *ofuro* had to be heated on the stove in cast iron cauldrons every evening. The bathing process also took a fair amount of time since I had to scoop the water out of the tub with a pan and pour it over my head in order to wash myself. Once again, I felt as if I had stepped back in time into another era.

≈

On December 27, I boarded a commuter train to Fukuoka and transferred to the *shinkansen* heading for Nagoya. We travelled through the armpit of Japan, passing Kitakyushu where black smoke belched from the smokestacks of the steel mills. Finally, we escaped into the tunnel under the Kanmon Strait and emerged at Shimonoseki on Honshu Island, where the air was clean once again.

I was sitting beside a Japanese businessman who started up a conversation, asking me all of the obligatory questions about my visit in his country. When he inquired, "Are you American?" I told him that I was Canadian.

"I'm sorry. I'm truly sorry," he repeated several times as if he had insulted me. The look of discomfort on his face was almost painful. After visiting Hiroshima and Nagasaki, I could certainly understand why some of the Japanese might not be particularly fond of Americans.

In Nagoya, I boarded the wrong train. Fortunately, I realized my mistake soon after we left the station. I examined my copy of the Japan Travel Bureau *Jikokuhyô*, a huge 1072-page volume including the schedules of all trains, planes and highway buses in Japan, and managed to change trains at Chikusa station for Suwa. I was spending *Oshôgatsu* (New Year's) with the Takadas so I called to let them know I would be arriving an hour later.

Kenji was at Shiojiri station waiting for me. Snow had fallen earlier in the day and I felt right at home. When I arrived at the Takada household, I was welcomed back as if I was a member of the family. Once again, their house was crowded with relatives during the most important holiday for the Japanese.

Generally speaking, Japanese homes do not have central heating. Even with portable kerosene and electric heaters, the rooms were somewhat chilly and I was given a traditional jacket to wear around the house. The first night, I couldn't figure out how to set the timer on the electric heater. So I crawled under the thick covers on Noriko's bed and went to sleep. When I woke up the next morning, the digital readout indicated a chilly 2 degrees Celsius (35 degrees Fahrenheit). Brrr.

On New Year's Eve, I helped with some of the special food preparations. Outside the house, the grandparents were pounding steamed rice in a wooden barrel until it was a gooey mixture. I quickly discovered that this was not an easy task since the wooden mallet was quite heavy. The glutinous rice is formed into small cakes, called *mochi*, which are served in a soup, called *zoni*. Today, most families rely on *mochi*-making machines to make these rice cakes. *Mochi* also has the dubious distinction of causing a number of casualties during the holidays every year, particularly among the elderly who choke to death while eating the sticky rice cakes.

While the women cleaned the house to welcome *Toshigami*, the deity of the New Year, I went cross-country skiing with Mr. Takada in the nearby mountains. He had managed to borrow the equipment from a friend and I marvelled that even the ski boots were the right size. The scenery was breathtaking, with Mount Fuji in the distance, majestic and snow-capped against the powder blue sky.

In the evening, we watched an annual musical gala on television. One of the soprano performers sang "Tonight" by Leonard Bernstein and Stephen Sondheim in English, though I didn't recognize a single word. The climax was the 5,000-member choir singing, in German, Schiller's "Ode to Joy" from Beethoven's Ninth Symphony. "Ode to Joy" is almost a national anthem for the Japanese and everyone knows the words to the song.

Before midnight, Kenji and I joined the crowds at a Shinto shrine where the stalls were doing a brisk business selling good luck amulets and lucky fortunes. Kenji bought me a *hamaya* (sacred arrow) to drive away evil spirits during the next year. The donation box at the shrine was filled with coins and bills from the faithful, who prayed for safety and peace in the New Year. Then we headed off to a nearby Buddhist temple to greet the New Year. At the stroke of midnight, the bells began to ring 108 times to exorcise the people of their 108 earthly passions so they could start the New Year with a clean slate. After the tolling of the bells, everyone greeted each other with "*Akemashite omedetô gozaimasu*" (Congratulations on the New Year) as we welcomed the Year of the Ram.

When we arrived back at the house, Mrs. Takada served a spectacular feast along with *toso*, spiced sake. Actually, the word "sake" is a general term for Japanese alcoholic beverages. The correct term for Japanese rice wine is *Nihonshu* (Japanese liquor).

Brewed from fermented rice, sake is relatively sweet and served in tiny ceramic cups called *sakazuki*, either warm to release its flavour and aroma or ice cold. The Japanese believe that sake is the drink of the sacred spirits of Shinto. Sake used to be drunk often, but now, the traditional drink is usually reserved for ceremonial occasions, such as weddings and funerals as well as numerous festivals throughout the year. We had our share of *toso* by 3:00 a.m. when it was time to go to bed.

Just before crashing for the night, Kenji informed me that we were going to a brief Moralogy meeting first thing in the morning and suggested that I dress in my Reitaku uniform. I'm sure Kenji heard me swear under my breath. But this was Japan and neither of us commented on the insane hour that we had to get up.

≈

On New Year's Day, I was sipping sake and eating *mikan* (tangerines) at 9:30 a.m. in a meeting room of a nearby office building with several other families. Even the young children were served a small amount of sake as we celebrated *Oshôgatsu* together. The rest of the day was devoted to traditional activities, visiting the local Shinto shrine once again and dropping in on relatives. I also played *hanetsuki*, a game similar to badminton, with Noriko and Mrs. Takada, on the parking lot next door. The *hago-ita* (paddles) are beautifully decorated with paintings of kabuki actors. The birdie gives the game the name "feather moon."

All of the New Year's postcards, including the one I had mailed three weeks previously, arrived on New Year's Day. The post office holds onto these special cards and university students are usually hired to deliver them. Children are also given *otoshidama* (gifts of money) in special red envelopes.

≈

The following evening, Kenji and his girlfriend, Takamoto-san, decided to meet for dinner in Chino, a nearby town. She was bringing Michael, a friend from New Zealand, who was teaching English at a local high school. So it was an unusual opportunity for two *nehtibu spiikah* (native speakers) to meet in the valley of Nagano Prefecture. I was looking forward to sharing experiences with another Westerner who had spent some time in the country.

When we arrived at the restaurant, Kenji couldn't find his shoes. He always drove with his oversized Mickey Mouse slippers and put on his shoes at his destination. Fortunately, a shoe store was still open across the street so Kenji trekked through the slush and snow in his slippers and bought a new pair of shoes.

We dined at a fancy French restaurant located in the corner of a nondescript office building. After chatting with Michael for a while, I wondered why he had bothered to stay in Japan. Michael had plenty to gripe about and most of his comments about his experiences were laced with sarcasm. He described our meal as "children's portions designed by an interior decorator." I laughed softly at this apt description. The servings were small, even by Japanese standards, but I didn't want to offend Kenji.

Japan bashing has become a popular sport when *nehtibu spiikah* get together. The communication barrier experienced by many foreigners living in Japan is not necessarily the Japanese language. In a culture dominated by duties and obligations to ensure social harmony, there is no opportunity to speak frankly or express frustrations. While I agreed with some of Michael's views, I found him to be bitter and resentful.

≈

One night, Kenji and I went to a local theatre to see *Total Recall*, starring Arnold Schwarzenegger. Western action films are very popular and the theatre was crowded. Thankfully, Hollywood movies were not dubbed. Instead, the dialogue in Japanese ran down the side of the screen.

The popular show had attracted a big audience and people sat in the aisles when all of the seats were taken. There was no central heating in the theatre, but the large kerosene heater at the back of the theatre was surprisingly effective.

The air was thick with cigarette smoke. Although smoking was strictly prohibited in all movie theatres in Japan, and signs were posted everywhere, it was common practice to ignore the restrictions. In a country where there is an almost obsessive duty to obey the rules, the ones relating to smoking were often broken. That's just the way it was.

There were a few comic moments in the film but Kenji and I were the only ones laughing. The Japanese generally do not laugh in public since it is considered impolite, even at a movie theatre.

≈

After spending two wonderful weeks with the Takadas, my winter vacation ended abruptly. A friend of the family drove me to a Moralogy retreat at Gotemba, near the base of Mount Fuji for a three-day leadership seminar for second-year boys. I couldn't summon much enthusiasm for another series of moral education seminars, but once again, I had no choice in the matter.

Unlike the summer session, we were formally dressed in our uniforms during all of the classes and outings. There were no girls so the *paatis* in the evenings were a bore. I spent most of my spare time reading in one of the Spartan *tatami* rooms set aside for sleeping.

Our mornings began with assembly scheduled at 6:30 a.m. With 12 of us sharing a room, it was impossible to get any sleep until everyone finally hit the sack. After breakfast, with all of us squinting at the blackboard, we sat through an "I told you so" session reprimanding us for our late night prowls. Several teachers were on duty to make sure we didn't fall asleep during the seminars. I was completely lost during most of the lectures probably because I was too tired to understand what was going on. Whenever I started to nod off, one of them was whispering, "Jon-kun, Jon-kun," in my ear.

Meals in the dining hall were a welcome break from the drone of the lecturers. The food was very good and the atmosphere was far more relaxed than at Reitaku. I was fascinated by a very elaborate cuckoo clock on the dining room wall, with a different window opening for each hour. But it was also a reminder of how each hour dragged on. I suspected that my classmates were just as bored as I was but no one complained and I didn't dare say a word.

The following day, we made a pilgrimage to Hiroike-sensei's modest timber dwelling on the Fuji River where he was inspired to develop his new field of study called Moralogy. On the front verandah, I noticed a strange sight, a small circular wooden bathtub, about three feet in diameter. Such bathtubs were quite common before World War II, though I could not imagine taking a bath in front of my neighbours in the small village. Even my classmates thought it was an odd spot for reflection on universal morality and the advancement of human happiness.

Just the same, nearby Mount Fuji is an inspiring sight and I never tired of the spectacular views of the snow-capped volcano against the clear blue winter skies. I'm not sure about the benevolent presence of the *kami* spirits during the seminar, but everyone agrees that Fuji-san is the soul of Japan.

On January 15, we boarded the bus for Reitaku. Only snores disturbed the silence in the bus as everyone tried to catch up on sleep.

Lessons Learned

They are naturally ingenious and have a high character of honesty and voracity. The mathematical and physical sciences are in their infancy but highly esteemed among them. Some of the arts and manufacture even surpass those of Europe.

Brookes' Gazetteer, 1843

Learning is the key to success in life... There shall, in the future, be no community with an illiterate family, or a family with an illiterate person.

Fundamental Code of Education, 1872

Be filial to your parents, affectionate to your brothers and sisters; as husbands and wives be harmonious; as friends be true; pursue learning and cultivate the arts, and thereby develop intellectual faculties and perfect moral powers; furthermore, advance public good and promote common interests.

Excerpts from The Imperial Rescript on Education, 1890

In Japan, education is a national obsession shared by everyone. The politicians, educators and parents all believe that children are the country's primary resource. Consequently, the goals of Japanese children are set very early in life and success can only be achieved by pursuing a formal education diligently, even before kindergarten.

Competition to get into the best preschool is fierce. As many as 80 percent of Japanese children are enrolled in a private preschool by the time they are four years old to ensure that they get into the right kindergarten. Much has been written about the careful ranking of Japanese schools and the critical path from kindergarten to university. In Japan, there is an overwhelming preference for a private school education as long as the families can afford the additional cost. The mother, who is referred to as *kyôiku mama* (education mama), carefully checks the standards of each school. With the family honour at stake, she takes her responsibility very seriously. The *kyôiku mama* is under tremendous pressure to make sure that the best avenues are open for her child. Otherwise, prospects for a good job and even a good marriage are ruined.

By the time Japanese children enter the first grade, they have been taught the importance of polite behaviour, social bonding and rote learning. Most of them can count to 100 and do simple math problems involving amounts under ten. They can also read and write the phonetic alphabet. Illiteracy is unacceptable in Japan and a source of shame for both students and their families. Still, no one is taking any chances. Even in the early grades, Japanese children are assigned serious homework. Rather than let their kids slip behind, mothers keep a watchful eye over their progress and help them when necessary. From early on, children know that the key to success is hard work.

Most mothers also get involved with their children's schools and participate in parent-teacher associations.

The Japanese educational system is hardly perfect. The pressure to succeed is intense. Not surprisingly, there are a few students who can't or won't meet their parents' and teachers' expectations and drop out. But such incidents are rare. If nothing else, the students have learned the importance of social conformity. For those who can't keep up with their studies, there are evening *juku* (private remedial schools) to help them. *Juku* has become one of the most lucrative service industries in Japan since so many students attend them. These schools also cater to students who are preparing for the university entrance exams or looking for enrichment. Generally speaking, the system doesn't provide any encouragement for highly intelligent and creative students. They are forced to advance in an orderly fashion from grade to grade with the rest of the class. No one gets ahead of the line.

The career path of Japanese students comes to a climax during *shiken jigoku* (examination hell). If they are accepted by an elite university, they are set for life. But failure can be both devastating and humiliating, seriously limiting their choices. Instead of giving up, they become *rônin* (drifters), the name used for the masterless samurai who used to wander around the country looking for work. These modern-day *rônin* spend the year at an expensive cram school authorized by the Ministry of Education, such as the Sundai Prep School in Tokyo, and try again.

In university, life changes dramatically for Japanese students. Their career path has been secured and the pressure to succeed has virtually disappeared. For the first time in their lives, they have found a haven of freedom previously unknown to them. The pace slackens and their mothers and teachers are finally off their backs. University students often skip classes and spend time on leisurely pursuits such as playing tennis, joining social clubs and browsing in the nearby shopping districts. Most of them don't work at part-time jobs or during the holidays since Japanese parents are expected to fully support their children until they complete their university education.

After graduation, the major Japanese companies recruit college graduates from the best universities and put them through an intensive six-month training course. During this period of time, the recruits usually live in communal company housing. Each day begins with vigorous morning exercises and the singing of the company song. Now, more than ever, the lessons they have learned are critical to their success: honour, respect, co-operation, loyalty and team spirit.

≈

By the third term, I was able to relax. I had become accustomed to the daily regimen of the school and I felt at ease in my surroundings. My language skills had improved substantially so communication was no longer a problem. I was living like the Japanese, even learning to think like the Japanese. When I stubbed my toe on the steel chair in my *bokusu*, I instinctively muttered "*K'so!*" (Shit!) under my breath. When I struck a pothole biking in Kashiwa, I yelled, "*Iya da!*" (No!).

I settled in comfortably after the winter holidays. Most of the third-year students left at the end of second term to study for the dreaded university entrance exams, or they took up residence in a six-man room at the end of the hall where they escaped from the daily dorm activities. Even

Takebe-san had gone home, so there was no one left to order me around. The dormitory groups were shuffled around, and I found myself in Dormitory 8, around the corner from my old dorm. Toyota-san, a second-year student, was appointed room leader, so we were equals. I could stretch out across the *tatami* mats in the sleeping quarters whenever I wished and I took full advantage of my new freedom. Life for the first-year students eased up as well, but they respected the rights of the second-year students and spent much of their Sunday afternoons hanging out in their cramped study cubicles.

Not everything was easier. We still had to do all of our chores. The teachers made it clear that the second-year students had to set an example by pitching in with the cleaning. Extra *kendô* practices were also scheduled almost every day at 5:30 a.m. I couldn't believe my ears when Miyamoto-san mentioned the time we were expected to be in gear, with *shinai* in hand. Full participation is a basic requirement in Japanese society and it was taken for granted that students would show up regardless of the hour. I confess that I didn't bother to get up for these early practices. Without question, my absences would not have been tolerated if I was Japanese. But my teammates never said anything. Nor did anyone suggest that I should be there. Perhaps they understood that a *gaijin* doesn't really understand the concept of personal sacrifice.

Instead, I was motivated by a more selfish desire to stay in bed. Imagine dragging my body off a comfortable futon at such an unreasonable hour. Hey, I was already putting in at least 15 hours of practice each week. I suspect that even the most committed jock at Trinity would have difficulties adjusting to such a brutal wake-up call in the winter. Even in the afternoons, working out on the icy floor of the unheated *kendô* hall was a real test of endurance since we practiced in our bare feet.

Winter had set in though it never snowed while I was in Kashiwa. Temperatures rarely dropped below the freezing mark and the days were sunny and crisp. All of the newer buildings at Reitaku had central heating, but the classrooms were much cooler than I was accustomed to. For the first time in my life, I wore a T-shirt under my dress shirt just like the rest of the students. Actually, long underwear would have been more practical. The gymnasium, like the *kendô* hall, was not heated at all. Our phys ed uniforms were barely adequate. With the poor lighting from the sodium lights in the ceiling, the freezing temperatures and the endless drills, the gym was more like a dungeon. I seemed to suffer more from colds than anyone else.

≈

Classes began on January 16, the day the United States declared war on Iraq. When Iraq invaded Kuwait on August 2, 1990, the Japanese were not terribly concerned, even though much of their oil was imported from the tiny Arabic country. While I was travelling during the summer, I never heard the crisis in Baghdad mentioned once. The first time I saw "Iraq" in the newspaper headlines was in late August when I returned to Reitaku. I went immediately to the university library to read back issues of the English-language newspapers.

As Christmas approached, war was imminent and the news coverage intensified. My dorm mates devoured newspapers with unusual interest and viewed television newscasts showing the Stealth bombers taking off from

Saudi Arabian soil. "*Sugoi!*" (Wow! Great!) was a common expression.

Psychologically, the Japanese never fully recovered from the *oiru shokku*, the previous oil crises in 1973 and 1979, which caught them off guard. Japan had suffered more than any other major economic power when the Arab states held the rest of the world hostage by cutting off oil shipments. When the Gulf War broke out, it was front-page news every day. Once again, oil prices skyrocketed.

The Gulf War became the *ôroka na sensô*, the foolish war. Nevertheless, Japan ultimately contributed $13 billion toward the UN effort, even if it was done grudgingly.

The attacks on Baghdad were also carried over the US Armed Forces Far East Network and we listened to the broadcasts on the radio in the English office. Robert, who had friends in the Marine Corps at the base outside of Tokyo, listened to reports all day long on his Walkman, even during one of his Japanese language tests.

But nothing changed as far as our classes were concerned. There were no lively discussions about the war. Only the same, boring routine, day after day.

≈

As soon as the teacher walked into the room, the classroom monitor ordered us to stand up and bow by shouting, "*Kiritsu. Rei!*" And we did so in army-like precision, exchanging greetings, "*Ohayô gozaimasu*," as we bowed respectfully in perfect unison. The custom of standing at attention when the teacher entered the class used to be common, even at Trinity. But we gave up such formalities years ago.

There was nothing casual about the atmosphere in our classes at Reitaku. Our teachers lectured for 50 minutes nonstop and then handed out homework assignments, which were due the following day. We didn't dare show up in class without our homework completed. There was no shortage of assignments either, as Japanese students log an average of 15 hours of homework each week. But there was nothing particularly demanding either. Japanese students are rarely, if ever, assigned special projects or asked to write an essay that requires creative, independent thought. Instead, schools rely on frequent tests, requiring one-word answers, multiple choice selections or responses to true and false questions. Tests usually lasted 50 minutes and it was almost impossible to fail them as long as we had done our homework on a regular basis. If we were having difficulty with a subject, we could arrange to meet with the teacher after classes for extra help. Reitaku also had an extensive video library with tapes covering all subject material.

During the lecture, however, students never asked questions nor challenged the authority of the *sensei*. And no one interrupted the teacher, asking to be excused to use the *toire*. Nevertheless, classroom discipline had its shortcomings. Some of the first-year students in my math class fell asleep as the teacher droned on and on. I could hardly blame them; the monotony was almost deadening. Sometimes, the teacher ignored them. Other times, he tapped a pointer on their desks or called out their names. A couple of the teachers had short tempers and often yelled at the students who were not paying attention in class. But no one had to be reprimanded for disorderly conduct.

Without question, there is more respect for teachers in Japan than in many Western countries. Still, Japanese students are like students everywhere. One day, Ito-san got up in front of the students before class and pretended he was Yamauchi-sensei, our homeroom teacher. Ito-san mimicked his low-speed monotone and blank stare perfectly and we all roared with laughter.

In Japan, the school year begins on April 1 and there are three terms: April through mid-July, September through December, and mid-January through mid-March. Holiday breaks include: Golden Week at the beginning of May; six weeks in the summer; three weeks for New Year's; and three weeks at the end of March. Classes were also held on Saturday, but that has been reduced to two days each month. Just the same, the demands of the curriculum have remained unchanged. Classes in Japanese public schools are large, with as many as 45 students. At Reitaku, however, the average class size varied between 25 and 35 students.

All schools in Japan follow the same basic curriculum set out by the Ministry of Education, Science, Sports and Culture, known as Monbusho. In March 1989, Monbusho revised its courses of study taking into account "anticipated changes in society and the resulting changes in the life and attitudes of young people." The basic aim of the revisions was to ensure the "development of people who possess richness of heart and strength of mind" and will be "capable of coping with the changes in our society, such as internationalization and the spread of information media." So far, values in Japan have remained intact. Just the same, the government was not about to take any chances. Some of the other objectives of the revisions were to "put more value on developing an attitude of respect for

Japanese culture and traditions, as well as an increased understanding of the cultures and histories of other countries" to prepare Japanese students for the 21st century.

Although Western schools do not place much emphasis on *dôtoku kyôiku* (morals education), instilling proper values in young people has been a critical component of the Japanese educational system since Emperor Meiji issued the Imperial Rescript on Education in 1890 setting the guidelines for national morals and ethics. From the very first day of classes, all students are taught to respect their parents and elders, to be kind to others and to think of the group rather than themselves. As far as the Japanese are concerned, the welfare of society as a whole is always more important than individual concerns.

When Japan was defeated in 1945, morals education was abolished from the curriculum by the Allied Forces because of the emphasis on loyalty to the emperor. But the spiritual vacuum after Japan's military defeat threatened the country's traditional value system. Crime committed by juveniles became a serious problem. "Today's youth lacks moral purpose, civil responsibility and national pride," reported a correspondent for *The New York Times*. In 1958, *dôtoku kyôiku* was put back on the school's curriculum and subject headings included: etiquette, proper conduct in respect to the community, general human relations and social behaviour between the sexes. In 1964, the program was strengthened and Premier Hayato Ikeda declared: "It is essential to use every medium available - radio, television, the home, the schools - to spread an awareness of responsibility to society." In 1972, textbooks were revised once again to stress national pride and responsibility.

Although the Japanese educational system recognizes the need to adapt to changes in society, schools still stick to the basics. Mathematics, science, social studies (history and geography), civics (contemporary society, politics and economy or ethics) Japanese, English, art (music, fine art, crafts or calligraphy), physical education and home economics (for girls) are compulsory. With 35 class hours each week, the schedule is very tight and there is no breathing space in between classes. Only third-year students have spare periods and a limited choice of elective courses, including religion and culture.

Many educators believe that the uniform and rigid system is obsolete and there is too much pressure on young people to get ahead. Problems with students at school have been on the increase in recent years, including violence against teachers, bullying of fellow students and truancy from classes. As a result, the Ministry of Education is proposing major changes for the year 2002, quite revolutionary ones at that, such as introducing a five-day school week, eliminating high school entrance exams and allowing gifted students in math and science to skip their final year of high school.

In our society, choice has become an integral part of life and often defines who we are and how we live. At Trinity, the only compulsory subjects in our final year were English, chaplain's period, art/music appreciation, health and university guidance. We were required to take six more courses from a choice of 29 subjects, including physical education. Unfortunately, the tremendous variety of options throughout high school presents problems for many students. By the time they enter their senior year, some of them do not have all of the required courses for the university programs they wish to study.

As an exchange student, I had the luxury of choice. Japanese, history, contemporary society and geography were taught on a private tutorial basis. I joined the other students for math, physical education and calligraphy classes.

Math was a disaster. I was taking the first-year course because the Canadian curriculum lags behind the Japanese curriculum by at least a year. Even so, I was completely lost. I spent a fair amount of my free time in the math office where Kawafune-sensei tried to teach me basic concepts in trigonometry. But it was a hopeless effort. Nobody could understand why I was having so much difficulty in the subject. I didn't dare tell anyone that I had scored consistently high on the standardized tests back home.

Everyone was just as surprised with my knack for calligraphy. Acquiring the technical ability usually takes years of practice and yet, I was able to do as well as the others in the class. Calligraphy is a creative but very disciplined art form, which attempts to express spiritual depth and beauty with *kanji* and *kana* characters. We used three different sizes of brushes, dipping them into black ink and applying the strokes onto absorbent rice paper with the characters flowing into each other. Calligraphy classes were a wonderful opportunity for individual expression and creativity, though the bold red lines across incorrect strokes from Kakei-sensei's pen constantly reminded us of the discipline required in her class.

The calligraphy classroom was as Spartan as the rest of the school. All classrooms were bare except for a blackboard and a closed-circuit television hanging from the ceiling. There were no drawings, posters or maps on the walls. Even the architectural design of the ferroconcrete buildings was very plain. Not a yen was spent on creating an atmosphere conducive to learning. The school did not spend money on any extras either, such as lavish facilities, expensive equipment and new technology. While I was at Reitaku, computers were not used as teaching tools and a small computer room was reserved solely for the use of teachers. When I visited the school again in the summer of 1995, a computer lab was finally being built on the campus as the Internet and CD-ROM were becoming essential tools for learning, even in Japan.

At Reitaku, phys ed classes are just as demanding as the rest of the curriculum. The Japanese are firm believers that exercise enhances the mutual development of the body and the mind. All students must participate in a rigorous athletic program as long as they are in school. There is no more tolerance for athletic ineptitude than academic failure. We were spending almost as many hours each week in the gym or on the tennis court as we spent in math class. Our phys ed classes were not designed to create outstanding athletes. Instead, the training regimen encouraged students to push themselves to the limit. In all aspects of school life, *gambatte* prevails. Persevere! Do your best! Hang in there!

Once a week, there was an opportunity to move away from the restrictive curriculum into a more progressive mode in our "long home room" class, which also lasted 50 minutes. Some assignments were quite unconventional. Toward the end of term, we conducted a popularity poll in our class. Such an exercise was very unusual since Japanese schools have a tendency to downplay competition among the students. Personal achievement, which is highly regarded in our society, doesn't receive the same recognition in Japan. Schools do not have an Honour Roll hanging in the lobby or even a system of ranking the top students in each class. Rather than singling anyone out, the schools strive to achieve the highest possible standard of conformity among its students.

At Trinity, the top ten students in each grade are ranked and the class average is also included in the term reports sent to the parents. Students in Group I of the Headmaster's Distinction List, who have an average of 80 percent or higher, are given extra privileges and invited to the Scholars' Dinner each term.

Needless to say, I was caught off guard when we were asked to write down the names of the three *besuto* (best) students in our grade. Votes were tallied up and the results were posted in the hallway of the classroom building. There were no surprises. In fact, the results were not any different than one would expect at North American schools. The most popular students excelled at sports and academics.

We were also asked to make comments on each person on the sheets of paper that were passed around to everyone. Some of the comments made about me were: "You are good at Japanese" and "You are good at English." There were also words of encouragement: "Try harder at *kendô*." Was that a reference to the early morning practices I skipped? Probably.

More often than not, Yamauchi-sensei took the opportunity to lecture us on the hazards of smoking, even though he was a heavy smoker, and other topics, such as time management. These classes had a tendency to be just as boring as the math lectures. Even I nodded off occasionally.

Sometimes, we watched videos on the closed circuit TV. I found it quite ironic that we were shown a video about the civil rights movement in America when the Japanese continue to discriminate against the *burakumin*. Originally, members of this class were known as *eta,* a word that means "much filth" because their livelihood was unacceptable to the purist notions of the Shinto and Buddhist religions. Essentially outcasts from society, they slaughtered animals, tanned leather, collected dung for fuel and buried the bodies of executed criminals. During the Tokugawa Shogunate, the *burakumin* were forbidden to marry outside their caste. Little has changed over the centuries. The abolition of the designation of these people as *eta* was ordered in 1871 in an effort to make everyone equal. But their plight remained unchanged. More often than not, descendants of the *burakumin* were forced to work in the same jobs because no one else would hire them. New laws were passed in 1970 to prevent further discrimination but racist attitudes continue to exist. Unfortunately, efforts by the government to integrate three million *burakumin* into the mainstream of society by getting rid of some of their slums have not been successful either. Change happens slowly in a highly regulated society with centuries-old prejudices. No one will risk jeopardizing their children's future for generations to come by marrying someone with ties to the *buraku* people.

≈

Despite all of the criticisms of Japan's draconian educational system, it works. Japanese students consistently test higher than American, Canadian and European students in math and science. They know more about our country, our culture and our language than we know about them. All of them can read music and the majority play at least one musical instrument, reasonably competently. Many of my friends don't know how to read music, let alone play an instrument. I spent three years in the band when I started at Trinity and my skills as a drummer aren't even worth discussing.

Why can't we be as good as they are? Actually, we can be, if only we have the same obsessive motivation, dedication and drive. I'm not convinced that the Japanese brain functions differently from ours. There are plenty of us who have the same dogged determination to get good marks so we can get into a university of our choice. Many of our top students also excel in sports. But most of us are not conditioned from the very first day we enter school that hard work is essential for success in life. In our society, many students manage to drift from grade to grade without really trying. *Gambatte* is not part of our vocabulary.

When I was 12 years old, my parents were not taking any chances with the public school system. Despite the financial sacrifice, they were prepared to pay for a private school education and sent me to Trinity, where the academic standards were high, sports were compulsory and discipline was taken seriously. They wanted an educational environment where the staff was willing to provide a lot of encouragement and support in all aspects of school life. The class sizes were small, no more than 20 students in each, allowing for individual attention from the teachers. My parents also wanted a school where there were no excuses about cutbacks to extracurricular programs because of budget restraints.

North American schools, both private and public, vary tremendously in the quality of education and the commitment to their students. Just the same, there is no question that our education system is far more relaxed than the Asian system. Children are not always challenged to pursue the highest possible standards. Instead, many teachers are content "as long as a child is working to the best of his/her ability." Still others contend that grades are not that important and should not appear on report cards. They also worry about pushing students too hard, particularly in the early grades. There are other concerns that distract from the three R's -- reading, writing and arithmetic. In some schools, the war on drugs begins in kindergarten and sex education isn't too far behind.

By the time we reach high school, the focus on the basics has weakened even further. Students are allowed to choose what they want to learn since math, sciences, history and geography are no longer compulsory subjects at higher levels. Some students become bored and others have trouble with their work. Instead of studying, they spend their evenings with their friends or work at a part-time job. Many drop out before graduating. Even the students believe that something is missing in their education. In a *Washington Post* survey at a Maryland high school, more than half of the students agreed that they had it "too easy" in school, compared with Japanese and European students.

There were plenty of lazy first-year students at Reitaku who read comics during study hour and fell asleep during class. Even some of the second-year students dozed off during a lecture. Teachers at Reitaku were always concerned about students who were falling behind and reminded them repeatedly about the importance of hard work. I wonder where some of them would be today if it were not for the persistent prodding of the teachers.

I was shocked that there was so much abuse of the study hour by the first-year students. However, by the time they entered their second and third year, all of them were concerned about their future. The academic pressure intensified and everyone hit the books with a vengeance.

≈

When I was asked to give a farewell speech at the closing ceremonies for first and second-year students, I made sure that I was well prepared. I hadn't forgotten the embarrassing silence the first time I was asked to speak in front of the students and teachers. After working on the speech for a full week with my Japanese tutor, I had everything down pat. Actually, I was more concerned about screwing up on the correct bowing procedure than the speech itself. I observed everyone else closely, watching as they bowed to each of the important individuals on the stage and in the audience, at the beginning and at the end of their speeches.

"*Mina-san* (everyone)," I began.

I told them how my biggest accomplishment of the year was getting a cold. I'm sure I caught them off guard but it was enough to get everyone roaring with laughter.

"In the first term," I explained, "I had one cold. In the second term, I had two colds. By the end of the third term, I had three colds." I had to pause for a few moments until the room was quiet again. I was relieved that the year ended on the same note it began, with good-natured laughter, even if it was about my shortcomings. Naturally, I talked about my impressions of Japan and how much I truly enjoyed my year at Reitaku. I also thanked them for their kindness and generosity. Since I had never been any good at giving speeches, let alone sentimental speeches, I kept it short.

I had a great year at Reitaku and suddenly, it was all over. Sure, I had my periods of frustration with all of the petty rules and the lack of freedom to come and go as I pleased. I didn't like the way third-year-students behaved like drill sergeants, ordering me around. And I didn't always like the food served in the cafeteria. I wasn't fond of the cold *soba* dish with a raw egg on top and I never developed a taste for *nattô*. But these were trivial complaints.

I am grateful for the many lessons the Japanese have taught me. The staff and students at Reitaku were always patient in spite of my shortcomings. Perhaps they expected less from a *gaijin*. Nevertheless, I have learned to appreciate more than ever, how sports activities help relieve the stress of the daily grind. The training was tough but the camaraderie was warm and genuine. I have tremendous respect for the dedication of my *kendô* team-mates who got up at 5:00 a.m., especially on Sunday mornings, for practice.

I also learned to appreciate the importance of the concept of "harmony." It's more than people getting along with each other. For the Japanese, it's a deliberate repression of negative feelings to protect the peace and harmony within a group. In the Land of the Rising Sun, strength of character is defined by the ability to conform.

Perhaps, most important of all, I have learned to appreciate the meaning of *gambatte* and apply it in my own life when the going gets tough.

Sayônara

The longer one stays in Japan, the more apparent it is that the Japanese people are basically unchanged, in spite of their very modern appearances and way of living.

Pearl S. Buck
The People of Japan, 1966

Under the heavy snow of winter,
The pine tree bends,
But does not break,
Or change its colour.
People should be like this.

Emperor Hirohito shortly
after surrendering to
the Allies in 1945.

Kyoto is Japan's cultural soul. The ancient imperial city is also known as the "capital of capitals." For the past 1,000 years, Kyoto has been a haven of skilled artisans and craftsmen who built more than 200 Shinto shrines, 1,600 Buddhist temples, 3 imperial palaces, 9 major museums and countless classic gardens.

Nikkô, another popular tourist destination, is even more spectacular than Kyoto. There is nothing simple and serene about Nikkô. All of the shrines, temples and mausoleums are intricately carved, brightly coloured and richly gilded with gold leaf. Perhaps the best descriptive word for its extravagant displays of religious architecture is gaudy, and even that is an understatement.

The Americans spared Kyoto and Nikkô during the bombing raids of Japan in 1945. On the other hand, the Japanese have come close to destroying their own cultural heritage. In a country with such magnificent temples and shrines, there is a callous disregard for beauty and grace among modern architects and city planners. Kyoto has become another disappointing city of steel, glass and concrete high-rise buildings along with hundreds of hotels, some with revolving restaurants on the top floors.

More than 30 million tourists visit Kyoto every year. In the summer, the serenity and harmony of the ancient capital is disrupted by the roar of buses and the loudspeakers blaring at many of the historical sites. McDonald's set a world record here for the number of hamburgers served in a single day.

Nikkô, which sits in a lush green volcanic valley, has been a sacred site since AD 782 when a Buddhist priest named Shôdô finally succeeded in climbing Mt. Nantai after several attempts. He founded Jungu-ji and the temple became a training centre for Buddhist monks. Nikkô also became popular with religious devotees of Ryobu Shintoism. In 1617, Nikkô was selected as the site of the mausoleum for Ieyasu Tokugawa, the founder of the Tokugawa Shogunate. There are many other shrines and temples in the city which have attracted both pilgrims and tourists over the years but none compare with the grandeur of the memorial to a warlord who devoted his life to conquering all of Japan.

During the Meiji Restoration, Japan was so keen on adopting Western ways that the religious and cultural heritage of the country was threatened. When the government ordered 144 castles be destroyed in an effort to eradicate symbols of "old Japan," the people of Nikkô organized a society to save their city from a similar fate.

≈

At the end of the school term, I spent a few days with the Sakunos in Kashiwa. One evening, Mr. Sakuno joined us for a game of Scrabble. A lecturer at the Moralogy Institute, his English skills were reasonably good but his vocabulary was another matter altogether. And Seijiro had spent a year at Trinity. The game was awfully close. Losing would have been rather embarrassing to say the least. Most of the time, however, Seijiro and I played endless rounds of Nintendo except for the day we dropped into a local pool hall after lunch.

I had a craving for curry so we headed off to the Bombay Restaurant, a favourite spot with Reitaku students. Curry dishes have been popular in Japan since the British introduced Indian cuisine during the late 1800s. Today, almost all Japanese restaurants serve at least one curry dish.

We were both fond of a concoction of hot peppers and curry mixed with rice and lamb with some finely sliced *daikon* as a garnish. The three choices on the menu were: Bombay (mild), Indo (hot) and Kashmir (fiery hot). Seijiro opted for the Indo but I asked the waitress for the Akatombo (red dragonfly), even though it was no longer on the menu. Within minutes, the cook was at our table asking Seijiro if I really wanted a curry dish so hot that it was red. I replied instead.

"*Hai*, *onegaishimasu*." (Yes, please.)

When the curry was served, I said *"Itadakimasu"* and prayed for the best. Even during casual meals with friends, we always said *"Itadakimasu"* before digging in.

I sweated throughout the meal, with both my eyes and nose running. By the end of the ordeal, I felt as if I was going to explode. But the Akatombo was fantastic. How was I going to survive back home without all of the wonderful exotic food I had become accustomed to eating on a daily basis?

We stopped in at *Saati-wan Aisu-kuriimu* (Thirty-One Ice Cream, known as Baskin-Robbins) for a Sweet Tofu cone. I was also going to miss the other refreshing flavours including Green Tea and Red Bean.

On March 15, my last night in Kashiwa, we celebrated my 17th birthday a day early. Birthday parties are another Western custom adopted by the Japanese since the Allied Occupation. Mrs. Sakuno served a fabulous *sashimi* meal with a variety of raw seafood including tuna, shrimp, salmon and squid, along with cucumber, processed egg, sticky rice and sheets of seaweed for us to roll our own *sushi*. We finished off the meal with Seijiro leading everyone in an enthusiastic rendition of "Happy Birthday" as Mrs. Sakuno presented me with a cake. I was touched by the fact that even Mrs. Sakuno, who did not speak any English, had learned the words to the song.

≈

The following day, I was standing on a crowded platform at Shinjuku station, one of the busiest railway stations in the world, waiting for the train to Suwa to visit the Takadas again. With two million people travelling through Shinjuku everyday, I spotted Mr. Takada who was waiting for the same train.

"Hi Jonathan," he said casually, when I approached him. There wasn't a hint of surprise in his voice.

After boarding the train, we chatted for awhile. But as soon as we pulled out of the station, Mr. Takada nodded off with the rest of the businessmen on the train.

In the evening, we watched a Japanese murder mystery on TV called "Murder at Kami-Suwa." Both Mr. Takada and I thought the plot was rather eerie, taking place on the same 3 p.m. train from Shinjuku to the same station as we got off, Kami-Suwa.

There was another birthday celebration with plenty of delicacies prepared by Mrs. Takada and another cake. Among my birthday gifts was a fascinating alarm clock which wakes me up in Japanese, screaming *"Yehhhh, okiro! Yehhh okiro!"* (Wake up! Wake Up!)

≈

When Kazuo arrived back from Canada, I went to Narita Airport with his parents to meet him. Even though they had not seen their son for a year, there were no hugs or kisses. His family greeted him the same way they greeted me whenever I showed up on their doorstep, with broad smiles and polite bows.

On our way back to Suwa, the conversation was in Japanese and I struggled to understand as much as possible. My fluency in the language had improved considerably during the year but I still had difficulty following casual conversations.

That night, we celebrated Kazuo's homecoming at a local sushi bar. Neighbourhood sushi bars are tiny and the six of us took up most of the stools at the counter. Actually, the Japanese always refer to sushi as *osushi,* using the honorific prefix for objects requiring a sense of reverence and respect. In the same manner, sake is often called *osake* and *furo* has become *ofuro*.

Back in February, I had called Kazuo to discuss our travel plans when he returned home. Not surprisingly, Kazuo was having a great time at Trinity and he presumed that I was enjoying myself as well. Especially with the rumours making their way to Canada that I had stolen his girlfriend, Aizawa-san. A true exchange, eh? But I tried to explain that we were just friends, casual acquaintances. After all, there was no opportunity to pursue a relationship with a girl at Reitaku. Kazuo should have known better. At least, that's what I thought.

We also talked about visiting Kyoto since I had hoped to see more of Japan's historical sites and treasures before leaving the country. Since Kazuo had never visited Kyoto, his parents agreed to our plans and also arranged for us to visit relatives who lived near Nikkô.

We travelled to Nikkô by train, standing all the way on the *shinkansen,* which was crowded during rush hour. Kazuo's aunt and uncle were eagerly waiting for us at Nasu-Shiobara station. They lived in a ranch-style house, which was huge, even by Western standards. The house had central heating as well as central air-conditioning, a real luxury in Japan. Even more unusual was the fact that there were two toilet rooms, one traditional and one Western-style. While many Western homes have two or more bathrooms, most Japanese homes have only one *toire*.

We were seated on comfortable cushions around a low table in an enormous *tatami* room and Kazuo presented his relatives with a large picture book of Canada. They were thrilled with the gift as he pointed out a number of the places he had visited, including Niagara Falls and the CN Tower of Toronto.

I'm sure Kazuo was relieved to be back in Japan when drinks were served, Suntory Whisky and Jack Daniel's, mixed with a sweet honey-lemon drink. Although he was a year older than I was, there were very few opportunities for him to indulge while abroad. As a minor, he would never have made it past the door of any respectable pub. Even restaurants would have asked him for I.D. Although Kazuo assured my parents that it was "O.K." for him to drink beer, they were not about to start an international incident by serving alcohol to a minor. Kazuo later admitted that my mother had finally given in and served him a grand total of two beers during a very hot week in July when they were vacationing in Cape Cod. Otherwise, Kazuo experienced a rather dry year while he was in Canada. If my parents had only known what was going on the other side of the world. From time to time, I wondered how they would have reacted if they discovered that part of my cultural experience in Japan included some degree of social drinking.

No doubt, there are numerous reasons why underage drinking is not a major concern in Japan. Forget the fact that beer is readily available in vending machines. Drinking alone is no fun. Getting together for a party at a friend's house, is almost, if not impossible. Unlike most of our homes, Japanese houses do not have a separate recreation or family room, which is isolated from the rest of the house. And I'm sure that the *tatami* room is out of bounds. Besides, mother is usually at home and she is more concerned about the homework schedule than recreational activities.

≈

The following day, we explored some of the main attractions in Nikkô, including the Sacred Stable, which is world-famous for its carvings of the simian trinity, the three monkeys in their "hear no evil, speak no evil, see no evil" poses. We also joined a tour for the Tôshô-gû Shrine for Ieyasu Tokugawa at the elaborate gold-smothered Yômeimon (Sun Blaze Gate). The most recent restoration of the Main Hall and other buildings in the complex, with their intricate carvings with gilt and lacquer work, cost $34 million.

After visiting several shrines, we drove along a narrow highway with hair-pin curves up the mountain to Kegon Waterfall. The 97-metre-high (318-feet-high) waterfall cascades in delicate rivulets over a huge horseshoe chasm, not quite as spectacular as Niagara Falls, but much higher and more beautiful.

The Kegon Waterfall has the dubious distinction of being a famous suicide spot, attracting close to 100 people each year who intend to follow the example set by an overwhelmed Tokyo high school student who jumped from the top of the cliff in 1893. A lot has been written about the high suicide rate among overworked students who can no longer cope with the intense pressures to pass the entrance exams for the best high schools and universities. And yet, the suicide rate in Japan is far below most Western countries, and less than half of the rate in Canada and the United States for the population ranging in age from 15 to 24.

≈

The scenery was magnificent as the train passed through the mountains on its way to Kyoto. I stared out the window, wondering when I would have an opportunity to return to Japan. Kazuo kept himself busy hacking out an essay on his father's old *wah-puro* (word processor) for Nonaka-sensei about his experiences abroad. At Trinity, Kazuo took advantage of the variety of sports and extra-curricular activities. But he had his problems adjusting as well. The school yearbook mentioned that he "finally stopped bowing at every turn." Kazuo also missed having girls on campus, since we were still an all-boy's school at the time. But he didn't appreciate the students who chewed gum in class and paid little attention to the teacher. Had he already forgotten how the first-year students at Reitaku fell asleep during lectures? Kazuo was also a big fan of Jim's pizza. Otherwise, he was not going to miss the food at Trinity, in particular the beef stew served on alternate Mondays and the shepherd's pie served on alternate Tuesdays.

Of course, Nonaka-sensei was expecting a similar essay from me. I had kept a journal but there was so much to say and I didn't know where to begin. Spending a year in Japan was a dream come true. The months had passed by quickly and I had learned a great deal, not only about Japan, but also about myself.

I thought about writing a book about my experiences and wondered about Nonaka-sensei's reaction. I had ventured into the inner circle and penetrated a closed society. I also discovered the enduring nature of relationships with the Japanese, particularly with the Takadas for their generosity, consideration and kindness while I was a guest in their home on several occasions. Even the families, who took me in for a few days, went out of their way to make me feel welcome. Then, there were the incidents at Reitaku that Nonaka-sensei, I'm certain, would rather forget. While Kazuo worked away on his essay, I wondered if I would have the courage to write an honest account, comparing the similarities of the two schools and talking about the differences as well without feeling an obligation to censor any potentially embarrassing incidents.

≈

The ugliness of the drab urban areas of Japanese cities was always a letdown and Kyoto was no exception. At the train station, Kazuo called the hotel to make reservations at a *bijinesu hoteru* (business hotel). As we approached Kyoto, we had looked through one of the popular Japanese transportation timetable books with advertisements showing pictures of hotels and their rates as well as a map giving directions from the train station. Mrs. Takada's only advice about lodgings in Kyoto was, "Do not stay at a love hotel."

Our *wa-shitsu* (Japanese-style room) cost ¥6000 per night. We were forced to pass up on the *yô-shitsu* (Western-style room with a decent bed) because there were no doubles. The two of us ended up in a room the size of a large closet, with a *tatami* floor so we left our shoes in the small *genkan* just inside the door. The room was bare except for a small table and a coin-operated television. Futons were hidden behind the sliding doors of the *oshiire*. Fortunately, the weather was still cool and we didn't need to use the air conditioner, which operated for an hour on a ¥100 coin. The bathroom was tiny with a door reminiscent of an airplane lavatory, but it was complete with a proper toilet, shower and tub. I felt right at home.

That evening, Kazuo and I searched for pizza. Three days in Japan and Kazuo already wanted some decent "za." Of course, we could have gone straight to Shakey's or to the Italian restaurant down the street from the hotel. But Kazuo had his heart set on a good, Western-style pizza. At a pay phone, he ripped out the page out of the telephone book with listings of pizza places. A year in Canada and Kazuo was corrupted. But he just shrugged his shoulders explaining that no one else would be looking for the same thing so the page was not a big loss. At least, not in a phone booth plastered with business cards with photos of scantily clad call girls, including a "very top class" gal charging ¥40,000. Prostitution was officially banned in 1956, but the world's oldest profession appeared to be thriving in the ancient capital.

We wandered around downtown and explored the narrow back streets with its teahouses and coffee shops. Finally, we headed to the west end of the city where most of the pizza joints were located and checked out several spots, but the menus were not very appetizing. When we spotted Shakey's, Kazuo surrendered. As soon as he took one bite out of a conventional green pepper, mushroom and sausage pizza, he realized that it was a mistake to expect the impossible. "This is the worst pizza I have ever had," he complained. Actually, the pizza wasn't too bad at all. Obviously, I had become accustomed to the Japanese version of the pie. But Kazuo was hoping for the real thing. To make matters worse, the Shakey's pizza cost three times as much as Jim's pizza back in Port Hope which was hard to beat by anyone's standards.

Back at the hotel, Kazuo went downstairs to the basement to get some cold beer from one of the vending machines. Instead of room service, most business hotels provided a wide variety of vending machines for their customer's convenience. We settled down on our futons and plugged in a ¥100 coin to watch the *Sony Music Video Hour* broadcasting the latest dance music from America. Porno movies were also available for ¥300 per hour.

≈

During the next two days, we explored Kyoto, cramming in as many attractions as possible. The weather was miserable with overcast skies and it rained most of the time. Cabs cost Kazuo a fortune, more than ¥10,000 per day, but we managed to see the most popular sights. The whirlwind tour overloaded my senses as one attraction blended together with another in my memory.

The gardens surrounding the main shrine at Heian Jingû were beautiful with its purple irises in full bloom. Even some of the *sakura no hana* (cherry blossoms) were out. Symbolizing purity, simplicity and fleeting beauty, the delicate pink blossom is the most beloved flower in Japan.

Within a week, Kyoto would be packed with thousands of tourists.

We had also hoped to visit Gosho, the old imperial palace where foreigners can apply to the Imperial Household Agency in the palace grounds 20 minutes before a tour by simply bringing along a passport. Much to our dismay, we discovered that the Japanese must apply months in advance for a pass. I wasn't about to join a *gaijin* tour with Kazuo waiting outside.

Kyoto was as exciting as it was exhausting. Kiyomizu-dera, one of the oldest temples in the city, is built into the side of *Higashiyama* (East Mountain) overlooking the city. Established in AD 792, the Temple of Pure Water is dedicated to Kannon and monks still bathe in the ice-cold waterfall. We climbed hundreds of stairs and steep paths at this sprawling complex of 16 exquisite buildings, which date back to 1633. Kiyomizu-dera was certainly the high point of my visit to Kyoto.

≈

When we returned to Suwa, I was faced with the challenge of packing my belongings, including dozens of books and other items that I had bought during the year. Kazuo had been faced with the same problem when he was returning from Canada, so my mother provided him with an extra large duffel bag, which I managed to fill as well. I didn't even want to think about the extra charge for an additional bag I couldn't even move by myself. My *shinai* and practice sword didn't fit into any of the bags but I didn't expect any problems with them at the airport.

The mood was festive during an elaborate farewell dinner. But I had mixed feelings about going home. Sure,

I was looking forward to seeing my family again. And yet, I was reluctant to leave. Venturing inside the *torii* gate had been an exciting adventure, and an opportunity of a lifetime. I will never forget the kindness of the staff at Reitaku and all of the people who invited me into their homes and even their hearts.

The following morning, the entire Takada family piled into two cars for the four-hour drive to Narita Airport to see me off. Kazuo was in good spirits as usual, keeping us entertained with jokes he had learned while he was in Canada. At the airport, we gathered for a final group photo before I said good-bye and walked to the gate. *Sayônara* was bittersweet, only because I knew I would return soon.

Glossary of Japanese words and expressions

aisu kôhii	iced coffee
aisu kuriimu	ice cream
aisu tii	iced tea
amae	indulgence or induced dependence
animé	cartoons
arigatô gozaimasu	polite thanks
ashigaru	foot soldier
banzai	ten thousand years
Basho	Japan's greatest poet (1644-1694)
beddotaun	bedroom community
bekka	the Japanese-as-a-foreign-language department
bekkasei	students of bekka
benjo	excretion place, toilet
bentô	boxed lunch
besuto	best
biiru	beer
bijinesu hoteru	business hotel
bokusu	study cubicle
burakumin	sons of small villages who were traditionally outcasts of society
bushidô	The Way of the Warrior
butsudan	Buddhist altar
cha-no-yu	traditional tea ceremony
Chikuro Hiroike	Founder of Moralogy
chônan	oldest son
daikon	delicious white radish
daimyo	feudal lord
damé	No! It's useless to do that.
deito	a date with a friend
denwa	telephone
dezâto	dessert
dômo	thanks
dômo arigatô	polite thanks
dômo arigatô gozaimasu	extremely polite thanks

donkô	local train in the country
dôtoku kyôiku	morals education
dôzo	please; be my guest
ero-guro	erotic and grotesque
ero-hon	erotic books
furai potehto	French fries
furii pasu	free pass
furii taimu	free time
fuyu yasumi	winter holidays
gaijin	foreigner
gambatte	preserve; do your best; hang in there
gaman-tsuyoi	strong stoic personality
genkan	vestibule; foyer area where shoes are removed
genshi bakudan	atomic bomb
gochisô sama deshita	that was a real feast
gohan	meal; rice
gomen nasai	I am sorry
gyôza	dumplings
ha	fast
hadaka no otsukiai	naked bonding
hagoita	paddles
hai	yes; I hear you; I'm listening
haito	fight
hakama	long divided skirt used in *kendô*
hakujin	white foreigner
hamaya	sacred arrow
hanabi	fireworks
hanami	cherry blossom viewing
hanko	personal seal
hashi	chopsticks
heiwa	peace
hibakusha	explosion affected persons
hikinuki	pulling out the threads in Kabuki theatre; onstage costume change
hiragana	Japanese alphabet
hiropon	amphetamines
hontô	Really? Is that so?

hotto kôhii	hot coffee
iie	no
ijime	bullying
inu	dog
irasshaimase	welcome
itadakimasu	I humbly receive
Iya da!	No!
jan-ken-fon	paper-scissors-rock
jidanhambeki	vending machines
jigoku	hell pools
jishuku	self-discipline
jo	slow
juku	cram schools; private remedial schools
kampô	Chinese herbal medicine
kanji	Chinese characters
karaoke	sing-along sound track; empty voice
karê-raisu	curried rice
karôshi	death from overwork
kasutera	sponge cake
katakana	one of two phonetic Japanese alphabet; used primarily for foreign words
kazoku	family
keigo	honorific form of speech
keigoki	tunic used in *kendô*
kendô	Japanese fencing; the oldest of the martial arts
kôban	police boxes
kôen	park
kôhai	junior
koi	carp
kokoro	heart or spirit
kombanwa	this evening
kombu	seaweed
konnichiwa	this day
kote	gloves used in *kendô*
K'so!	Shit!

kun	suffix used for persons of equal or lower age or status
kurisumasu kehki	Christmas cake
kyôiku mama	education mama
kyû	faster
machigatta	what a mistake
mainichi	everyday
Makudonarudo	McDonald's
mama-san	female bar manager
manga	comic book
men	helmet used in *kendô*
mikan	tangerines
mina-san	everyone
mirin	sweet white rice wine
mochi	pounded rice made into small cakes eaten at festive occasions
monogatari	tale
Moralogy	a new moral science developed by Chikuro Hiroike who believed that true happiness can be achieved by applying high moral standards to one's life regardless of religious beliefs
mugi-cha	barley tea
nakôdo	matchmaker
nattô	partially fermented soybeans
nehtibu spiikah	native speakers of English
neko	cat
Nihonshu	Japanese liquor
nintai	patience
nore	seaweed
oden	stew made from fish and vegetables
ofuro	bathing room; bath tub
ohayô gozaimasu	it is early; good morning
oiru shokku	oil shock caused by OPEC countries in 1973
oishii	delicious
okonomiyaki	cook what you like
okyakusama	customer

omawari-san	police officer
omiai	arranged meeting possibly leading to marriage
omiai kekkon	arranged meeting marriage
omiyage	gifts
onée-san	older sister
onegaishimasu	please do me a favour
onigiri	rice balls wrapped in seaweed
onsen	hot springs
oseibo	special year-end gifts
oshibori	hot towels
Oshôgatsu	New Year's
oshiire	large closets with sliding doors
otearai	toilet (literal translation: honourable hand wash)
otoshidama	gifts of money
oyasumi nasai	rest well
paati	party
pahsonaru	personal
rabu hoteru	love hotel
ramen-ya	bowl of noodles store
renai-kekkon	love marriage
romaji	Japanese Roman script
rônin	"masterless samurai"; reference is usually made to students who must rewrite university entrance exams
ryôtei	gourmet Japanese cuisine
sakazuki	tiny ceramic cups
san	suffix which shows respect to a person
Sankei Shimbun	a national newspaper
sarariman	salaryman; a male, white-collar employee, usually with a large firm
sashimi	raw fish
satori	enlightenment or the awakening of the "True Self"
sayônara	good-bye
seikô	success; immaturity; sex
seiza	sitting in a kneeling position

sembazuru	a chain of 1,000 organic paper cranes
sembei	rice crackers
sempai	senior
sensei	teacher
sentô	public baths
seppuku	suicide by disembowelment
seppun	kiss
shibui	cool; sophisticated
shinai	bamboo sword
shiken jigoku	examination hell
shinhatsubi	newly on sale
shinjinrui	youth who reject parental and traditional values
shinkansen	new express lines; bullet train
shitsuke	sense of fair play, loyalty, self-discipline and honour
shôyu	soy sauce
shusse	success
soba	buckwheat noodles
soroban	abacus
Sugoi!	Wow! Great!
sukiyaki	stew consisting of thinly sliced beef, tofu, leeks, shittake mushrooms and noodles
sumimasen	excuse me
taibatsu	corporal punishment
tatami	tightly woven floor matting made from rice straw
tenko	roll call
Tennô	emperor
tesuto	test; exam
Tôdai	Tokyo University
toire	toilet
tokkyû	express
torendi na	trendy
torii	gate to a Shinto shrine
toso	spiced sake
tsuyu	rainy season

umeboshi	pickled plums
unagi	eel
uyoku	right-wing nationalists
wa-shitsu	Japanese style room
wah-puro	word processor
wakarimasen	I don't understand
wakarimasu	I understand
warashita	sauce made from soy sauce
wasabi	pungent green horseradish
yakisoba	stir-fried noodles
yakitori	chicken kabobs
yakuza	Japanese "mafia"
yakyû	baseball
yehhh okiro	wake up!
yô-shitsu	Western style room
yôkan	sweet soybean paste
yûbin-kyoku	post office
zanshin	stop
zoni	a soup served at festive occasions
zubon	pants
yen	Japanese currency; during 1990 the average cost of ¥100 was $0.81 Cdn or $0.69 US.

Order Form

I wish to order ____ copies of ***Inside the Torii Gate*** at $19.95 each (US$13.95 each) plus $4.00 for the first book and $1.50 for each additional book for shipping and handling charges. Canadian residents, please add 7% GST or 15% HST for each copy.

Please make money order payable to:

The Beresford Press
400 Walmer Road, Suite 724
Toronto, ON M5P 2X7
Phone: (416) 922-0202
Fax: (416) 934-1331

Name______________________________
Address____________________________
City_____________**Province/State**_____
Postal/Zip Code____________________
Country___________________________